The Match:
Althea Gibson and
Angela Buxton

The Match:

Althea Gibson and Angela Buxton

How Two Outsiders—

One Black, the Other Jewish—

Forged a Friendship and

Made Sports History

BRUCE SCHOENFELD

Amistad

An Imprint of HarperCollins*Publishers*

HarperCollins books may be purchased for educational, business, or sales promotional use. For information, please write: Special Markets Department, HarperCollins Publishers Inc., 10 East 53rd Street, New York, NY 10022.

Grateful acknowledgment is made for permission to reprint photographs in the following chapters: chapters 4 and 16, courtesy of the ITA Women's Tennis Hall of Fame; chapter 1 and chapters 4 through 8, courtesy of the International Tennis Hall of Fame. All other photographs courtesy of Angela Buxton.

FIRST EDITION

Designed by Amy Hill

Printed on acid-free paper

Library of Congress Cataloging-in-Publication Data
Schoenfeld, Bruce.
The Match: Althea Gibson and Angela Buxton / Bruce Schoenfeld.—1st ed.
p. cm.
ISBN 0-06-052652-1
1. Gibson, Althea, 1927–2003   2. Buxton, Angela, 1934–   .
3. Tennis players—United States—Biography.   4. Tennis players—
Great Britain—Biography.   I. Title.
GV994.A1S42 2004
796.342'092'2—dc22
[B]   2003065380

04 05 06 07 08   ❖/RRD   10 9 8 7 6 5 4 3 2 1

To Julie Selene and Theodore Samuel

We pray to be conventional. But the wary Heaven takes care you shall not be, if there is anything good in you. Dante was very bad company, and was never invited to dinner.

—RALPH WALDO EMERSON

Contents

Acknowledgments

THIS BOOK would be far less informative, interesting, or historically accurate without the contributions of each of the following: Art Anderson, John Barrett, Flo Blanchard, Shirley (Bloomer) Brasher, Louise Brough, Maria Bueno, Angela Buxton, Gordon Buxton, Bud Collins, Rosemary Darben, Billie Davis, Mayor David Dinkins, Joel Drucker, Margaret du Pont, Derek Dutton, Alice Dye, Kirk Ellerson, Richard Evans, Daphne (Seeney) Fancutt, Beverly Fleitz, Steve Flink, Allen Fox, Shirley Fry, Adeline (Matthews) Gittens, Ralph Gonzalez, Doris Hart, Dr. William Hayling, Jeff Heckelman, Pat Hird, Deacon Lawrence Howard, Bob Johnson, Simon Jones, Judge Robert Kelleher, Billie Jean King, Peggy (Lebair) Mann, Desmond Margetson, Alastair Martin, Edwina Martin, U.S. Rep. Carrie Meek, Mary Mills, Angela Mortimer, Fay Muller, Gardnar Mulloy, Robert Mungen, Gordon Parks, Jack Phelps, Renee Powell, Betty (Rosenquest) Pratt, Hamilton Richardson, Bob Ryland, Dick Savitt, Ted Schroeder, Eugene Scott, Vic Seixas, Audrey Snell, Randy Walker, Nancy (Chaffee) Whitaker, Rev. Dino Woodard, Pat Yeomans, and Mark Young.

Contemporary accounts and information from the *New York Times* and the *New York Amsterdam News*; from *World Tennis* magazine and an array of other national magazines; from England's *Dunlop Annuals*; and from the tennis coverage provided by the London newspapers of the day all proved invaluable. In addition, several books must be cited:

most notably, Althea Gibson's own *I Always Wanted to Be Somebody*, now unfortunately out of print, and the fourth edition of Bud Collins's *Tennis Encyclopedia*, which has since been superceded, but also autobiographies by Alice Marble, Angela Mortimer, Hubert Eaton, and others.

I am indebted to the talented Amistad/HarperCollins team, including Dawn Davis, Darah Smith, Nicole Revere, Amy Hill, and Rhoda Dunn, that proved publishers do have hearts and souls. And to Andrew Blauner, whose tireless efforts made this project a reality.

Special thanks to Scott Price, a terrific writer and editor, and an even better friend.

The Match:

Althea Gibson and
Angela Buxton

Angela

INSIDE THE KITCHEN of her fifth-floor condominium unit, part of a forest of similar buildings clustered atop glorified swampland in this faceless stretch of South Florida, Angela Buxton is sautéing onions for Sabbath dinner. She has the brisket marinating in the icebox, the chicken soup simmering in a pot, carrots on the cutting board. She's hardly the type to settle for a hastily prepared Friday night, a few scraps of this and that, apologies along the way.

It is the middle of the last decade of the twentieth century, and Angela is sixty-one years old. Propelled by ambition and a healthy dose of impatience, she has marched through the world at her own pace. She has a suitcase full of scrapbooks and a modicum of fame; people of a certain age remember her name, especially in London, where she lived most of her life, until the man who had become her life's partner died, and then her son, and finally her cat. That confluence of *tristesses* drove her to sell the old house and take on this part-time refuge by the Florida shore. The memories lingered, but she isn't one to grieve for too long. She took up golf and pursued it with her customary zeal. Ambition and impatience conspired again, and they made her a pretty fair golfer almost right away.

The complex where Angela lives exists as a city unto itself that pushes north from the Hollywood line, poking a finger of squat, green-gray buildings and lushly carpeted fairways into deepest Pompano Beach. The condominiums are filled with retirees and snowbirds, many of them widowed or divorced women. Sabbath dinners are being prepared inside one after another of the nearly identical units on this March afternoon, up each hallway and down the next. The hallways smell like every Jewish grandmother's kitchen.

Just as Angela's onions are approaching the crucial juncture, at which a moment of inattention will fill the kitchen with the acrid smell of burnt carbon, the telephone begins to ring. This in itself is worrisome, for calls at the complex often include news with overtones of mortality. Without warning, the virtues of air-conditioned semiretirement in the subtropics can be overshadowed by details of a relative's myocardial infarction, a friend's metastasized tumor, a neighbor's untimely passing. The chances that a particular call will carry such tidings rise as the years pass, and the range of potential maladies swells, until some elderly residents are terrified to answer the phone at all. There is nothing but bad news left to hear.

Angela is rarely spared the details. She is an empathetic woman, though she hides it behind a brisk manner and distaste for idle chatter. In truth, you could almost call her a soft touch. She is immensely popular in the condominium complex, in part because she knows how to get things done. She persists until nobody has the will to deny her. She can get the condo committee to replace a broken lightbulb, convince the clubhouse restaurant to serve the matzoh ball soup without salt if that's what the residents want. She is something of a hero here, almost a cult figure. She has been asked to represent the floor at the association meetings, but she tells them that she simply doesn't have the time. She is still teaching tennis, and writing pieces for tennis magazines and the occasional British newspaper, as well as locating housing and arranging travel for foreign players who come to play at the local Junior Orange Bowl tournament. The work keeps her going, in more ways than one. And then, every April, she gives a farewell wave and departs for home. She is a British citizen who takes pains never to stay on this side of the Atlantic for an hour more than her legally allotted time, working out the dates carefully on a yellow pad to ensure that she doesn't exceed the limit.

For all those reasons—onions sizzling, worrisome scenarios about the health of neighbors pecking at her consciousness, an innate distaste for casual conversation—she hesitates to pick up the phone when she hears it that Friday afternoon. But few of us can resist the insistent ring that reminds us we're wanted by someone, if only a salesman, in this precarious world. Angela carefully places the spoon on a dishtowel, casts a cautious eye on her onions, wipes her hands, and hurries reluctantly—if such a thing can be imagined—into the living room.

She knows at once from the hum on the line that the call is long distance. She knows from the first word that it is a voice she has been hearing on and off for forty years. They exchange greetings, an obligatory prelude to the business at hand. It is evident to Angela that Althea Gibson isn't calling for a chat.

"I really am down," Althea acknowledges. "I can't take it. I'm calling to say good-bye."

"Now, just a minute. What's going on?"

"I've got bills mounting up. I don't know what to do. No money coming in. No money for my medication. I feel dreadful. I just can't carry on anymore." Then Althea forces out the words: *I'm going to commit suicide.*

Through the years, Angela has learned to function best in moments of crisis. With the life of an old friend all but hanging in the balance, she is absolutely certain that she can form a plan, implement it, relieve this distress. Her head is as clear as the March afternoon. Not a thought is out of place.

"Let's talk this over," she says. "Hold on just a minute while I turn off the onions."

AT ONE TIME, Althea Gibson had been the most famous tennis player in America. During the summers of 1957 and 1958, as Henry Aaron and the Milwaukee Braves were winning consecutive National League pennants, and the rock 'n' rollers were making their initial inroads on the crooners, and Eisenhower was keeping the country a step ahead of the Russians, Gibson's face filled the newsreels. She'd come out of Harlem at just about the time Jackie Robinson was breaking in with the Dodgers: a tall black woman with arms and legs like a spider and an inscrutable smile. She'd battled against the infrastructure of a sport that had no inclination to support her, invented her own techniques when she couldn't master the existing ones. She struggled to earn enough money to survive, thought of quitting to join the army's Women's Auxiliary Corps when success didn't come her way. Instead, she persevered, tapping reservoirs of confidence she didn't know she had, and ended up riding down Wall Street in an open car as ticker tape filled the air like snowflakes. She won Wimbledon twice, won twice at Forest Hills, where the United States championships were played until 1978, then abandoned competitive tennis to cash in as best she could. She cut an album, sang on *Ed Sullivan*, toured with the Globetrotters. She joined the golf tour, integrating the LPGA. For a time, anything she did made news. The world knew her name.

But by 1995, she was old and forgotten. Old in a way she could feel in her bones, holed up in her ramshackle apartment in East Orange, New Jersey, with bills unpaid and the gasman threatening. She'd had a stroke, her blood pressure was well into the danger zone, her memory was beginning to play mean tricks. She had no money to pay for her prescriptions, and could see nothing ahead but a road leading down. She was too proud to live this way, old and broken like a junked car up on cinder blocks in a barren yard. What was the point of being some-body if the end was illness and poverty and despair? She told Angela, "This is the quickest and easiest way out. I don't want to be a burden. I just want to say farewell."

Angela was one of the oldest friends Althea had, one of the few who'd stuck with her through the twists and turns. They'd visit with each other during the U.S. Open every year, and Althea had even made it all the way to London in 1984 for the centenary of women's competi-tion at Wimbledon. But now travel was out of the question; Althea barely wanted to get out of bed. There'd be no more Wimbledons, no more cheering, precious little joy. Why go on?

Angela assumed her manner of brisk competence. She asked Althea to calculate how much money she needed to keep the wolf at bay. Add up all the bills, including back debts, and come up with a total. The answer was fifteen hundred dollars a month, which seemed paltry. Save her friend's life for fifteen hundred? Angela could handle that.

Althea may have been ailing, but she was still a stubborn and proud woman. She wouldn't accept such assistance without at least a perfunctory fight. But Angela wouldn't listen. She and Althea had been doubles partners, and the credo is that your partner didn't let you down. How many times had they played deep into a point, each covering for the other, sliding from ad court to deuce court and back again as the play unfolded? They knew just where to be to keep the ball alive, until Althea could get an angle for that windmill forehand or unleash an overhead from just inside the service line, her arms and legs flying in all directions, her eyes bugging from her head like Olive Oyl. They'd turn in unison, as if choreographed, and walk back to position with the knowledge that their unlikely partnership was working. During those moments, they believed they were destined to win.

Angela came from a prosperous and loving family, though her parents had divorced in her childhood. She knew her father, an entertainment impresario, would always be there to lend support. Althea never had such emotional security, and her financial safety net was nonexistent. Never had two nickels to rub together is how Angela would put it, watching Althea improvise as she went along. Now Althea, who had always been less adept at figuring out how to live a life, needed help. More than that, her accomplishments—and, by extension, *their* accomplishment—had faded from view. Jackie Robinson was an American icon, Billie Jean King epitomized women's tennis, but nobody knew Althea Gibson anymore. She was a name from the history books, someone the students were probably reading about right now at her old elementary school in Harlem—even as she lived on in her apartment day after day, too poor to get her teeth fixed, too ill to drive a car.

Angela mobilized. The Lipton was coming up, arguably America's most important tournament after the U.S. Open, held each March at nearby Key Biscayne. So she drove down I-95 to a ceremonial tennis dinner and saw Bud Collins, the writer and commentator, hawking his new book at a table. Decked out in his customary pinks and greens like a Margaritaville Beau Brummel, Collins was easy to recognize, and Angela wasn't shy. Althea had helped teach her that. She marched up and introduced herself.

Collins didn't need to be told about Althea Gibson; he had literally authored the *Tennis Encyclopedia*. There she is, on page 403: "No player overcame more obstacles to become a champion than Althea Gibson, the first black to win at Wimbledon and Forest Hills." He knew Angela as soon as she said her name. Her connection to Althea linked them together in his mind. He hadn't been aware of Althea's situation, but he *had* wondered why she never answered the phone anymore. He volunteered to ask everyone he knew for help, and he knew everyone. Thousands of dollars were collected from tennis champions of every era. Martina Navratilova gave money. So did Dick Savitt, who had won Wimbledon in 1951. Angela was overjoyed, yet at first Althea didn't receive a dime. It was a mystery, one of many that marked Althea's life. Maybe the checks were never sent, maybe the money ended up in the wrong hands, nobody ever knew for certain. Althea didn't get any of it, not the first time around. Time passed. Angela continued writing checks.

A year after Althea's call to Angela, a freelance journalist and author named Paul Fein took up the banner. "I call upon tennis lovers and men and women of good will and compassion to help Althea Gibson before it is too late," he wrote in a letter to the editor of *TennisWeek*, published on June 8, 1996. "[S]he's financially destitute and emaciated (barely 118 pounds on her 5'11" frame) and dispirited. She may not last much longer." He asked that contributions be sent to a post-office box that Angela had opened in East Orange on her behalf.

It was the second time an epistolary plea would change Althea's life. In 1950, former Wimbledon champion Alice Marble wrote an editorial in *American Lawn Tennis* magazine, wondering why a gifted Negro like Althea Gibson couldn't test her skills against the best amateurs at the U.S. Championships. This was three years after Jackie Robinson, four years before Rosa Parks. Blacks would apply to play in tournaments, and the tournaments would mysteriously be canceled. Or they'd be told that they didn't meet the proper criteria, though it was never explained precisely what that meant. It was a shell game, and the directors of country clubs throughout America were the con men. They would do what it took to ensure that no Negro set foot in the place.

Marble's editorial shamed the sport's hierarchy. The USLTA, which used the avoidance of controversy as an operating principle, was forced to reconsider. That September, at the age of twenty-three, Althea battled the reigning Wimbledon champion in a match that will be remembered for as long as anyone who saw it is alive. After that, no one could seriously consider keeping Althea Gibson out of any tournament. Yet it was the beginning of the hard road, not the end of it. She wouldn't win the title at Wimbledon or Forest Hills for another seven seasons.

Paul Fein's letter some forty-five years later tapped into the collective guilt of the wealthy whites, country-club Republicans and limousine-liberal Democrats, who populate the tennis community. They sent checks for fifty dollars, a hundred dollars, whatever it cost to buy a clear conscience. When checks started arriving in East Orange, Althea called Angela. She made it sound like an affront—how dare anyone meddle in her affairs?—but Angela knew she was grateful. Angela feigned ignorance, but Althea knew the truth, and Angela knew she knew. That's how they were together.

Drawn by the sudden attention being paid to Althea, someone made a film. It debuted at the U.S. Open in 1999, a chronicle of her life and times. By then, Venus Williams was winning tournaments. Althea's fame was dusted off and presented as the direct antecedent. She started to give the occasional interview. She bought a car and fixed her teeth. She'd go for a drive on Fridays, head down to the post office and pick up her mail. She was hopeful again. Her doubles partner had saved her.

NOW GO BACK FIFTY YEARS, to a warm afternoon in postwar London. Fifteen-year-old Angela Buxton leaves her school on Fitzjohn's Avenue, near Regent's Park, and steps onto the number 74 bus. She is headed for Queen's Club, a tennis facility across the Thames where she, a middle-class Jew, holds a membership. Unlike the other clubs in London in those days, Queen's doesn't care who you are or what level of tennis you play. The war has taken its toll on the economy. If you have the money, Queen's Club lets you in.

Angela has read in the newspaper that Althea Gibson is competing in the London Grass Court Championships, a tournament that serves as a warm-up to Wimbledon. Angela carries a backpack on the bus, which occasions some curious looks and even a few snickers; nobody but hobos wears backpacks in those days. She is traveling alone, which also marks her as peculiar, but she doesn't care. Already, she calibrates her pace to some inner rhythm.

She is interested in Althea because Angela is also a tennis player, a rangy girl with powerful strokes, though rather deficient in pure athleticism. Beyond that, she has been attuned to blacks since she lived in South Africa as a girl, waiting out the war with her mother and brother. She wondered then why everyone considered it a scandal that she brought home a black girl to be her playmate. Even now, she doesn't have an answer to that.

As a Jew at the convent school in Johannesburg, she was an outcast. In England, too, both blacks and Jews are perceived as irrevocably outside the norm of a white, Anglo-Saxon world. Now here is a black woman coming to play tennis against the whites at Wimbledon. That, thought Angela, is something to see.

Passing through the Queen's Club gate, she encounters a throng, or what passes for one at a tennis tournament in 1951. Spectators in shirtsleeves are standing three deep in some places, straining for a view. It is Althea, more a curiosity than anything else, playing her first-round match. Angela can't see a thing. She works her way toward the front and catches a glimpse. At first, she figures she must be mistaken, for surely this is a young man holding the ball on the baseline. Althea is wearing a sleeveless vest over a polo shirt. When she serves, her arms extend far above her head. She has an expression on her face of absolute stoicism; it is impossible to tell if she is winning or losing, excited or glum. She hits the ball like no female Angela has ever seen. Her arm emerges from the puffy clouds overhead and her serves fly over the net with alacrity, not the arcing, pitty-pat deliveries even the champions seem satisfied with on the newsreel.

She has not seen a black person this close since South Africa, and now Angela is transfixed. Althea Gibson is *different*. In form and substance, she is utterly unlike every other tennis player Angela has encountered. More than that, she is a celebrity. Angela has read about Althea, and now here she is: beads of sweat forming on her upper lip, moving like a cat as she comes to net to win the match. The prospect of using tennis to make a name for herself has never occurred to Angela, but it does now. She studies Althea coming off the court as if she is trying to memorize the scene in case someone tries to convince her later that it hadn't happened.

At the last moment, as Althea brushes past, Angela asks for an autograph. Althea turns toward her, a pen and paper materialize from somewhere, and the transaction is completed. The two women don't make eye contact, but Angela never forgets this moment. Althea, though, forgets it in the time it takes to work her way through the crowd.

FIVE YEARS LATER, these two outsiders teamed up to win the Ladies' Doubles competition at Wimbledon, which was as stuffy and pretentious—and traditional and prestigious—as tennis tournaments got.

Then their paths diverged. Injury ended Angela's career shortly after Wimbledon, and she channeled her ambition into fashion design, journalism, marriage, motherhood. Althea became a champion, the finest female tennis player in the world. She affiliated herself with the Globetrotters, playing tennis exhibitions before their games. She became a recording artist, a celebrity, a professional golfer. She lost all her money, even as Angela deftly managed hers.

They seemed to have less in common as time passed. They had come from dissimilar backgrounds and were living disparate lives. Yet Althea still stayed with Angela when she came to London. She enjoyed having a home away from her home, somewhere she could throw her clothes in the hallway without reproach and sing in the bathtub if she wanted to. Much later, once she had started coaching and resumed traveling to tournaments, Angela would place a call to East Orange before the U.S. Open each year, reestablishing contact, heralding her impending visit. They'd meet for an afternoon, watch the matches together, reminisce.

Such is the raw data of a friendship between two women, each singular in her own fashion, over the arc of fifty years. What began with an autograph request was turned on its end when Angela, perhaps quite literally, saved Althea's life. Time is the great equalizer, but their relative status along the way was not always as it must have seemed. From the beginning, Althea was the more renowned. Yet at Wimbledon in 1956, when they teamed to win the doubles in what would stand as the crowning achievement of Angela's life, it was Angela, not Althea, who advanced to play in the Ladies' Singles final that same day.

Althea would win five major singles titles, Angela none. Yet Angela and her family supported and even sponsored Althea, folding her into their home for weeks at a time. If we know about Angela today, it is because of her association with Althea. But if we remember Althea, it is due, in large part, to Angela, who beat the drums for her four decades later, reminding us of who she was and all she had accomplished.

Althea was among the most inscrutable of recent sports champions. She was difficult to know, harder to understand. Her accomplishments are set in type in the tennis annals and impossible to refute, yet those who saw her play offer conflicting assessments of her talents. Intimidating, athletic, the precursor of a new breed of female athlete, she languished in relative obscurity until the generation of talented players that preceded her had retired. In her middle twenties, an age at which most players are in their prime, she submitted an application to the army and almost gave up tennis for good.

Credited as being the first player to crack her sport's color line, she scorned such an achievement, refusing to be identified by her race. Sugar Ray Robinson bought her a high school ring, Joe Louis paid for a trip to England, the city of New York threw her two ticker-tape parades, countless Halls of Fame have inducted her as a member, yet to her dying day in 2003 she felt unappreciated as a tennis player. In her personal life, too, Althea was not always as she seemed. In her Fred Perry polo shirts on the court, she was often mistaken for a man, yet when crooning ballads at the Wimbledon ball in makeup and evening dress, she was a portrait of femininity. One of the most famous athletes in the world in her day, she had few close friends; with her life in the balance, she turned to her former doubles partner, whom she'd seen only a handful of times in decades. Lauded as an American hero, she has had no serious books written about her life except her own.

Those who knew her best often hardly knew her at all. "It's always been a fault of mine that I don't let many people get close to me, and not many of those people had any way of knowing what I was really like or what made me that way," she wrote in her autobiography, *I Always Wanted to Be Somebody*, published in 1957. Angela was an exception. Althea and Angela traveled together, played together, lived together. She referred to Violet Buxton, Angela's mother, as "Mom," and considered their apartment at Rossmore Court in London her second home. When Althea finally won the Ladies' Singles title at Wimbledon in 1957, after nearly a decade of frustration, she thanked Angela in her speech. "How could I forget my good friend and former partner Angela Buxton, whose friendship I shall always treasure?" she said. Then she added a postscript, in typical fashion: "Although she always forgets to bring the cold milk in, so that by the time I get up to drink it I really have warm milk. So, Angela, please, next time let's have the milk real cold, huh?"

That Althea was an African-American and Angela a Jew is not incidental. "The story of blacks and Jews was a story of mid-century America," Columbia University's Samuel G. Freedman wrote in the *New York Times* in 2003, "of alliances made in the Scottsboro Boys case, anti-lynching legislation, the creation of fair-employment commissions and, of course, the civil rights movement." He did not have in mind two tennis players, broadening and, in the process, enlightening this moderately popular sport, but he well might have. It was their status as outsiders that helped imbue Angela and Althea with the determination necessary to succeed, and that same status that ultimately brought them together as doubles partners. And though they played together during only a handful of tournaments in 1956, from the Paris indoors in February through Wimbledon in early July, the friendship that they formed colored the lives of each from then on.

Some objects are more profitably viewed obliquely than straight on. So it is with the sun, as reflected off the moon, and so it is with Althea Gibson. Unencumbered by the glare cast by latter-day mythologizers, her relationship with Angela limns her inner life in a way previously unseen.

CHAPTER 1

Althea

ALTHEA GIBSON was born in South Carolina, but at three years old she was bundled off to Harlem to live with her aunt Sally, who sold bootleg whiskey. That's the story as she tells it in *I Always Wanted to Be Somebody,* and we have no reason to doubt it. Althea's memory faded by the end; she was said to be unable to recall the details of a single tennis match she played. "I don't remember everything I did, or when, or how," she said in a lucid moment not long before her death. But there is enough verifiable fact already on the record to get us where we need to go.

She was born in Silver, South Carolina, on August 25, 1927, to parents Daniel and Annie. She weighed eight pounds. She spent much of her youth in Harlem with her younger brother and three sisters, and a couple of years in Philadelphia—most likely 1934 and 1935—with her aunt Daisy. This was not unusual at the height of the Great Depression. Families dispatched their children to live with relatives who still had work, and food to eat.

In Harlem, beginning in about 1936, Althea lived at 135 West 143rd Street, between Lenox and Seventh Avenues, in what are now called the Frederick E. Samuel Apartments. The brick is red from a new coat of paint, but in those days it was brown. Fire escapes run up the front of the building, as they did when Althea lived there.

She and her friend Alma Irving would spend hours at the playground shooting baskets, or at the Apollo Theater watching movies. School was hardly a priority. Althea would go truant for days at a time. She'd ride the subway all night rather than head home and face the whipping she knew would follow. Her mother would walk the streets at two in the morning, calling Althea's name. Her father couldn't control her, even when he used his fists. At one point, she spent a night at the Society for the Prevention of Cruelty to Children, on 105th Street, showing off welts on her back where her father had beaten her out of frustration. It wasn't his fault, she allowed; she just couldn't stay home. It wasn't drugs, or sex, or anything more serious than stealing fruit from the Bronx Terminal Market that kept her away. She had a restlessness in her soul.

Before the war, Harlem wasn't yet a slum. That happened later, when New York's outer boroughs opened up for blacks, and then suburbs, such as Mount Vernon in Westchester County, did. White flight from urban areas is well-chronicled, but plenty of blacks flew, too, the moment the cage door opened. Why wouldn't they leave the congestion of Harlem, the crumbling pavements, the rusted fire escapes where children would waste away steamy summer nights, if they could? Many of the wealthiest, the most successful, and the most creative abandoned Manhattan for, quite literally, greener pastures. Count Basie left for St. Albans, in Queens. Cab Calloway, too.

Harlem wasn't a slum in the 1930s and early 1940s, but it *was* a ghetto. It was insular, a world of its own. Like the Jewish ghettos of central Europe, it housed people of all economic strata. An entire sepia-toned cross-section of American life lived on the latticework of city blocks, from river to river, from about 110th Street up to 155th. There were millionaires on Sugar Hill and bums in the gutter. There were preachers and housepainters, small businessmen and card sharks. There were blacks up from the Caribbean and blacks from the American South, two wholly different categories of people that often regarded each other warily.

There's Joe Louis in a famous picture from 1935, striding down a Harlem sidewalk in a three-button camel's-hair coat, looking majestic. Down there on the left, wearing a leather jacket and high boots outside

his blousing pants, is the young Desmond Margetson, who had con-
nived to work his way to the front row of the assembled crowd as Louis
walked past and the photographer snapped, and now is grinning for
posterity like a madman. Margetson would later play tennis at New
York University and, in 1954, partner with Althea in a doubles tournament at the Seventh Regiment Armory. It isn't merely coincidence that
the same names emerge repeatedly at different points in this story. The
world was smaller in those days, and exceptional people found a way to
achieve—or at least to catch a glimpse of Joe Louis if that's what they
wanted. Margetson would surface again in 1957, when his engineer's mind
conjured up the idea for the tennis bubble, which covered an outdoor
court and enabled enthusiasts of all races to play in inclement weather.

Harlem had its own nightclubs, of course; those were famous. Whites
came uptown to see acts at the Apollo. But it also had good neighborhoods and bad neighborhoods, restaurants, clothing stores, art galleries,
even soda fountains like Spreen's, where black kids would squander a
nickel on an egg cream or chocolate soda, just as the white kids were
doing on the Lower East Side and in Brooklyn Heights.

In those days, government organizations took an active role in urban
life. Centralized solutions hadn't yet been discredited. The Police Athletic
League was empowered to close entire city blocks to traffic. Each summer,
it commandeered blocks all over Harlem and called them Play Streets.
There weren't many playgrounds in Upper Manhattan and even fewer
parks, so the pavement became stickball fields and hopscotch and paddle-
ball courts. Fire hydrants were routinely opened to keep kids cool. The
police, those benevolent peacekeepers, supplied all the equipment; all you
had to do was show up. It was like summer camp, except that you could
hear the mothers at their apartment windows, one after another calling
their children in to dinner.

The PAL regularly closed off a portion of 143rd Street. Althea wandered by one day and began to play paddle tennis, which utilized a short
wooden paddle and a rubber ball, like a Spaldeen. She was tall and
lanky, with long arms. Soon, if we are to believe what we hear, she was
winning match after match, holding the court until darkness fell, challenging all comers and never losing. She became the best player on the

block, and when the PAL matched their 143rd Street kids against those from the other Play Streets, she won nearly all those matches, too.

That talent at hitting the paddle ball would eventually manifest itself in a life in tennis. But for now, Althea was an athlete; any sport would do. At some point, her father began to give her boxing lessons, teaching her to duck a punch as well as to throw one. He was preparing her not merely for defending herself, but for a professional career. (That was before the sport of women's boxing was outlawed, though it has since been legalized again.) She played softball with the boys at Mount Morris Park on 121st Street. She played basketball in the schoolyards, and later, as womanhood approached, with an organized team called the Mysterious Five, which would compete against teams of female nurses and teachers and various other groups.

The girls of the Mysterious Five had known each other for years. Althea and Gloria Nightingale became friends in elementary school, and early on Nightingale introduced her to Bea Jenkins. Agnes Polite was a friend of a friend who joined them along the way. Adeline Matthews had been enrolled in the same junior high as Althea, P.S. 136; the difference was that Matthews bothered to attend class. Althea was almost never there. Her attitude was severe and simple. Nobody could make her do anything she didn't want to do.

Several times, early in her teenage years, Althea had confided to Matthews that life at home was difficult. Her father was strict and beat her when she misbehaved. Her siblings ran underfoot. The apartment was cramped, and Althea wanted desperately to be on the street, where life was actually taking place. At a certain point, her parents all but gave up on her. They didn't have the energy to keep fighting. She was fourteen years old when she graduated from junior high in 1941, not knowing how she managed such an accomplishment but pleased to have triumphed over the system. She headed off for a desultory attempt at vocational school, then soon stopped going altogether. She waited out the years until society would let her live on her own. She didn't know what her future held, but she was certain it was something more interesting than listening to teachers drone on for hours at a time about how to hem a dress. She wasn't averse to learning, just to sitting still.

Over time, the Mysterious Five came to be the most organized
aspect of her life. She may have been irresponsible in most other matters, squandering the coins her mother gave her for family groceries on
soft drinks and a hot dog for herself, but she never missed a basketball
game. The coach of the team was Marsden Burrell, and he also acted as
its sponsor. He bought uniforms with distinctive red-and-white shorts.
He booked the dates, at times four or five games in a week, against
teams from all over the city—most of them black, but some of them
white. He'd get the word out somehow, telling one of the girls to tell
another, and they'd gather. Win or lose, they'd repair to Spreen's afterward for a malt and a ham sandwich, which served as dinner. Then
Althea and Nightingale would usually go bowling, and the other girls
would head home. They didn't often visit each other's apartments; the
small walkups barely left room for families, let alone visitors.

As basketball players, these girls were sure of themselves. They
thought they could beat any women's team in the city, and probably
most of the men, too. Friends would come to see them play—it didn't
cost anything. The *Amsterdam News*, which served Harlem and the
remainder of New York's black community, would occasionally write up
the results. It never occurred to Althea or any of the others that all the
professional athletes they read about were white, and most of the college athletes, too. They were living in a cocoon, as teenagers often do.

Nightingale was the leader. She was the loudest, the one you had to
notice. She was forceful, full of braggadocio. A little shorter than the
others, a little stockier, perhaps the prettiest, depending on your taste.
She'd bring the ball up the court, shout out instructions, laugh the
loudest when something struck her as funny. Looking back, she's the
one you'd have picked to make a name for herself, on the force of that
personality. Or maybe you'd have picked Jenkins, a true tomboy who
had the most athletic ability on the team and led it in scoring. Not
Althea, anyway. So scrawny she looked almost emaciated at times,
those big eyes bugging out of her head, she could shoot the ball, and
she knew how to throw a fake and send a defensive player sprawling in
the wrong direction as she drove past. But she was just a schoolyard
basketball player transplanted to the indoor courts of the city, all

dressed up in striped shorts on a winter's night. There was no indication she'd ever be anything more.

After a while, Matthews noticed Althea trying to pattern herself after
Nightingale. Nightingale was a star in Althea's eyes, and Althea tried to
act like a star, too. She'd talk a little louder than before, bark out instructions. It was almost comical; she couldn't quite pull it off. At other times,
she was quiet and shy, almost moody. She'd have to be talked into going
to parties, and she sometimes went her own way when the crowd gathered at Spreen's. She cultivated her independence, remembers Billie
Davis, who was getting to know her in those days and would remain a
friend and tennis partner for decades. There was always part of her that
was antisocial, even in her own group.

At one point, after she'd turned eighteen, Althea moved into the
Nightingale family's apartment, paying nominal rent to a grandmother.
By then, she'd worked a sequence of jobs, from elevator operator at the
Dixie Hotel to waitress. She'd play basketball late into the night, then
go bowling with Nightingale until four in the morning. There was no
one to bother her if she came home late, or never came home at all. It
was, she'd later recall, one of the happiest times of her life.

LONG BEFORE THEN, blacks were playing tennis across America. They
were playing it at exclusive clubs and on city courts. They were playing
on campuses, competing intercollegiately for a black national championship, and in informal tournaments in small towns. But like so many
other aspects of American life at the time, black and white tennis
existed in parallel universes. Whites and blacks rarely stepped on the
same court together, and almost never with official sanction.

In 1916, Talley R. Holmes—Dartmouth, '10—founded the American
Tennis Association (ATA) as a governing body for black tennis. In an
idealistic leap, he called it the American Tennis Association and not the
Negro Tennis Association or the Colored Tennis Association. He had
the notion that enlightened whites ultimately would play under its auspices for a genuine national championship. It would be easier to get
whites to play in a black tournament, he figured, than to try to integrate
the existing white power structure. It never happened. Though the ATA

lingered on into the twenty-first century, it eventually faded into near oblivion, in large measure because Althea had rendered it redundant.

By 1917, the ATA was sponsoring national championships. The first event was held in Baltimore, and the men's singles tournament was won by Holmes, who was stationed on domestic soil while serving as an intelligence officer in the army. After World War I, Holmes returned to Washington and taught German, French, Latin, and math to high schoolers. He owned Washington's Whitelaw Hotel, the largest of its day to admit Negroes. He had the time, talent, and inclination to win ATA singles titles in 1918, 1921, and 1924, and eight doubles titles.

The ATA also held a women's championship in Baltimore in 1917. The winner was Lucy Diggs Slowe, a Howard graduate who would become the first dean of women at Howard in 1922. These were formidable people, achievers. Winning the 1917 ATA women's singles title made Slowe the first African-American woman to win a national title in any sport.

None of this had any impact on Althea Gibson, who was playing paddle ball on the asphalt of 143rd Street on hot summer days. She had never heard of Tally Holmes or Lucy Slowe, or any black tennis players at all. It is also difficult to imagine that she knew anything of substance about Bill Tilden, Fred Perry, Suzanne Lenglen, and Helen Wills, the dominant white players of the 1920s and 1930s. It wasn't like today, when you can watch a player on *SportsCenter* and then imitate him on a playground or a ball field. For Althea, tennis was something to compete at of an afternoon, after stickball and before basketball. Which game she was playing almost didn't matter. Teach her the rules—cards, pool, tackle football, or anything else—and she'd try her best to beat you. Most often, she did.

Her climb from that teenager playing stickball and paddle ball on the street to a Wimbledon champion was accomplished with the aid of a succession of patrons. It began in Harlem, with black men who took an interest in her as a potential talent and helped her climb the ladder. Getting by as a black in a white man's world wasn't easy under the best of circumstances, so those who had accomplished something often did what they could to lend a hand. They offered their time, their knowledge, and even their resources, meager as those might have been. Part of the motive was altruism, and part of it was projection. They lived in a time of limits and limitations; they wanted the next generation of African-Americans to have greater opportunities. Buddy Walker, a part-time bandleader and salaried recreational supervisor, was never going to be a world champion at anything, he well knew. But this young Althea Gibson he saw strutting along the sidewalks, whipping every girl and boy in the area in paddle tennis—well, she just might be.

Walker worked for the Police Athletic League by day and played music at night. Later he'd be almost famous, his band appearing at many prominent Harlem weddings, but at the time he still had to supplement his income supervising Play Streets. He saw Althea playing paddle tennis and admired her coordination and competitiveness. He couldn't help wondering how she'd fare at the real thing. So he purchased two used rackets from a secondhand shop, five dollars for the pair, and started hitting with her against the wall of the handball court at Morris Park. He liked the way she smacked the ball with everything she had, though her form was terrible. And why wouldn't it be? She had never seen a real tennis match before, just weekend players hacking around at the Harlem River Courts on 150th Street.

Walker talked her into walking the seven blocks to the courts to play a real match. It was no easy feat. Nobody was going to tell her what to do, especially not a figure of authority. She made her way there on her own time, but she eventually arrived. Buddy set her up on one side of the net and stationed himself on the other. Soon she was keeping the ball in play for long rallies, and even winning some points.

It was an impressive exhibition for someone who had never played the game before. One of the men watching her there, Juan Serrall (or perhaps Serrell), took an immediate interest. Serrall was a schoolteacher and a friend of Walker's. Walker could get Althea off 143rd Street, but Serrall could get her out of the neighborhood. He knew members at the Cosmopolitan Club, at Convent and 149th on Sugar Hill, where the one-armed tennis pro Fred Johnson made his living giving lessons. Serrall delivered her to Johnson and disappeared from the story, having played out a small but critical role.

Years later, in the ABC television series *The Fugitive*, a different one-armed Fred Johnson would bear the guilt for the murder of Helen Kimble, the wife of a Stafford, Indiana, pediatrician. The name of our one-armed Fred Johnson adorns the tennis courts at 150th Street, the Cosmopolitan Club being long gone. As a young teenager, Johnson lost an arm in a factory accident, yet he gravitated toward teaching tennis. His playing technique was impressive to watch. He'd hold the racket in his only hand—and the ball there with it. He'd manage to toss the ball skyward, then swat at it on its way back down. He didn't have a second hand to balance the racket while he rotated it a quarter-turn to hit a backhand, so he used a Continental grip, which stayed the same no matter which face of the racket you were using. That's what he knew, and that's what he taught, so that's what Althea learned.

The Cosmopolitan Club consisted of five clay courts and a club-house. Every so often, a famous white player would pass through and play an exhibition there. But for the most part, the Cosmopolitan was New York's center of black tennis, the only place in town for serious black players to play. It was run, in large measure, by Caribbean-Americans, from islands like Barbados and Trinidad and St. Kitts, and had a certain colonial air. Perhaps that explains the popularity of cricket and tennis among the members. Harlem's social elite filled its halls and its courts, but courts could also be rented by the hour by nonmembers if they weren't in use. The club had a junior program, and occasionally money was raised to send promising junior members to ATA events across the country.

Des Margetson was there the day Althea arrived and remembers seeing a marvelous athlete who had no idea how to hit the ball. Her shots were far from sound, but her timing was so good that it hardly mattered. Her ability to run like a sprinter and belt the ball over the net with such force, to leap high and cut off lobs or turn tail and run them down deep in the backcourt, impressed everyone who saw it. Almost instantly, the club decided to sponsor her. They paid for her membership, bought her rackets. From being underprivileged, she became privileged, at least in comparison with the other young players who were on the outside looking in. In return, Althea helped out retrieving balls, laundering towels, that kind of thing. She was happy to do it. She had barely heard of Forest Hills, let alone Wimbledon. In her world, the Cosmopolitan Club was the big time.

In 1944, two years later, Alice Marble played an exhibition match at the Cosmopolitan Club. She and Bob Ryland, a future ATA champion, were matched against Reginald Weir and England's Mary Hardwick, a formidable player who had advanced to the Wimbledon quarterfinals before the war. These were genuinely mixed doubles, with a white and a black on each side of the court. Years later, Marble would write the letter that gained Althea entrance into the U.S. Championships, but in those days she was simply the finest female player in the world. She was blond and trim, the picture of femininity, but she played the game like a man. She socialized like a man, too, drinking and smoking with impunity. Over a cocktail at the Cosmopolitan Club bar, a small victory for race relations in itself, she asked Ryland about this young Gibson girl she'd heard about from various members of the club. That discussion evolved into the beginnings of a plan to get Althea or another black player into Forest Hills. It wouldn't come to pass for six years.

For her part, Althea had never seen a woman play tennis so well. "I can still remember saying to myself, Boy would I like to be able to play tennis like that!" she wrote in her autobiography. It was the same reaction that fifteen-year-old Angela Buxton would have seven years later, watching Althea play at Queen's Club.

IT CERTAINLY WASN'T athletic ability keeping African-Americans from playing championship tennis in the mid-1940s, nor even a lack of exposure to the game. Public courts were numerous, perhaps more numerous than today. But adequate coaches were scarce. "There were no truly great teachers, or places to go to get a first-class tennis education, with due respect to Fred Johnson," Margetson remembers.

It was fine that Johnson used the Continental grip; England's Fred Perry had won Wimbledon with it in the '30s. But Johnson hadn't mastered the techniques necessary to generate any power in the forehand. There was no torque on his balls, no muscle, no spin. The truth was, Johnson himself had never taken a lesson. He'd go to tournaments, watch some of the better players, take mental notes, but he wasn't really seeing what he had to see. Althea became good enough, but later she'd have to unlearn almost everything technical that Fred Johnson taught her.

Even so, she progressed quickly. Johnson taught her rudimentary strokes, but he also taught her to learn from her mistakes. Each time she lost a match, she tried to figure out why, instead of threatening to slug the winner in the mouth, which is what she was tempted to do. Pure athleticism went a long way in tennis then, as it does today, and Althea was able to chase down shots and get them back with power. Her speed and range made her one of the better players at the club before long. In the summer of 1942, when she was almost fifteen and had been playing tennis for about a year, she entered the New York State Open Championship in the junior division.

The event was sponsored by the ATA and held at the Cosmopolitan Club. It was largely black, though not entirely so: a white girl named Nina Irwin was also entered as a junior. Irwin's mother, a Russian immigrant, had learned tennis from Johnson at the 143rd Street Armory years before, and now Nina was traveling each week to the Cosmopolitan Club from Inwood, near Fort Tryon Park at the top of Manhattan, for lessons. She was welcomed there, and not merely because the Irwins paid their bill on time. Members were proud to think that their club was truly cosmopolitan.

Irwin was a friendly girl with a sunny smile, but she longed to beat Althea, the emerging standout in their age group. As it happened, they each advanced to the tournament final. Althea won it easily, her first significant victory. It tasted all the sweeter because she perceived that many of the Cosmopolitan Club members watching from the grandstand had been rooting for Irwin, though Althea was black and Irwin was white. In fact, Althea would spend her entire career believing that the spectators on hand were mostly against her—and, in many cases, they were. Sometimes it happened because of her skin color, but often it was caused by the confidence bordering on arrogance that infused both her play and her body language. It made a neutral observer want to see her defeated.

Even as a teenager, Althea wanted to win her matches more than anyone she knew. It showed in how she behaved on the court, especially after losing a match. More than once, Johnson cautioned her to subdue her histrionics and act like a lady. In that amateur era, tennis wasn't taken as seriously as it would be later, with millions of dollars on the line. It was a pastime, not a livelihood. The finest players were future doctors, lawyers, and other professionals, and they played as an avocation, between their work and their studies. This held true for blacks even more than for whites, who could at least grow up fantasizing about Wimbledon. Blacks knew they weren't going far, so they cast their ambitions in other directions. Weir, who played for City College of New York, won five ATA titles between 1931 and 1942 while studying to be a dentist. Margetson, the future engineer, went on to captain the NYU tennis team. He wouldn't have traded his college education for the chance to be the finest tennis player in the world. "Tennis, unlike the true professions, is not a college-degree subject," he said. It was an engaging game, but a game nonetheless.

It did help integrate society. Every mixed-race match struck a small blow for equality and open-mindedness. Margetson played against whites as a high schooler at DeWitt Clinton, and he did it again at NYU. Sonny Jackson played in the Eastern Scholastics against whites, winning some matches. One can easily imagine the sons of New York's privileged getting their first real exposure to Negroes at such tournaments and realizing they had more in common with these burgeoning preprofessionals than they ever realized.

Still, most of the United States Lawn Tennis Association's tournaments, including the U.S. Championships at Forest Hills—also called the U.S. Nationals, and the precursor to today's U.S. Open—were held at private clubs that excluded blacks by fiat. The effect this had on black tennis was deadening. Ora Mae Washington, born in 1898, won eight ATA titles and went undefeated in ATA events from 1924 to 1936, when not playing on a barnstorming black basketball team called the Philadelphia Tribunes to earn a living. She was a phenomenon, possibly one of the most talented tennis players in the world for as long as a decade, and undoubtedly among the most successful in terms of tournaments won. Yet she was unable to test her talents against the finest players of the day under championship conditions. She was black, and they were white.

ON THE OTHER SIDE OF THE WORLD, the democratic precept of the fundamental equality of all men and women was faring even worse. In the newly independent Union of South Africa, the official languages remained English and the Dutch variant of Afrikaans, though the vast majority of citizens spoke neither one. Blacks, Cape Coloureds, and Indians, grouped together as nonwhites, were stricken from that country's voting rolls and denied basic liberties, such as the right to travel freely between towns or attend schools, or even to emigrate to a better life. A tiny percentage of land was set aside for them, though they far outnumbered the former colonials.

At the same time, immigration was limited to those who would easily assimilate into the white minority population. That description didn't include Jews of any color. They were legally barred from entering South Africa with an intent to stay, as the Buxton family was strictly warned when it arrived by steamer from Liverpool in 1940 with Europe already at war.

Violet and Gordon Buxton with Angela

CHAPTER 2

"Put Her in Tournaments"

During the middle months of 1940, as U-boats plied the trade routes of the Atlantic and the possibility of a German invasion drove some English families to the countryside and even into exile, South Africa existed as an idyll, a world of its own. Under the warmth of the afternoon sun, a small girl with skin colored like coffee with cream took to playing in an alleyway off St. John's Road in Cape Town, behind a house of stone and stucco. The house was situated at the end of a steep street that led up the back slope of Table Mountain, a panoramic spot. You could see the Indian Ocean from the yard, and that majestic, cloud-shrouded landmark loomed out the back door.

The girl's mother worked as a domestic at one of the bigger houses on Ocean View Drive, and her family may have even lived there, in the servants' quarters of some grand white man's residence. One day the girl had materialized, as if by magic, in back of the house that Violet Buxton had contracted to rent on a monthly basis for herself and her children. After that she was waiting each afternoon when young Angela, who was almost exactly the same age, returned from the day school she was attending. The girl had long black hair that she wore very straight. She had bloodlines going back to the Indian subcontinent. Angela wore pigtails and ribbons in her light-brown hair. The girls would skip and play hopscotch together outside the Buxtons' kitchen door until sunset, as six-year-olds are wont to do.

This happened only a few times before a neighbor stopped by with advice. White children in South Africa didn't socialize with Cape Coloureds, she told Violet. Perhaps in England it might be done, but not in this part of the world. "Do not encourage this friendship," the woman said. "Stop the two girls from playing together now."

Violet Buxton was only five-foot-two, but very feisty. She had a stubborn streak that bordered on the contrary. Tell her not to do something, and she was all but certain to do it. But living as a single mother, with a husband two continents away, she wasn't prepared for a battle. Her life was difficult enough in South Africa without making enemies. She had sailed south from England with her son and daughter, temporary exiles seeking a safe haven to wait out the war. They spent the journey terrified that the U-boats would sink their ship, then arrived in the midst of the chilly Cape winter and promptly fell ill with a strain of pneumonia. As Jews, they were welcome in South Africa only on a temporary basis. They were unwanted guests required to leave the moment the hostilities ceased back home—or before that, if the government decided to evict them. Their standing was nothing if not precarious.

Accordingly, Violet had no appetite for trouble. She warned Angela not to see the girl again. She's not like we are, Violet said, and that offends certain people here. We're guests and we have to abide by their rules. Ever the obedient daughter, Angela nodded, but she was crestfallen. It had never occurred to her that skin color might have anything to do with friendship.

HARRY BUXTON had sent his family to South Africa to escape the buzz bombs that would soon be plummeting from the sky, and perhaps to mend a ruptured marriage. Though he loved Violet and adored his children, Angela and Gordon, he wasn't meant to be a husband. He couldn't stay still. Home meant a suitcase in a hotel room, usually in the best hotel in town. Later, once his money had multiplied, he'd maintain a suite at the Grosvenor Park in London, another at the Hotel de Paris in Monte Carlo, and one behind the gilded facade of the Midland Hotel in Manchester, right off St. Albans Square.

The marriage to Violet had been on the verge of disintegrating. Now husband and wife were thousands of miles apart and getting along far better by writing letters than they had face to face. Harry remained in England, a burgeoning entertainment mogul: dashing here and darting there, adding movie theaters to his growing empire, and regularly mailing out money orders to Violet, who was now on the move herself. She and the children left Cape Town for rural life in the Little Karoo, then journeyed on to Johannesburg, searching for a climate that wouldn't exacerbate Gordon's asthma. By then, seven-year-old Angela had come to understand that some people were considered different. Her school in Johannesburg was attached to a convent, and she was one of the few Jews enrolled; they'd stand outside in the hallway during prayers, talking quietly.

The Buxtons lived in a bed-and-breakfast, sharing a bathroom at the end of a hall with other guests. Violet took her time doing her hair in front of the mirror; preening a bit, if truth be told. It was hardly egregious, and she needed some diversion. She usually left the door open to assuage the stifling heat, and once the wrong man walked past. He looked at her disapprovingly, as if he'd come across a wild animal in heat. "You bloody Jews, you're all alike," he said. This time, she didn't hesitate. She slapped him hard with the comb, then told the children to start packing. They were gone that night.

Young and attractive, Violet wasn't about to wait out the war alone. She might have had a tacit agreement with Harry that she could see other men—or not. It hardly mattered; they were miles apart and on uncertain terms. She began dating a man named Bennie Tessel. He was unattractive but extraordinarily generous to an exiled family that felt disconnected from the dauntingly different city in which they'd arrived. And he was Jewish, which made them feel comfortable. They celebrated the same holidays, ate the same food. It was a vestige of home.

Tessel kept a country estate outside Johannesburg where he'd often bring the three of them on a weekend afternoon. He had blacks working there, and he treated them as though they were animals. He'd literally play with them in the same way you might train your puppy. Go on, into the corner, he'd say, expecting them to get down on hands and knees and crawl there. And they would do it. It was the oddest thing, the Buxtons thought. He'd loom over them and pretend to kick them as though they were disobedient dogs. Stay in the corner, he'd say, looking stern. That's where you belong. And then Bennie Tessel would let out a roaring laugh, and whichever laborer happened to be folded against the wall at the moment would laugh, too. It was just Bennie, playing his games. He didn't mean any harm. He gave them work, which was hard to come by with the trade routes blocked and the economy failing, and he fed them well. But Angela, watching this play out from across the room, was sickened. She couldn't reconcile it with the gentle way he treated her.

Violet sat her down and spoke to her like an adult. "We don't condone it," she said, "but we won't rock the boat." Violet figured the war would be ending soon. She refused to follow the example the white South Africans were setting, but she didn't want to make trouble. They were Jewish, and life was hard enough. Keep your head down, don't get noticed, don't get involved. For Jews during wartime, especially, those were words to live by.

ON JULY 19, 1891, Charles deVille Wells spent eleven hours at the roulette table at a Monte Carlo casino and parlayed a 100,000-franc holding into more than twice its value. He nurtured his winnings and eventually had another run of luck, which netted him a million francs. At that point, the casino ran out of chips and temporarily closed. Later that year, composer Fred Gilbert wrote a song about Wells that was sung all around England, in the music halls that were fashionable at the time:

> As I walk along the Bois Bolog' with an independent air
> You can hear the girls declare
> He must be a millionaire
> You can hear them sigh and wish to die
> You can see them wink the other eye
> At the man who broke the bank in Monte Carlo

The renowned performer Charles Coborn, whose real name was Colin McCallum, debuted the song at the Trocadero in London. It became wildly popular around the British Isles, and later in the United

States. It was a song for the parlor-room piano; assembled friends and family were urged to sing along. Everyone knew the lyrics, but the story that inspired it had faded into obscurity.

Decades after Wells, Harry Buxton broke the bank at a casino in Nice, just up the coast from Monte Carlo. The date is uncertain, but it must have been around 1928, two years before he would propose to Violet Greenberg. He won so much playing roulette that the casino laid black velvet over the tables and closed its doors until additional chips could be procured. The song followed Buxton for the rest of his life. People around Manchester, where he eventually cut quite a profile, came to believe it must have been written about him, though it had been popular more than a generation before. It fit his precariously glamorous lifestyle so well: *I to Monte Carlo went/Just to raise the winter rent/And I've now such lots of money I'm a gent.* They could envision Harry Buxton thinking just that way.

He was no longer a salesman on the make from a low-class family of Orthodox Jews in Leeds, standing on a crate in the marketplace, hawking whatever he could to get by. He was smart and ambitious, and the run of luck in Nice had brought him a small fortune. He made the most of it. He briefly traded in the stock market, segued into jewelry, then found his niche in the entertainment industry. He bought movie theaters in Manchester and beyond, all over the north of England. He bought the Gaiety in downtown Manchester, and the famed Royale, erected in 1845, which stood directly across the street. He'd stride over from his suite at the Midland, stand off to the side, watch the crowds file in one theater and then the other, count profits in his head.

When *Gone With the Wind* came to England in 1940, Harry felt he was in a position to capitalize. This maudlin love story set in the distant American South provided an ideal respite from a world at war. But the three-hour film, which had cost a fortune to make, arrived loaded with egregious taxes. The taxes were so high that the agency representing the cinema exhibitors flatly refused to book it. They were making a stand. Harry shrugged and ordered the film for the Gaiety: an extraordinary decision, and not merely because he was arousing the ire of the exhibitors' association. For a movie of such renown (ten Oscars, including Best Picture) to open in the provinces before it had been seen by Londoners would be peculiar even today. At the time, it was scandalous. The representative of the association called Harry and threatened to dispatch picketers to Manchester. They would parade around the theater in sandwich boards labeling him unpatriotic. "How many picketers are you planning to send?" Harry asked. Told that it might be as many as half a dozen, he asked them to make it twelve. He understood that the publicity from such a scene would attract intense interest, and so it did. The picketers came, and then the crowds. Harry played the film for an entire year, until most of Manchester had seen it twice.

At times, Harry was the embodiment of the cartoonish Jew. He was the loudest man in the room everywhere he went. He was ostentatious and made money easily. He had none of the reserve that characterized most Englishmen. If he saw a friend on the other side of the street, he'd cross it to greet him. "How're your bowels?" he'd bellow, loud as a foghorn. After the war, he would buy a white, chauffeur-driven Rolls-Royce that had belonged to Queen Wilhelmina of Holland and still had her crest on the door. The car would ease up to the exclusive Church Road entrance at Wimbledon when Angela was playing. Harry would wave confidently from the back seat and be let on through, though he was the furthest thing from anyone they'd allow to be a member. Such harmless hoaxes were part of his nature, but he also played loose with the truth when reporting his annual income to the Inland Revenue. When Angela began to make a little money, she would be viewed with intense suspicion by the tax authorities because she was Harry Buxton's daughter. She must be hiding something, they'd figure. The apple doesn't fall far from the tree.

Harry wasn't suited for Violet from the start. That was clear to anyone who knew them. He was an irresistible force and Violet an immovable object, and they clashed on almost every issue. Neither would take a subordinate role in the relationship. But she was almost an old maid when he proposed to her, all of twenty-four, and her father urged her to accept. Here was this man of means who wanted to marry her, and she was being choosy. How many more chances did she think she would get?

Violet had her flings in Africa, Bennie Tessel and some others. But when she and the children returned to England in May of 1946, they moved with Harry to a rented house in Sussex. They'd left a man with pretensions, but in the intervening years he'd become a VIP. Days prior to their arrival, he bought the pier at Bogner Regis, on the other side of the English coast, near Brighton, which is like someone purchasing the Atlantic City boardwalk. Actually, he bought the right to build a new pier, for the old one was gone. It had been destroyed by English troops to help thwart a potential German invasion. England did that with all its piers, all along the coast. The idea was to make a landing more difficult for the enemy troop ships and U-boats if they stormed the shore. With the war over, the government sold the rights to rebuild the piers to private individuals for a pittance. It was the quickest and most efficient way to get them rebuilt. In April of 1946, Harry purchased the rights for Bogner Regis, then built a new pier with a white clapboard music hall and started booking some of the top acts in England.

The reconciliation with Violet only lasted a few weeks. She couldn't stand him being away so much, and liked it even less when he was home. She threatened to expose his secrets to the tax collectors unless he agreed to a divorce. In the end, nobody seemed terribly upset about it except sixteen-year-old Gordon, who was just old enough to see his world coming apart. That July, just two months after arriving back in the United Kingdom, Violet and the children moved to bucolic North Wales, where her parents had fled from Liverpool during the war. Harry stayed behind to mind his empire.

IN JOHANNESBURG, Angela had picked up tennis. She was tall, well on the way to the five-foot-nine she would reach as an adult, and aggressive compared to the proper South African girls. By the time she was eleven, in 1945, she was getting instruction from the national coach, George Demasius, who also served as the South African correspondent for *American Lawn Tennis* magazine. International competition had ceased during wartime and he had little to do. He'd come to their little convent school and give lessons to any girls who wanted them. As a result, when she returned to England the following year, Angela was a far better player than her peers, most of whom had barely played the game.

England had all but abandoned tennis during the war, which had lasted for more than half the sentient lives of these twelve-year-olds. Indoor courts were bombed or requisitioned, while outdoor courts had fallen into disrepair. The Championships at Wimbledon's All England Croquet and Lawn Tennis Club hadn't been played since 1939. Rackets and balls and nets were deemed superfluous to the war effort, so their manufacture was halted. By 1946, few remained in any useable form.

Violet's parents in North Wales had a four-bedroom semi-detached house. There was a public tennis court directly opposite, but nobody ever used it. Instead, Angela would play tennis alone against the rough, pebbled wall of the house, using the rose hedge to approximate a net, hitting a ball for hours. Sometimes she'd hit the rose bushes, and her grandfather would come out and scold her. He believed that a young woman should be reading books, not soiling her clothes with sweat. That fall Violet sent Angela to Gloddeath Hall, a boarding school near the English border, an hour from Liverpool. Each week, she'd get thirty minutes of tennis lessons, shared with another girl. Tennis balls were hard to come by, and many coaches had turned to other work, or hadn't come back from the war intact or even alive. Half an hour a week was all that could be managed.

She was a weekly boarder, and she'd go home each Sunday to spend a day with her mother and brother, then return that evening for tennis. A coach named Bob Mulligan would travel in from Liverpool and hit balls at the two of them, one after another. There was little talk and almost no instruction. Half an hour and it would be over, and then she'd wait until the following weekend to do it again. But Angela showed promise. Eventually, Mulligan informed Violet that her daughter had talent for the game, and she needed to do something about it. This flummoxed her.

"Like what?" she said.

"Put her in tournaments."

"Like Wimbledon?" She wasn't being flip; it was the only tennis tournament she knew.

"No, not Wimbledon. In junior tournaments. Not here, but 'round where I live."

Near Liverpool, on England's west coast, a series of tournaments were held every summer. They were just starting up again after the war. As it happened, Violet had a sister in Southport, which was the end of the line for the Liverpool train and not far from Mulligan's home. Mulligan offered to meet up with her on the train each day and travel with her to the various events.

The following summer, 1947, Angela went to Southport for three weeks, one to train and two to play. Having not hit a ball in a month, she showed up rusty. Everyone was eager to see this potential champion Mulligan had been talking up. She tossed a serve, missed it entirely, felt an utter fool. But she rallied. She played 18-and-under events against ranked players, but she'd get a handicap. In one match, she started off each game up 40–0, which is like beginning each inning of a baseball game with a man already on third. Soon she was beating some of her opponents without the handicap. With it, she was unstoppable. She won both tournaments she entered.

Violet came to visit for the week in the middle, and they stayed at a fancy hotel. By then, Angela was entertaining the idea that she was rather good at tennis. She was eager to show off for her mother, who had never seen her play. She acted condescending on the court, hardly deigning to pick up the balls; she figured it was the way champions carried themselves. Violet was mortified. "If you ever behave like that again on the court, I'm walking right out and getting you," she said.

Like Althea, Angela had no role models and no sense of the history of the sport. Because of the war, England hadn't fielded a national tennis team for seven years. A generation of players—in sports terms—had come and gone. For the same reason, the country's coaches and tennis administrators had little idea which young players might have potential. To find out, Dan Maskell, the national coach, was dispatched around the country with former Wimbledon champion Fred Perry, an English icon. They traveled by train throughout England, Scotland, Wales, and Northern Ireland, looking for future standouts. Perhaps because of her summer success, Angela found herself invited to one of these siftings, as they were being called. It was in Colwyn Bay, Wales, a tourist town. Like the rest of the hopefuls, Angela hit briefly with

Maskell as Perry manned the microphone and observed. Afterward, she heard nothing for months. Then word came that she was among several dozen who had been invited to show their skills in a grand sifting at Wimbledon.

She traveled by bus to London, her ambition making her heart pound the entire way. She had never seen Wimbledon, much less played there. (The sifting was held on courts adjacent to the All England Club, but Angela figured that it counted as Wimbledon, nonetheless.) She toured the grounds, spent time hitting, but it was quickly evident that she didn't have the natural talent that some did. These were the best of the best, after all. She was given a hearty handshake and a sincere thanks, then sent back to "her little corner of the world," as she thought of it, where she tried to put tennis out of her mind. She commenced studying for her school certificate, which she duly passed.

It gave her no joy. She remained resolutely uninterested in schoolwork. She couldn't help it, she said to herself. Talented or not, she wanted to play tennis.

HARRY BUXTON was constantly on the move, one city to the next. Occasionally, he'd stop by for a family visit, and they'd all take a drive. One day, he and Violet rumbled off to discuss Angela's future. Harry proposed sending her to Switzerland for finishing school, which would give her the polish and poise that few Jews of her generation had been able to obtain. Violet didn't think that was a bad idea—funny how they got along so well now that they were apart—but remarked that Angela wanted only to hit tennis balls, hour after hour. To her surprise, Harry didn't object. "I'm told you meet some nice people in tennis," he said. He was thinking of Hollywood and leisurely matches he'd read about, as played by the likes of Charlie Chaplin and Katharine Hepburn. As usual, he had stars in his eyes.

Harry didn't know a thing about the game. He couldn't even keep score and never bothered to learn. Sitting at Wimbledon in 1956, watching his daughter play in the singles and doubles finals, he'd lean over to her boyfriend at the time and ask how the match was progressing. He could see the scoreboard as clearly as anyone else, but he couldn't decipher whether she was winning or losing.

He did know that if a daughter of Harry Buxton wanted to play tennis, she would have the opportunity to do it right. It was decided that Gordon would come and live with Harry, while Violet and Angela would move to London, which afforded far more opportunity for tennis instruction than anyplace else in England. Angela would attend a year of school there, to learn to cook if nothing else, and play all the tennis she could. Harry would pay for everything. The idea thrilled Violet, who saw it as a new start, and when Angela heard, she was beyond joy. Lying in bed that night, she decided that she had the most wonderful parents, even if they happened to be divorced. Her mother looked after her like a baby, and her father paid for it all.

Violet and Angela alighted at 97 Rossmore Court, NW1, near the Baker Street tube stop, little realizing that Angela would live there for the most memorable decade of her life. She was fifteen that summer of 1950, about to turn sixteen in August. She wanted to be finished with school, but Violet wouldn't allow it; that was part of the deal. Violet found her a small, private academy in Hampstead run by the mother of a national skating champion.

Gladys Lyne Jepson-Turner, known as Belita, had a long run as the featured attraction in the Ice Capades, then turned to movies. She would appear in *Invitation to the Dance* in 1956, and *Silk Stockings* in 1957. Her career gave her mother's school a certain cachet. Mrs. Jepson-Turner's school, called Queens House, looked like the setting of a Dickens novel. It was dark and foreboding, with a chimney that often blocked the sun. There was a decrepit tennis court in the back that was too far gone to use, but Mrs. Jepson-Turner promised to make arrangements nearby. It was part of the curriculum of the school that athletes and artists were able to practice on school time. Skaters could skate, painters could paint, dancers could dance, and Angela could play her tennis.

Mrs. Jepson-Turner wore a feather boa and reeked of perfume. She carried herself with an artistic air, as if she couldn't be bothered with details. But, true to her word, she worked out a deal with a teaching pro at the Cumberland Club, several blocks away. Three times a week, she drove Angela to the club, a stream of ostrich feathers flying out of the car each time she rolled down the window to signal for the left turn at the top of the hill. She waited in the car until the hour was up and the instruction over, then drove Angela back to school.

From the outside, the Cumberland Club looked like a tenement house. Though it backed against the Hampstead Cricket Club and its fields of billiard green, it had peeling paint and a tiny, faded sign. Inside, however, the Cumberland Club was quite posh. At the time, it was the best tennis club in North London, and it arguably remains that today, though it has barely received a new coat of paint in the intervening years. Bill Blake, the coach at the Cumberland Club, was a charmer in white flannel pants. He welcomed this young player who seemed to have some promise, and, after a few lessons, gave her an application to join the club. She filled it out: name, address, parents' names, religion, all the details. Weeks passed, and nobody mentioned her status. Others would have let it pass, but it was Angela's nature to probe and push.

Each time she stepped inside the club for a lesson, several days each week, she inquired about her application. Am I going to join? Have they had a committee meeting? Am I suitable? Finally, Bill Blake couldn't stand it any longer. "Look, you'll never make it," he told her.

"Why not? Aren't I good enough?"

"You're perfectly good, but you're Jewish," he hissed. "We don't take Jews here."

Back in the car, Mrs. Jepson-Turner was more exercised than Angela. She couldn't believe that such prejudice existed in postwar London, especially after everything the Jews had suffered. She wanted to write a letter, make a fuss. Angela told her not to bother. "I've other clubs in mind," she said airily.

Several times in the years that followed, Angela would win the London championships, played at the Cumberland Club. She never failed to remind them that she was Jewish. And years later, her son Joseph Silk umpired a tournament there that happened to be held during Passover. They handed him the requisite meal tickets for lunch and tea, but he turned them down. "I'm Jewish," he said, well aware of how such words would resonate inside those walls. "I have my own matzoh."

THAT FOLLOWING JUNE OF 1951, just as the spring term was ending at Queens House, Angela read in the newspapers that Althea Gibson was coming to Queen's Club. She pulled on her backpack and a boater hat and made the trip to see her. In the nine years following Althea's first tournament, when she'd beaten Nina Irwin in that interracial match at the Cosmopolitan Club in 1942, she had gained a measure of fame. But she was still considered more of a novelty act than a champion. She hadn't won anything, still hadn't even played at Wimbledon. She was famous because of what she represented, not for anything she had managed to accomplish.

Althea's journey from the Cosmopolitan Club to Queen's Club had begun with the Irwin match in the summer of 1942. Buoyed by her success, the wealthier members of the Cosmopolitan Club had pooled their resources and sent her by bus to the ATA's national championships that August. They were held that year an hour's drive outside Philadelphia, at Lincoln University. It was an act of faith, for nobody knew how good she might actually be. She had only been taking lessons with one-armed Fred Johnson for a year.

At Lincoln, Althea advanced to the girls' final before losing to a promising player named Nana Davis. No championships were held the following summer, because of war travel restrictions, but by the time they resumed in 1944, Althea had emerged as the best female among all ATA juniors. She still had received no formal instruction beyond Johnson's flawed pointers; still positioned her feet incorrectly when striking the ball; still had scant sense of court strategy, still chased down balls with a frenzied gait. But she retrieved so well, served so hard, and advanced to net in such intimidating fashion, none of it mattered. She was a formidable athlete, and she played each match with the insouciance of someone slapping a paddleball on 143rd Street. She won the ATA junior championship in 1944, and again in 1945.

During the year that followed, she would meet three more men of means who would guide her toward opportunities. All her life, Althea was able to entice others into taking an interest in her. She exuded something compelling. Without expectations, she carried herself as if she had little to lose, was afraid of no one, ashamed of nothing, though she never tried to hide her naïveté. There was a ferocious honesty to everything she did, a lack of artifice that contrasted sharply with the well-mannered reserve cultivated by many Southern-bred, churchgoing black women of her generation, even those whose families had migrated north. Some of those whose lives intersected Althea's ended up offended, for such honesty was polarizing. To others, it came off as immensely appealing.

CHAPTER 3

Help from Her Friends

IN THOSE DAYS, Althea carried herself with great bravado. When she met boxer Ray Robinson for the first time during the winter of 1945–46, she couldn't help informing him that she was the defending ATA champion among female 18-and-unders, while he was a mere *contender* for the welterweight title. Robinson had fought professionally since 1940, and had been anointed the Fighter of the Year in 1942 by the prestigious *Ring* magazine, but he wouldn't win his first championship until the following December, when he whipped Tommy Bell.

Still, everyone in Harlem knew Robinson and his wife, Edna. Born Walker Smith Jr. in Ailey, Georgia, in 1921, he'd been moved to Detroit while still an infant, then on to midtown Manhattan with his mother and sister after his parents divorced. Eventually, the fragmented family gravitated to Harlem, where Smith started boxing under the tutelage of the Salem-Crescent Athletic Club's George Gainford, and the Ray Robinson name.

At the time, boxing was one of the few sports in which blacks could compete on an equal basis with whites. It had been that way since Jack Johnson defeated Jim Jeffries to win the heavyweight title in Reno, Nevada, on July 4, 1910, the first "fight of the century" in a century that ultimately would offer up maybe a dozen. Unlike the best black baseball, basketball, and tennis players, black boxers such as Joe Louis were not merely the Negro champions, they were world champions.

Althea's achievements meant little in comparison, and not only because she was still competing as a junior. Tennis just wasn't on the radar screen in Harlem. She was getting more attention locally for paddleball, basketball, even tackle football. Tennis required rackets and new balls, and a permit to use city courts, which could cost as much as two dollars a season, a formidable sum. The sport was an abstract concept for someone living in Harlem in 1945, not a recreational reality. Aside from Cosmopolitan Club members and habitués of the few public courts scattered around the city, most blacks didn't consider mastering it among the realm of the possible. "You had to wear uniforms in tennis," recalls Deacon Lawrence Howard of the Abyssianian Baptist Church, "and even those uniforms were white."

But a top welterweight contender living in your neighborhood—now, that was reason to be proud. Before long, Robinson had a bar-and-grill on Seventh Avenue, between 124th and 125th Streets. You could walk in and see him there, behind the bar or greeting customers. Stay long enough and you might spot Bill (Bojangles) Robinson, the famous dancer, wandering in, or Nat King Cole, who was married right there off Seventh Avenue at the Abyssinian Baptist Church, the Reverend Adam Clayton Powell presiding. The confluence of famous names was a product of the times. There was a limited number of places for a wealthy black man to go.

Althea was bowling with Gloria Nightingale when she encountered Robinson late one night. She didn't ask for an autograph as others might have done, or to pose for a snapshot. Instead, she challenged him to bowl against her. The outcome of the game or games is unrecorded, but by the end of the night, the two athletes were fast friends. Beginning almost immediately, Althea would spend as much time as she could with the Robinsons, often sitting on the floor of their Harlem apartment and talking late into the night. "She was unhappy," Edna Mae Robinson told *Time* in 1957. "She had a gaunt build, and she felt she was the least good-looking girl she knew. She had insecurity and went into herself. She used to talk wild. I tried to make her feel she could be something."

Althea would also benefit from the Robinsons' financial largesse.

Ray Robinson encouraged her growing interest in jazz by buying her a saxophone, fed her at his restaurant, frequently put her up at his home. In 1950, he would send her to Detroit to take tennis lessons with a white woman named Jean Hoxie, a stern disciplinarian who teamed with her gentler husband, Jerry, to coach future pro Jane (Peaches) Bartkowicz and fifteen other Michigan high school singles champions. On that trip, Althea would stay in a luxurious downtown apartment, courtesy of another benefactor, Joe Louis.

THE SUMMER OF 1946, the reigning ATA junior champion entered the organization's championships at Wilberforce, Ohio, as an adult. Althea, not yet nineteen, had little trouble advancing to the final to play Roumania Peters.

Peters and her sister Margaret, known in the black tennis community as Pete and Repete, were the ATA equivalent of today's Williams sisters. If one didn't beat you in a tournament, the other likely would. They'd started playing in the early 1930s while growing up in the Georgetown section of Washington, D.C., at the colored courts at 26th and O Streets. Later, they both played varsity tennis at Tuskegee Institute in Alabama. During World War II, entertainer and tennis buff Gene Kelly was stationed in Washington, and he paid at least one visit to 26th and O to play with the Peters sisters.

In the first ATA national championship she entered, in 1936, Roumania reached the women's final. (In 1938, Margaret followed as an ATA finalist, losing to Flora Lomax.) By 1946, Roumania Peters was considered the ATA's finest female player, yet Althea matched her almost point for point at Wilberforce. Peters won the first set by a single service break, while the second set in the best-of-three match threatened to last all day before Althea finally won it. With an ATA open-bracket title within her grasp on her first try, Althea began to swing wildly, launching balls wide of the net. Peters won the third set and the championship. It was the last ATA tournament match that Althea would ever lose.

By the time it had ended, two black doctors watching from the grandstand had plotted Althea's future. The first was Dr. R. Walter

Johnson of Lynchburg, Virginia, known as "Whirlwind," a general practitioner and surgeon who had dedicated his life to black tennis. Johnson was a skilled natural athlete. He'd played football at Lincoln University in the early 1920s, played it with such verve that the governor of West Virginia made a trip to West Virginia State in 1922 to watch Johnson compete for Lincoln. Johnson must have been something to see on the football field, for Southern politicians of the day did not often attend sporting events contested by Negroes.

After college, Johnson coached football and baseball for several years across three states, then went to medical school. While doing his internship at Prairie View A&M in Texas in the early 1930s, he played his first game of tennis. He didn't play it well; in fact, this renowned athlete had trouble finding anyone who would stand across the court and hit him balls. Ultimately, he prevailed upon a woman named Agnes Lawson to teach him the basic strokes. Later, Lawson would come to Lynchburg to train with him. She won the ATA's women's singles title in 1939, then again in 1940. Johnson had a keen eye for spotting and nurturing talent. His guidance helped Katherine Jones upset Roumania Peters to win the ATA women's singles final in 1945.

Johnson was no technician, but he was a natural teacher with an easy manner, and a selfless benefactor. He'd salt away money in a Christmas Club account so he'd have savings for the warm months, then fill his old green Buick with as many players as it could hold and set out for an ATA-sanctioned tournament somewhere. He'd be in Ohio one week, Pennsylvania the next, Kentucky after that, an endless summer of serves and volleys and match points. He was single then and his children were grown, so he was responsible for nothing but his patients and his tennis. With his bald head and steel-rimmed glasses, he was a familiar sight at black tournaments up and down the East Coast.

Dr. Hubert Eaton, a successful surgeon from Wilmington, North Carolina, watched the Gibson-Peters match from the grandstand seat beside Johnson. Eaton had been the ATA's doubles champion with George Stewart in 1943, and he would win again in 1949, 1951, and 1956. Like many of the black champions of his day, he was impeccably educated. After spending his entire childhood in a segregated community and attending college at all-black Johnson C. Smith in Charlotte, he matriculated at the University of Michigan in 1937, intending to get a master's degree in zoology. When he arrived there, the only black in his graduate class, he could not distinguish between the various white faces he saw.

More than two dozen times during his years in Ann Arbor, which also included medical school, he traveled home to North Carolina. Each time the bus reached Bluefields, Virginia, the driver halted his vehicle, stepped from his seat, faced the passengers, and made the following announcement: "We are about to enter the state of Virginia. By law, all colored persons must move to the back." Eaton was a lifelong Southerner, the son of a doctor, a quiet man who loved fishing and reading, and no revolutionary, but hearing this legal endorsement of inequality made him determined to use his talents to help redress it.

Eaton developed a thriving practice in Wilmington and made money. He built a tennis court beside his house, and it quickly became one of the few places in the state where interracial matches were played. England's Fred Perry, that iconic champion, competed there once, as did some of North Carolina's best white players. In a self-published autobiography titled *Every Man Should Try,* Eaton described his tennis philosophy as taught to him by his own mentor, Dr. Charles W. Furlong of Smithfield, North Carolina: "I played a controlled game of tennis, as I had learned to live a controlled life. Dr. Furlong taught me to place the ball carefully, to be consistent, and to wait for my opponent to make a mistake."

The Althea Gibson he watched lose to Roumania Peters at Wilberforce could not have played any less like this description. Inconsistency was her hallmark. She would show flashes of brilliance, then fade into a stupor. She didn't have solid strokes to fall back on when her timing was off, and she tried to hit the ball as hard as she could on most every shot, except when she came to net. She'd usually commit far more unforced errors than her opponent, but she almost always hit more winners, too.

Even before the Peters match, Johnson and Eaton knew all about Althea. She was, they figured, about the most naturally talented

African-American player of either gender to come along in years, perhaps ever. You could tell that by how little she knew about the game yet
how well she played despite her ignorance. While watching her play
that week in one match after the next, the two doctors concocted their
plan. Althea would spend the summers riding from state to state in
Johnson's Buick, with nothing to divert her attention from tennis. She
would spend each school year in Wilmington, North Carolina, with the
Eatons, getting the high school diploma she lacked, and learning the
work ethic and discipline that a structured life imposed.

In Althea Gibson, Eaton and Johnson saw a reclamation project, but
they also saw something more. The World War had ended the year
before, and the black servicemen who had fought alongside America's
whites (in theory, if not so often in the foxholes) were returning home
having tasted a certain amount of equality. Already back-channel negotiations were taking place between ATA executives and the USLTA
about one day integrating the major white tournaments. It was 1946,
and Jackie Robinson was starring for the Montreal Royals, one step
below the major leagues. The following spring, he would be a Brooklyn
Dodger. Eaton and Johnson saw his potential equivalent in this
scrawny competitor from Harlem. Unlike Robinson, she was more than
a year away from being able to compete against whites on the national
level—but then, the whites were more than a year away from letting her
do it.

Johnson approached Althea after the Peters match and unveiled
their plans for supporting her. She was sitting in the grandstand alone,
"at life's darkest moment," she would later write, when a man
approached and asked if she might like to play at Forest Hills.

"Of course I'd like that," she said. "But you know that's impossible."

"It is impossible now," Johnson said, "but if you are willing to work
hard enough, I believe you are the key to unlock the door."

Johnson asked her to stay where she was and excused himself. Minutes later, he returned with Eaton. Together, they presented their vision
of her future. When they finished talking, Johnson asked her if she was
interested. "Who wouldn't be interested?" Althea replied. She had nothing to lose; her life of late-night bowling and recreational basketball

was at a standstill. According to Eaton, she then returned home to New York to get a signed letter from her mother. Bobby Johnson, Whirlwind Johnson's son, distinctly remembers Althea riding back to Lynchburg with them that night and returning to New York from there.

In any event, Althea arrived in Wilmington that September on the morning train, carrying two cardboard suitcases and the saxophone Ray Robinson had bought her. She was anxious and hungry, but ready for a new life.

IN WILMINGTON, Althea would mature from a teenager into a woman. It wasn't easy. At first, the Eatons made her eat in the kitchen, not the dining room, because her table manners were abhorrent. And upon entering Williston High School, an adult in the eyes of the ATA and the law, she didn't qualify academically even for the freshman class. She hadn't attended school in years.

Outside the Eaton house, Althea was exposed to a North Carolina of the late 1940s, which was relentlessly segregated. Blacks such as the Eatons were successful by any reckoning, but they lived separate lives from whites. The object of the laws was to eradicate all contact between blacks and whites that whites didn't initiate. Blacks were welcome in a white home, but only in a subservient position such as cook or domestic, in which they would speak only when spoken to. The Eatons had a butler and a chauffeur—black, of course—and that tennis court in their yard, but they still couldn't sit at the Woolworth's lunch counter and eat a hot dog.

As a New Yorker, Althea was accustomed to going where she wanted whenever she pleased; she could ride the subway to Midtown and not engender a curious glance. She could drink from whatever water fountain, eat at whichever restaurant, use any washroom she wished. In actuality, she spent most of her time with other blacks, but little was stopping her from living as integrated a life as she chose to.

Though she'd fought against regulations all her life, she was smart enough to realize that segregation wasn't her battle to win. So she moved to the back of the bus, ate her hot dogs on the street, watched her movies from the balcony. But she wasn't happy about it.

In Harlem, she could step into a poolroom, shoot a game, and think nothing of it. She could drink a beer or a gin-and-tonic, smoke a cigarette, and disappoint nobody. She was no one's charge but her own. Living with the Eatons, she had to conform to the Southern ideal of femininity. She was barred from poolrooms, had to wear dresses and lipstick, and when she excelled at sports, her classmates whispered disparagingly that she threw a ball just like a man would. She played saxophone in the school marching band, and in a local jazz combo, and she played basketball for Williston, breaking the school single-season scoring record—as far as anyone knew; in that era, few records of women's sports were kept. In her three years in Wilmington, her team didn't lose a game.

Althea also needed time to adjust to the regularities of academic life. Dr. Eaton's goal was to get Althea through high school so she could win an athletic scholarship to a black university. To do that, she needed to attend school daily, something she hadn't done in a decade. She persevered. By the time she graduated at twenty-one, she ranked tenth in her class.

Once school had ended each June, she would pack her clothes into her cardboard suitcases, grab her saxophone, and travel to Lynchburg. She spent the summers of 1947, 1948, and 1949 on the ATA circuit, traveling with Dr. Johnson and his other pupils. They were mostly college students at that time, though later he would come to specialize in coaching youths with some potential: a sort of black Nick Bollettieri, decades early, but spending his own money and working for nothing. When he could get away from his practice, Eaton would meet his players at the various tournaments, the majority of which Althea won.

At some point, Althea found herself at a segregated dance near Camp Story, Virginia, up the river from Newport News. She shared a dance with a soldier, just eighteen, who was down from the Aberdeen Proving Ground. Smitten, Kirk Ellerson invited her to a recreation camp that was being prepared for soldiers returning from Europe. "There's a Congressional inspection team coming that week," he told her. "They need volunteers to show off the facility."

They could play softball, ride horses, swim, shoot baskets, run laps on the beach, he said, and Althea agreed that it sounded enticing. Accordingly, they met one morning later that week and staged a mini-Olympics. As it developed, everything that Ellerson did, Althea managed to do better. He'd been swimming all his life but was astonished to see her swimming faster. He didn't know about the Mysterious Five, but he wondered where she'd learned to shoot a basketball so well. "I had just never encountered a female with those kinds of abilities," he says now. "We went swimming, we played softball, we went horseback riding. Everything she did, she did as well as any boy."

Ellerson was mesmerized by this woman from the big city whom he found so attractive and compelling. Who was she? Where would her talents lead her? He wrote her name and address in a little book he kept of women who interested him, but he never tried to contact her. Years later, working in Europe, he opened a newspaper to see Althea's face staring out at him as the Wimbledon winner. He dug out the book and found her name, and the memory of that idyllic day came flooding back. He was married by then, and his wife could plainly read the emotion in his face. "She was upset with me for a good while," he recalls. "That was how strong an impact Althea had had on me."

ON THE COURT IN HIS YARD, Dr. Eaton tried to teach Althea discipline. Her game at that time veered from dominating to catastrophic, tethered to her mood. Down 4–1 in a set, she'd rarely fight back. If she wasn't winning, she wasn't enjoying herself. Instead, she'd fall into a sulk that could last for hours.

"On the days she won she was all smiles; on the days she lost her face went blank and she seemed depressed," Eaton later wrote. She was the same way about cards, basketball, and any other game she tried. She wanted to win more than her opponent, and, as a result, she usually won. "I can't remember ever beating her at a single thing," Bobby Johnson would recall. "We played tennis through the years, and I never won so much as a set." Later, Eaton would realize that Althea's single-minded emphasis on winning was the mark of a champion. She carried it with her the rest of her life.

Traveling with Dr. Johnson, she avenged her 1942 loss to Nana Davis to win the ATA singles championship in 1947. She would win it each of the next nine years in succession, finally choosing to skip the event in 1957, when she was the reigning Wimbledon and Forest Hills titleholder.

Althea graduated from Williston High in June 1949, and a proud Ray Robinson paid for her class ring. That fall, at age twenty-two, she entered Florida Agricultural and Mechanical University in Tallahassee on an athletic scholarship, her room, books, and tuition paid. Tallahassee was as segregated as anywhere in the country. No restroom facilities existed for blacks anywhere in the downtown shopping district. Blacks were forbidden to try on shoes or hats in downtown stores. Carrie Meek, who later served in the U.S. Congress, grew up in the city and recalls her mother telling her to immediately step off the curb if she saw a white person approach. "They don't want you on the same sidewalk as them," she'd warn.

Meek attended Florida A&M because state law prohibited a person of color from attending another state school. "We'd had a strong women's athletic program, but when Althea came, she was the entire program wrapped into one woman," Meek says. "She was so outstanding, so skilled in every form of women's sports, she was the epitome of what you would call a superstar." Florida A&M didn't have a women's tennis team, so Althea stayed sharp by practicing with the men, though she wasn't allowed to compete with them against other schools. In a yearbook photo of the day, she stands in the center of the tennis team photograph, as tall as the tallest man. She is thin but muscular, and her hair is cut far shorter than the prevailing fashion. If you don't look closely, you'll mistake her for a man. And yet, Meek recalls, she had a strong sense of her own femininity. Excelling in athletics was perceived as a masculine pursuit in the Tallahassee of that time and in society at large, but Althea made an effort to always carry herself like a woman—and beyond that, a lady. She had learned from the Eatons. For a time, she went out on dates with a student from Miami named William Burrough. She'd dress up for him, even wear perfume.

At the same time, she constantly fell afoul of basketball coach Julia Lewis, not because of anything that happened on the court, but because of her transgressions off of it. When the Florida A&M team traveled to play other all-black institutions throughout the South, the team behaved under very strict guidelines. These were females between adolescence and womanhood, and they had to be chaperoned in the fashion that their parents would expect. Althea was three years older, the age of a typical senior when she arrived as a freshman, and she'd walked the streets of New York since childhood. She wasn't going to sit in a hotel room in someplace like Birmingham or Atlanta when there was a world to be seen.

"She would break curfew and she would smoke, and some of the girls would go tell the coach," says Edwina Martin, a teammate. "Coach Lewis could hardly manage her, because she always had an answer back. Althea was a very strong person in that way." The same infractions would have sidelined any other player, but not Althea. She knew she was good enough to break the rules and not face punishment. The same aggressive attitude carried over to the court. "She was a rough player, which was why she was so good," Martin says. "Most of the girls were timid." Althea was so competitive that her friends stopped playing tennis with her, until she agreed to let them win occasionally. It wasn't so much to keep their spirits up as to defuse the competitiveness that she brought to every activity she attempted. They wanted her to learn that one could stand across the net and hit the ball to a friend and not worry about who was winning—or even keeping score, for that matter. Althea agreed, but she didn't see the purpose of it.

She was popular, but on her own terms. "She didn't go out seeking anyone's company," says Robert Mungen, a classmate who later coached tennis at Florida A&M for thirty-two years. "She had more men friends than women friends, because the women didn't really understand what she was all about. She was an athlete, more than anything, and ahead of her time. You just didn't see women athletes like that back then."

AWAY FROM COLLEGE, Althea continued to focus on her tennis. In early 1949, while still in high school, she had integrated two USLTA-sanctioned tournaments in New York. Any tournament could theoretically make its own decisions regarding whom to admit, depending on the qualifications necessary to enter and the rules of the facility where it was being played. On March 11, 1948, Reginald Weir had played in the men's bracket of the U.S. Indoors to officially break the USTLA color barrier. To the sport's more progressive element, it was about time. *American Lawn Tennis*, which would serve as Althea's champion in the years that followed, began its report on the event with a sarcastic description of its repercussions: "The first Negro has played in an American tennis championship," Harold Rosenthal wrote, "and, at this late date, there have been no reports of any worlds having split asunder as an aftermath."

In 1949, Althea became the second black and the first black female to compete with USLTA sanction. She lasted until the quarter-finals of the Eastern Indoor Championships, held at the armory on 143rd Street, then lost in straight sets to Betty Rosenquest. She remained in New York the rest of that week, and the whole of the next, for the U.S. Indoor Championships. It is impossible to say whether she stayed with her family while in New York, or if they even bothered to attend her matches. She hadn't broken with her parents, but neither was she regularly in touch with them. It is known that she spent most of her free time in New York with the Robinsons, at their apartment or the bar-and-grill on Seventh Avenue. She wasn't quite a conquering hero, but as the best female tennis player in the country among blacks, she'd come home with far more cachet than she'd left with.

The U.S. Indoors were played at the hulking Seventh Regiment Armory, which filled an entire block of Park Avenue between 67th and 68th Streets. At that time, before the advent of artificial surfaces, indoor tennis was contested on shiny wooden floors, like basketball courts. This all but ruled out backcourt rallies; you'd serve the ball and rush the net to try to force an error. The terrain suited Althea's serve-and-volley tendencies, and it also aided those who had learned the game on the fast concrete courts of Southern California. At the same time, the substandard lighting of the armory cast an iridescent blue glow and made the ball difficult to see. Althea won her first two matches, losing just one game to Ann Drye, then beating Sylvia Knowles in three sets. This put her into the quarter-finals against Nancy Chaffee of Ventura, among the most talented of the Californians.

Chaffee would later marry Baseball Hall of Famer Ralph Kiner, and then sportscaster Jack Whittaker. She was often compared to one movie star or another (though she didn't especially resemble any of them physically), and she comported herself with a flair uncommon to tennis players of that day. ("Tennis Didn't Come Easy for Nancy Chaffee, It Had to Compete With Parties!" ran the headline over a feature on the gregarious Chaffee in *This Week* magazine.) But she remembers seeing Ray and Edna Robinson sitting beside Jackie Robinson and his wife, Rachel, in the bleachers at the armory—the only black faces in evidence—and feeling intimidated knowing such celebrities were rooting for her opponent. Chaffee calmed herself with the thought that Althea was doubtless more nervous than she was. If she beat Chaffee, Althea would advance into the semifinal against Gertrude Moran, "Gorgeous Gussy," who had titillated Wimbledon with the half-inch of lace trim on the panties beneath her tennis dress the previous summer. A Gibson-Moran semifinal would be a newsworthy event.

It didn't happen. Chaffee's fierce ground strokes neutralized Althea's acrobatics at the net. Althea hit the most spectacular shots of the day with volleys and backhand winners, but the more consistent Chaffee had little trouble winning, 6–2, 6–3. In the other half of the bracket, Helen Germaine beat Nina Irwin, whose own game had come quite a distance from the Cosmopolitan Club, in three sets. And in the doubles competition, Rosenquest and Irwin beat Althea and Germaine. It was a small universe of talented players. Althea may not have been the best of them, but she was holding her own. "She can hit like a boy," the former U.S. champion Sarah Palfrey Cooke, who would later befriend Althea, was moved to note, "and cover the court with huge cat strides."

Chaffee, who would win the event from 1950 to 1952, remembers the Althea of that time as confident to the point of cockiness. "I think she was trying to convince herself she was a great player," she said shortly before her death in 2002.

Althea wasn't yet great in 1949, but she was on her way. She had developed one of the best serves in women's tennis, and a deft touch at the net, though she still flailed at ground strokes as though she were trying to swat a bumblebee. It was the propensity to move to net that led onlookers to remark that she played like a man, not the substantial velocity with which she usually hit the ball. There were other hard hitters among the women of the day, but nobody who combined such strength with a nimble athleticism. "She was very light on her feet," Chaffee said. "It reminded me of Alice Marble."

Jack Kramer, the standout amateur and professional player and tennis promoter, would make the same connection at about the same time. He said, "She has the best chance to be a champ in the manner of Alice Marble that I've seen."

ANY COMPARISON TO MARBLE would have been distinct praise. By 1949, Marble had retired from amateur tennis with eighteen singles and doubles titles from Wimbledon and the U.S. Nationals alone. She'd also already lived enough in her thirty-six years to fill three lives. Growing up a tomboy in San Francisco, she caught someone's eye at thirteen and found herself serving as a mascot for the Pacific Coast League's San Francisco Seals. She shagged flies with Joe DiMaggio, played catch with Lefty O'Doul, then turned to tennis as a viable substitute for her real desire, which would have been to play professional baseball. In 1929, at age fifteen, she reports being violently raped by a stranger. She developed a friendship with Clark Gable and Carole Lombard, and William Randolph Hearst bought her a green Chevrolet. She recovered from anemia and pleurisy—and a misdiagnosis of tuberculosis—to win U.S. singles titles in 1936, 1938, 1939, and 1940. She even had a brief singing career, appearing once at the Waldorf-Astoria. After losing a baby to a miscarriage because of an automobile accident, she learned that her husband, Capt. Joseph Crowley, had been killed when his plane was shot down over Germany. An attempted suicide by overdose was thwarted when her friends discovered her unconscious but still breathing.

At about that time, fact and fantasy begin to blur. As detailed in her 1991 autobiography, *Courting Danger,* she claimed to have rekindled a prewar romance with a Swiss banker at the urging of the U.S. State Department. While staging a series of tennis clinics in Switzerland, she writes, she surreptitiously photographed a ledger of Nazi investments, and was shot in the back trying to flee. Marble's astounding revelations are impossible to verify. "It was terribly meaningful for her to have been accepted as having served her country as a spy, and I suspect she believes that she did," says Judge Robert Kelleher, a Californian since the 1950s who served as the USTA president and America's Davis Cup captain, and knew Marble well. "But I think you'll search in vain for any evidence." According to a spokesman, the U.S. State Department has no record of an Alice Marble having been in government employ during the war.

Marble had always been a strong and independent woman. She returned home from her espionage work—or whatever else she might have been doing in Switzerland—having sharpened her already keen sense of justice. It seemed absurd that a player of talent should be denied a place in the USLTA's national championships merely because of skin color. Having been exposed to other sports, Marble was able to understand that amateur tennis was insulated from real life, and all the poorer for it. "She had a streak of fairness, of empathy for the under-dog," said Billie Jean King, who, while she was still Billie Jean Moffitt, received instruction from Marble in the late 1950s. "You measure if you can make a difference in certain battles, and Alice knew she could in this one."

The editorial she wrote in *American Lawn Tennis*, championing Althea's cause, changed the history of the sport. In a small way, it also changed the course of American history. Who knows which courageous act tipped the balance away from segregation, toward a free and equal society? Perhaps blacks would ultimately have played in the U.S. Championships, just as they eventually integrated the National Basket-ball Association, the Augusta National golf club, and the modern incar-nation of the United States Senate. But without Alice Marble, it certainly wouldn't have happened in 1950.

CHAPTER 4

Breaking Through

In THE SUMMER OF 1950, Alice Marble was a revered former champion, Althea Gibson a rank outsider. Yet beneath the veneer their lives had accumulated, a few levels deeper than skin color, they shared common traits. Neither fit the contemporary stereotype of a female tennis player: a nice girl who used the game like she used the foxtrot—as a social skill.

Like Althea, Marble was a tomboy during childhood, excelling in athletic competition against boys. Her body language as an athlete was routinely described as masculine; over the course of their careers, both women heard that they played tennis like men more often than they could count. Yet they'd wear silk dresses when the occasion warranted, and could cut a glamorous figure. In an undated photo of Marble standing alongside Carole Lombard on the tennis court, the only way to tell the athlete from the movie star is Lombard's thickly applied eyeliner and lipstick.

Both Marble and Althea often set themselves apart from the crowd, yet they were crowd-pleasers who loved to perform. Marble had a brief singing career in 1941, while Althea would release a long-playing album and appear on the *Ed Sullivan Show* sixteen years later, each rather overestimating her own level of vocal talent. (Althea was a passable singer; Marble, by most accounts, objectionable.) Both were forthright and funny, and unmindful of the consequences. Both would nurse life-long beliefs that they hadn't received their due credit as tennis players. Marble was the first female player to routinely follow her serves to net.

Shirley Fry, Doris Hart, and Pauline Betz

Two decades later, that serve-and-volley strategy would propel Althea to the upper echelon of world tennis.

Marble hadn't met Althea as of early 1950, despite playing that exhibition match at the Cosmopolitan Club. But she may have been aware of some of the commonalities and connections. More than that, she nurtured a strong belief that tennis was headed in the wrong direction. A sport run by and for the country-club set could hardly succeed as popular entertainment. It had to be integrated, aired out, thrown open to all.

Marble was unaware of the negotiations that Bertram Baker, the ATA executive director, and Arthur Francis, his lieutenant, had quietly initiated after World War II with some USLTA members in an attempt to integrate the U.S. Championships. Harold Lebair was their most important supporter at the USLTA. Tall and thin, sporting a small mustache and rimless glasses, usually wearing a rounded collar beneath his suit coat and occasionally adorning himself with a straw hat, he looked like a nineteenth-century daguerreotype, but his thinking was thoroughly modern. A graduate of the University of Pennsylvania with high honors, he is remembered as intelligent, scrupulous, precise, and fair. For many years, he worked as a national advertising salesman for the *New York Times*, and served the USLTA as its chairman of umpires and, later, its treasurer.

Liberal and Jewish, Lebair was an anomaly in an organization that was nearly as averse to change and homogeneously WASPish as the clubs at which most lawn-tennis tournaments were played. Without fanfare, he put the first women in umpire's chairs at Forest Hills. By 1950, he'd come to see integration of the U.S. Championships, which were played there beginning at the end of every August, as both necessary and inevitable.

Perhaps because of the dialogue with Lebair and others, or else because of the strides being made in other sports and the first stirrings of the civil rights movement, a sense was growing within the ATA that getting a black player into the nationals might soon be possible. At the same time, it had become evident that Althea was ready for better competition. In August of 1949, she had beaten Nana Davis, the second- or third-best African-American woman playing at the time, by 6–0, 6–0 at the Cosmopolitan Club. Then she returned to Wilberforce to again defend her ATA title and didn't lose a set in the tournament. In the final, she made short work of Mary Fine of Kansas City, 6–3, 6–2. A succession of such matches were stunting her growth. "In second-rate company, where the ball is set up for her, she is dynamite," Hamilton P. Chambers, a veteran sportswriter who had seen her play at the U.S. Indoors in New York, was quoted as saying. "Against a hard hitter, and once on the defensive, she is lost."

At Wilberforce, Dr. Eaton again had asked Althea if she would be interested in playing at Forest Hills, should the occasion arise. It wasn't a moot question. If the treatment of baseball's Jackie Robinson was any example, the first black player entered in the U.S. Championships would be subject to severe scrutiny, perhaps ridicule, sabotage, even death threats. While the tennis community was hardly as rural, Southern, or uneducated as big-league baseball was, it was far more closed and elitist. Whoever would attempt to integrate that society would need to be strong enough to concentrate on playing matches despite a maelstrom of distractions, for a poor showing would hurt the cause considerably. "I'm ready," was Althea's steeled reply.

But the USLTA wasn't ready, and it had a convenient out. No player, black or white, could be invited to Forest Hills until proving his or her mettle at several of the grass-court tournaments that led up to the national championships. And because those tournaments were held at private clubs, the USLTA believed it was under no obligation—indeed, had no authority—to mandate which players should be allowed to enter them. Nearly all of these clubs were officially segregated, which gave Althea no recourse other than the legal system, a path the ATA had vowed not to take. Beyond that, female players were usually housed during tournaments at the homes of individual members, the pillars and paragons of the local social and business communities. It served as a point of distinction for some chamber of commerce type to announce to his colleagues that the likes of Sarah Palfrey Cooke was staying at his home for the week. In the vast majority of those homes, Althea would not have been welcomed.

Still, she continued to play as the only nonwhite at the USLTA-sanctioned tournaments that would have her. She played the Eastern

Indoors again in late February 1950, and beat Millicent Lang 6–3, 6–1 for the title. At the U.S. Indoors that followed, she advanced to the final with a three-set victory over Midge Buck. Her rival for the title was Nancy Chaffee, who had missed most of the previous season with an ailing back. Althea had clearly improved since losing to Chaffee the year before, and expectations for a memorable match were high. Instead, Althea played poorly, winning just two games in two sets.

Nevertheless, she managed to impress Howard Cohn of *American Lawn Tennis*, who praised her serve and, "when she has it under control," her powerful forehand. "Miss Gibson obviously needs more competitive experience," he wrote, but how was she to get it? April became May, May became June, and Forest Hills was less than three months away. Althea waited for a sign. She left Tallahassee after her first year of college and headed to Wilmington, knowing she might well end up back in the Buick with Dr. Johnson, traveling to the same segregated tournaments she'd dominated during previous summers. Forest Hills seemed closer than ever, a theoretical possibility for the first time, yet in practice it remained unreachable.

Such was the atmosphere when an editorial by Marble appeared on page 14 of the July 1950 issue of *American Lawn Tennis*, occupying most of a densely packed page. It read, in part:

> *For every individual who still cares whether Gussy [Moran] has lace on her drawers, there are three who want to know if Althea Gibson will be permitted to play in the Nationals this year. Not being privy to the sentiments of the USLTA committee, I couldn't answer their questions, but . . . [w]hen I directed the question at a committee member of long standing, his answer, tacitly given, was in the negative. Unless something within the realm of the supernatural occurs, Miss Gibson will not be permitted to play in the Nationals. . . .*
>
> *I think it's time we faced a few facts. If tennis is a game for ladies and gentlemen, it's also time we acted a little more like gentlepeople and less like sanctimonious hypocrites. If there is anything left in the name of sportsmanship, it's more than time to display what it means to us. If Althea Gibson represents a challenge*

to the present crop of women players, it's only fair that they should meet that challenge on the court, where tennis is played . . . but if she is refused a chance to succeed or to fail, then there is an uneradical [sic] mark against a game to which I have devoted most of my life, and I would be bitterly ashamed.

We can accept the evasions, ignore the fact that no one will be honest enough to shoulder the responsibility for Althea Gibson's probable exclusion from the Nationals. We can just "not think about it." Or we can face the issue squarely and honestly. It so happens that I tan very heavily in the summer—but I doubt that anyone ever questioned my right to play in the Nationals because of it. Margaret du Pont collects a few freckles—but who ever thought to omit her name for such a reason? The committee would have felt pretty foolish, saying "Alice Marble can't play because of that tan" or "We can't accept Margaret du Pont; she gets freckles across her nose." It's just as ridiculous to reject Althea Gibson on the same basis. . . .

The entrance of Negroes into national tennis is as inevitable as it has proven to be in baseball, in football, or in boxing; there is no denying so much talent . . . I've never met Miss Gibson but, to me, she is a fellow human being to whom equal privileges ought to be extended.

The editorial resonated. Within days, it had been mentioned prominently in the pages of the *New York Herald Tribune,* the *New York Post, Life,* and *Time,* among other influential journals. But despite its eloquence, the obdurate Maplewood Country Club refused to allow Althea into the USLTA-sanctioned New Jersey State Championships, which it was hosting. She was crestfallen. The best players in America and Althea were on parallel paths that seemed destined never to meet. On July 8, 1950, for example, Althea sleepwalked through a 6–0, 6–0 demolition of her good friend Rhoda Smith in the New York State Championships at the Cosmopolitan Club, while Margaret Osborne du Pont, who had married one of *those* du Ponts, was winning a USLTA event at the all-white Essex County Club in Manchester, Massachusettes. The following week, Althea beat a white woman, Isabel Troccole, 6–2, 6–2, in an open event in New York. But she couldn't gain admission to any of the tournaments that would prove her standing for the USLTA, and she wasn't a member of any USLTA-affiliated club because none would have her. It was an old story, this de facto segregation, and it was frustrating her.

Then came a breakthrough. A truck salesman named Jack Rosenquest had a talented daughter named Betty, who, as Betty Rosenquest Pratt, would rise as high as fifth in the USLTA rankings in 1954. (Althea had lost to Betty Rosenquest in the quarterfinals of the 1949 Eastern Indoors.) One of Betty's practice partners was a Jewish boy named Dick Savitt, several years her junior. They'd ride their bikes to the local courts and hit there for hours, Savitt roaming the baseline to retrieve everything Rosenquest hit his way. Then Savitt spent a year in Texas with an uncle and emerged with an explosive serve. "After that, I wasn't much of a practice partner for him," she remembers. In 1951, Savitt would win the Gentlemen's Singles title at Wimbledon.

The Rosenquests also happened to live across the street from the Orange Lawn Tennis Club in South Orange, New Jersey, where the Eastern Grass Court Championships had moved from Rye, New York. Using the Marble letter to open the dialogue, Rosenquest managed to convince the officers of the Orange club to issue an invitation to Althea. It would be good for the image of the club, he said, and for the image of tennis in the United States. The invitation was the first crack in the armor, a major step. But Althea played poorly at South Orange, the first tournament she'd ever contested on grass. She lost in the second round, which left her fate unresolved.

Shortly thereafter, Althea received and accepted an invitation to the National Clay Court Championships at the River Forest Club near Chicago. She did better there, beating the light-skinned Mexican champion Mela Ramirez before advancing to the quarterfinals. There, she lost 6–2, 6–3 to Doris Hart, a premier player who would rank No. 1 in the world the following year.

Though the tournament had been contested on clay, not grass, her results seemed to provide information—as the USLTA called it—that Althea could be at least competitive on the shamrock-green lawns of Forest Hills. On August 5, 1950, the *New York Amsterdam News* wrote that Althea was ready and waiting. "A more seasoned Althea Gibson is all set to compete in the National Tennis Tournament [*sic*] at Forest Hills, L.I., later this month, if she receives an invitation," the article read. It quoted the latest unofficial reports saying that Althea "is slated to receive a bid."

Ten days later, the thirty-six-member USLTA championships committee—under the chairmanship of Alrick H. Man Jr. of Kew Gardens, Queens—received Althea's application for the nationals at Forest Hills, which were scheduled to begin on August 28. By then, Marble's letter had become a cause célèbre. At the closed-door committee meeting that followed, it is easy to imagine Lebair and the other progressive members carrying the day against reactionaries such as Bill Clothier Jr., the Philadelphia department store magnate. ("The most conservative man I've ever met," Alastair B. Martin, who was a committee member at the time, says now of Clothier.) Change was inevitable, they argued. The best the organization could do was attempt to control it in such a way that participating clubs and institutions would not be forced to suffer.

After the meeting, a terse statement was released announcing that Althea had been accepted on her merits. What emerged eventually was an alteration to the entrance procedure for the U.S. Championships. Each year, the male and female winners of the ATA national tournaments would be included no matter what level of tennis they were judged to be playing. No longer would success in each summer's grass-court tournaments be considered a prerequisite for admission. In essence, blacks would be qualifying on a parallel course, which meant that integrating the grass-court tournaments held at exclusive clubs would not be necessary.

The ruling unknowingly employed the doctrine of "separate but equal" that had formed the original legal basis for segregation. In 1896, the U.S. Supreme Court's *Plessy v. Ferguson* decision upheld a Louisiana railroad company's right to separate blacks and whites into different cars, providing facilities and conditions were similar for both. In practice, of course, separate seldom meant equal, and the entire concept was offensive to a race of people guaranteed freedom of opportunity by the Bill of Rights. In this instance, however, such a policy suited the ATA's short-term aims almost as well as full integration. Althea was in; it hardly mattered whether she'd be coming to Forest Hills by the main road or a side road.

The fact is, apart from Althea, no other black women would have been qualified in 1950 to make the field of fifty-two—and only one or two men would have been, on their finest days. Getting more blacks the opportunities to better themselves by playing the best whites would be the next challenge, but the excitement caused by seeing an ATA champion compete at Forest Hills might well create the momentum for that on its own.

ATA executive secretary Bertram Baker made the stirring announcement on August 26 at the organization's annual championships, held again at Wilberforce. Hours after Althea had overwhelmed Nana Davis 6–2, 6–0 for her fourth consecutive ATA title, and teamed with Dr. Johnson to win a third consecutive doubles title, Baker said: "Many of us have worked untiringly for years to witness the day when our players would be accepted for competition in the national championships of the USLTA. That day has come."

Now Althea, who had never seen Forest Hills' storied West Side Tennis Club, had to play well. She asked Sarah Palfrey Cooke to take her into the facility at some point before competition started. It would help Althea to know where the locker rooms were, how far she'd need to walk to an outer court, and all the other logistical details that players had to divine for themselves at a time when few had traveling coaches and none had managers or agents. Even better would be an hour's practice time so she might gauge the feel of the courts. Cooke had won the U.S. Championships twice during the war, then retired from amateur tennis. A social-register Bostonian, she was a protégé of American tennis doyenne Hazel Hotchkiss Wightman, yet she had a progressive mindset. "She was calmly persuasive [and] had clout as an ex-champ," said Gladys Heldman, later the founder of the women's professional tour. Cooke wasn't a member of the West Side Tennis Club, but she prevailed upon its executives to allow her, as a former champion, to escort Althea to the courts. They even managed to practice together briefly, which worked wonders toward steadying Althea's nerves.

Little more than a week later, a photo of Althea decorated the main

sports page of the *New York Times*, the first time of many. She'd beaten
Barbara Knapp 6–2, 6–2 on August 28, 1950, in the first mixed-race
match ever played at the U.S. Championships. For whatever reason,
benign or not, the Knapp match had been held on Court 14, the one with
the smallest capacity for spectators, tucked away on the farthest edge of
the ground. The passageway leading to the court was so crowded, the
players were unable to push through without assistance. In the end, only
a few hundred fans—most of them black—were afforded the chance to
see her play. They stood four-deep and clapped politely whenever
Althea won a point, but not if she won it on a Knapp error or double-
fault. Althea raced to a 5–1 lead and served out the set at 6–2, then took
control of the second set at 2–2 and didn't lose another game.

It had unfolded without incident, and the tennis had gone easily
enough for Althea. But her next opponent was Louise Brough, the
Wimbledon titleholder, and that match would be played on the Grandstand Court, the second-largest. This would be the showcase that
Althea—and much of the growing antisegregation movement—had
been waiting for. Temporarily, at least, women's tennis became one of
black America's favorite sports.

It is tempting to infuse a coincidence with prophetic or revelatory
meaning, but happenstance is often just happenstance. Consider two
tennis players, each gifted at birth with the unusual name of Althea.
One is experienced, the other raw. One the Wimbledon titleholder, the
other playing—and, for that matter, attending—just the second match
of her life at the premier tennis facility in the United States.

Despite having the same uncommon name, a powerful serve-and-
volley game, and a balletic touch at net, the two women could not have
been more different. Althea Louise Brough, pronounced to rhyme with
"tough," had long since abandoned her given name in favor of the more
mellifluous Louise. She was a tall, quiet blonde with a history of
remarkable success. She had won the singles title at Wimbledon in
1948 and 1949, and at Forest Hills in 1947. (She would ultimately win
thirteen championships, singles and doubles, at Wimbledon alone.)

Born in Oklahoma in 1923, Brough was moved at age four to Beverly

Hills, where her father worked as an executive in the grocery business. She learned tennis from the same coach who taught Jack Kramer, who was two years older, and her volleying skill mirrored his. Like Kramer, she relied on her serve to put opponents on the defensive. Then she'd rush to net and try to intercept the ball and quickly win the point. In 1940 and 1941, she won the U.S. 18-and-under title, just as Althea would do among blacks two years later. By August 1950, Brough already had won three singles titles at Wimbledon and another at Forest Hills, as well as too many important doubles titles to list. She was at the top of her game. More than that, she sat firmly at the crux of the tennis establishment of the day, along with her doubles partner (and best friend) Margaret Osborne du Pont.

The top women's players at the midpoint of the twentieth century were like members of an extended family. They shared similar backgrounds and had similar motivations. Nobody was getting rich from tennis in 1950, and few players were getting famous. Du Pont traveled for years as a player and, later, the captain of the U.S. team in Wightman Cup competition, and says she never received a bit of adulation. There were no gold medals to be had, no endorsements or other money following an amateur career unless you were one of the fortunate few to turn professional and play exhibitions. Margaret Osborne had married the fabulously wealthy Will du Pont, a close friend but—by all accounts—hardly a lover, and several of her peers wondered aloud if it wasn't at least in part to fund her career.

What this generation of players enjoyed instead was the quality of their lives. They'd travel the world together as friends, getting hosted at tournaments and feted at cocktail parties, the darlings of the society page in whichever town they happened to be in. They'd see the sights, the Eiffel Tower in Paris and the Colosseum in Rome, while practicing and playing a game they enjoyed. When they weren't in Europe or on the Caribbean circuit, the backdrop of their competitions was likely to be the stately country clubs of America's best neighborhoods. The most important tournaments were played on grass, which had to be grown in a prescribed manner, and only the poshest clubs had the means to maintain such courts at competition level. The draw for each tourna-

ment would often be made in a back office of the club, far from the pry-
ing eyes of outsiders, and in many cases it was based on social standing
as much as anything else. "'Let's let this girl in,'" longtime umpire Flo
Blanchard recalls one East Coast tournament director saying,
"'because her mother is so nice.' That's the way it was in those days.
You got in if you knew somebody."

For these women, propriety counted. Mistakenly given an envelope
of tickets meant for Gussy Moran, whose display of frilly panties had
shocked Wimbledon in 1949, Margaret du Pont acted as though she'd
smelled a skunk. "I doubt Louise or I will be seeing Miss Moran," she
said, handing them back with her arm extended. She wanted nothing to
do with Moran, or anyone who would so publicly flaunt the conventions of the sport.

The players were mostly in their twenties, some extending this fantasy life into their thirties, but they acted like sorority girls. The tennis
circuit was a moveable slumber party, with matches during the day and
dinner dances at night. They'd play poker, bridge, and gin rummy
together, then compete fiercely against each other on the court. When it
was over, they'd come to net and offer up platitudes. "You were simply
the better player today," the loser would say, while the winner
demurred. Because the Americans had continued playing during the
war and the English and the Europeans hadn't, this group of perhaps
half a dozen superior American players won nearly all the important
events for at least a decade, beginning in 1946. The USLTA ran the
sport, but these insiders ruled it, just as the clique of popular girls rules
a high school. "Their tennis was a part of their life," says Judge Kelleher, the former USLTA president and Davis Cup captain, "and the life
they led was white, and above-average socially." They weren't overtly
prejudiced, these women, or they hid it well if they were, but they had a
keen awareness of oneness and otherness. "Louise and I were against
the world," du Pont says. Then she tellingly adds of the other prominent women's doubles pairing of the day: "Shirley Fry and Doris Hart
were our great enemies—but also our dear friends."

Althea viewed life through vastly different eyes. She still had the
competitive drive of that schoolgirl paddle-ball player, and she lacked

the niceties that would help make such competitiveness palatable to others. Dr. Eaton had tried to educate her in the social graces, but in that sense he had failed. She'd come to net after a match and all but spit on her opponent. "I'll get you next time," she'd say if she lost, or she'd say nothing at all. It didn't always work in her favor. "You were lucky if you caught her hand after a match, and things like that can irk you into competitiveness," said Betty Rosenquest Pratt. Althea's behavior was so distasteful to two-time U.S. singles champion Doris Hart, for example, that Hart made certain never to lose so much as a set to her. It is a point of pride for her even today that she never did.

Althea wanted to win so badly, she didn't know what to do when she didn't. In 1955, at the end of Hart's career, Althea approached her after a match at an English tournament, while they were drinking their tea. "What am I doing wrong?" she pleaded. "How come I can never beat you?" Hart looked at her, astonished at the impudence of the question. "Althea, you've got to be kidding," she said. "You don't think I'm going to help you, do you?"

Yet Hart was always available to help Fry, whom she considered something of a younger sister. As doubles partners, they'd travel and practice together. And they even discussed strategy before matches that they played against each other. In 1951, when they met for the Ladies' Singles title at Wimbledon, they spent two full days before the match in the company of no one but each other. "I did help Shirley, a lot of matches," Hart admits now. "But I didn't consider her a threat." Hart may have had a point; she won that 1951 Wimbledon final by 6–1, 6–0, in a mere half hour.

Althea arrived on the scene like the interloper at the country-club ball—because she was black, but also because of her attitude. She held her head high. She had a grand opinion of her own ability, regarding herself as a champion though she'd only ever won ATA events. "Her whole manner and demeanor was really much more imperial than the rest of those youngsters," says Judge Kelleher. "At that time, she had an overemphasized view of her own importance." That would later help sustain her during the bleak years between 1951 and 1955, but it didn't make her many friends.

Not that she wanted friends. Althea was a precursor of champions like Steffi Graf, Monica Seles, and the Williams sisters, who, especially when young, seldom offered more than a passing nod to other players inside a locker room and had little interest in forming social relationships with players they'd have to compete against on the court. "Althea would draw a curtain around herself, shutting out the others," recalls Shirley Bloomer, a British player of the day. "It was almost like pulling a blind down." By the professional era, such focused intensity, while not necessarily appreciated by other players, was acknowledged as appropriate. With a million dollars on the line, you did what you had to do in order to get your share. Not in 1950, though. The stakes weren't high enough. If these insiders were barely going to make enough to continue playing, and they weren't going to be on the cover of magazines, they might as well be comfortable in their surroundings.

Althea challenged that assumption. In that sense, she was the first modern athlete to play competitive tennis. For better or worse, her actions and attitudes were decades ahead of their time.

ALTHEA KNEW THAT THE VAST MAJORITY of the spectators at Forest Hills would be white. In her mind, it would be a hostile environment. Accordingly, she arrived each day with a retinue in tow. She'd bring two or three of her New York friends—including Rhoda Smith, at whose house she was staying on 154th Street—and they'd insist on crowding into the small women's locker room, which was so small that only players and club members were technically allowed.

We can envision them there: stuffed around a wooden bench in the cramped space between one row of lockers and the next, inadvertently blocking the passage of the players who, with rackets and presses in hand, were trying to push past to their own lockers, drawing cold stares, reinforcing all the stereotypes these white women might be nursing about who belonged in such settings, and who didn't.

Her camp followers may have been the only ones in attendance who figured Althea might have a chance against Brough, yet a swell of interest had filled the grandstand court to its capacity of two thousand. Hundreds more fans were angling for a view from outside the fence.

The lure of this match transcended mere novelty. Word had already started to spread that, skin color aside, Althea was worth watching. She had a big serve, a hard backhand, an overhead that seemed to whip down from the clouds, and she played the net instinctively, like the table tennis enthusiast she'd once been. She probably wouldn't have the consistency to beat a player of Brough's caliber, the feeling was, but she was sure to go down fighting.

CHAPTER 5

From Forest Hills to Wimbledon

A<small>NYONE WHO WAS THERE</small> will remember Althea's match against Louise Brough on the Grandstand Court at Forest Hills on the afternoon of August 29, 1950. A corps of newspapermen and newsreel cameramen had assembled for the occasion. Shortly before 3:30, Althea worked her way through the overflow crowd, with Alice Marble—whom she apparently had met in the interim—at her side. After a brief warm-up, play began.

In the second set of her first-round match the previous day, Brough had been extended to 11–9 by little-known Laura Lou Jahn. But when she broke Althea's serve early in the first set and cruised to a 6–1 victory, that sign of weakness was quickly forgotten. Althea's problems were tactical. Brough moved her around the court like a pool shark deploying his stripes and solids, inevitably drawing Althea into the blank area between the baseline and the service line, a court's equivalent of No Man's Land. Time after time, Althea would start to come to net, reconsider, then be forced into a weak, defensive volley from too far away. Brough had enough of a forehand to routinely capitalize. Althea was overly ambitious against an opponent as formidable as Brough. She was trying too hard to hit winners that weren't there to be hit.

The day had dawned clear, but by the time they'd finished the first set, a wind was whipping through the stands. Trains would rumble past on the elevated track and be mistaken in the stands for thunder, or perhaps it was thunder after all. The sky had darkened ominously. Years later, all Brough remembers about the match is wanting to get safely into the clubhouse with a victory. But somehow, the first set had given Althea confidence, and she started the second a different player. With Brough serving, they played a long first game that swung back and forth between deuce and Brough's advantage before she finally managed to hold.

Althea's serve, suddenly sharp and powerful, sliced through the gusts. At 3–3, she began to dominate. Brough double-faulted to hand Althea the seventh game, and Althea held her service to win the eighth. Brough was down 5–3 when the thought crossed her mind for the first time that she actually might lose the match if she didn't raise the quality of her game. The realization didn't seem to help her. The set ended with Brough double-faulting twice, then missing a simple backhand volley. She was playing like the newcomer, Althea like the champion.

There were six thousand fans in attendance at Forest Hills that day, but only two thousand could fit into the Grandstand. After the unbalanced first set, many of those had wandered off to other matches. But as the second set unfolded, talk of Althea's play spread to the outer courts. Soon the Grandstand was full again. In the minutes that followed, thousands more spectators packed into the adjacent Stadium Court, turned their backs on the action before them, and proceeded to watch play from there.

Between sets, a report arrived that a fierce rainstorm had halted play in the third inning of the second game of a doubleheader at Yankee Stadium, which was not far away in the Bronx. Forecasts had the weather heading east, due to strike Forest Hills in perhaps half an hour. Accordingly, Althea and Brough began the final set with a sense of urgency. Brough broke Althea's serve twice to take a 3–0 lead, and Althea responded by taking chances. The same strategy had undermined her effort in the first set, but now her timing was on and she started converting them into winners. In the fourth game, she used her lob to get Brough away from the net, then followed it in to win points on volleys. She broke Brough's serve, but Brough immediately broke her back to take a 4–1 lead.

At that point, someone began to heckle Althea from the grandstand. It was no racial slur, nothing untoward, but Althea heard the heckling and it inspired her. Her face hardened. She countered with another break in game six, then held to pull within 3–4. By the reaction that followed one shot, a fierce overhead that won her a point, she realized that much of the crowd—aware that it might be witnessing a historic upset—was actually cheering *for* her.

Brough labored to hold serve in game eight and take a 5–3 lead. She was panting as she chased Althea's lobs all over the court, but she stood just one game away from victory. Althea held serve for 4–5, then won the first three points of the tenth game. Brough methodically worked her way back to deuce, controlling play with her serve and keeping the ball away from Althea's backhand, which was her stronger side. She was two points away from winning the match. But Althea returned what seemed a certain forehand winner with a hard forehand of her own, then slammed a winner off a Brough serve. It was 5–5.

Althea won the eleventh game to move ahead for the first time in the match, but Brough held her service to equalize at 6–6. As she did, the sky darkened. A flash of lightning was seen, but play continued. Althea held to move ahead, 7–6, and the first fat drops of rain began to fall. A plea crackled over the public address system for all spectators to remain in their seats, but as it did, the heavens opened and the rain came down in walls of water. At that point, a bolt of lightning struck one of the sizeable stone eagles that sat atop the corners of the stadium, toppling it to the ground with a force that sent an echo throughout the grounds. In years to come, the symbolism of such divine intervention would be discussed, but at the time the deeper concern was getting safely under cover. After a short wait, play was canceled for the day.

ALTHEA RETURNED TO Rhoda Smith's apartment on 154th Street in Harlem just a single game from upsetting the reigning Wimbledon champion. She was thrilled, and almost beside herself with nervousness. She couldn't help but wish that the rain had held off for a few minutes longer. If it had, she felt, she could have completed the upset, but a night's rest would unquestionably alter the dynamic. Smith tried to defuse the tension. "Even if you lose tomorrow, honey, it won't make a particle of difference," she told Althea, but Althea knew that wasn't true. Beating Brough could put her on course to win the entire tournament in her first try.

Brough, too, remembers spending a nervous night. She'd gone back to her room, cleaned up, and eaten dinner with Margaret du Pont— "There were no coaches in those days, so that's who I talked to," she says—then tossed in her bed until morning.

By then the storm had passed. Fifteen photographers and five newsreel cameramen arrived to record the end of the match for posterity, as well as profit. But the 1:45 start time came and went without a sign of Althea. Brough stood beside the umpire Harold Ammerman, holding her racket, looking as though she'd been stood up by a date.

Nearly a decade into her career, she'd become skittish, prone to tossing the ball in the air several times and catching it during her serve. "I got more nervous as the years went on," she remembers. Now she stepped to the baseline and began to hit practice serves to alleviate her nerves. Ammerman called out to stop her, as the rules stated that neither player was to have an advantage in warm-up time. Brough protested that, since she was there and Althea wasn't, she should be able to do what she liked. At that moment, a tournament referee walked on the court and concurred with her, so Brough served for a few more minutes. Then she paced the sideline. If it was a mind game that Althea was playing, it was working. Still, Althea was risking disqualification with every minute that passed.

Finally Althea arrived amidst a crush of photographers, like a movie star walking into the Academy Awards. She'd been warming up with Sarah Palfrey Cooke, then had difficulty fighting her way past the media hordes to get to the court. Nineteen minutes late, the match resumed at the point at which it had been stopped the previous day. It lasted a mere eleven minutes more.

Brough was harboring so much nervous energy that she slugged her first practice volley almost to the grandstand, which was again filled to capacity. "It was not my nature to be calm," she recalls. But she steadied herself, followed her serves to net, and won game fourteen to tie the set, 7–7. Althea then proceeded to double-fault, smack a volley to the edge of the grandstand, and fall behind 15–40 before fighting her way back to deuce. An astonishing twelve more points then followed, the advantage swinging back and forth like a pendulum. On the last one, Althea double-faulted on Brough's advantage to give away an 8–7 lead.

That was all Brough needed. Althea was rushing her shots, making mistakes. Brough made a concerted effort to keep the ball in play, figuring that would be enough. At 15–15, Brough hit a hard forehand and Althea slapped it into the net. Down 30–15, Althea stepped back for an overhead off a Brough lob and directed that into the net, too. She saved one match point, but at 40–30, Brough unleashed her best serve of the truncated day and Althea returned it wide.

It finished 6–1, 3–6, 9–7. Althea stood still for a moment, her head cocked in disbelief, then started slowly toward the net. A newspaper reporter reached her as she was walking off the court and actually put his hand on her shoulder. "Look at it this way," he said softly. "Your picture is going to be all over the world tomorrow." For the moment, it was small consolation.

DOCTORS HUBERT EATON AND R. WALTER JOHNSON were disappointed by Althea's defeat, yet overjoyed by what had transpired at Forest Hills. Over the course of two matches, one of which would live on in the history of tennis, Althea had integrated the sport at its highest level. It was the culmination of an effort that had started on the hard bleachers at Wilberforce four years before. She'd lost that match they'd been watching against Roumania Peters, and lost this match, too—but what Althea had accomplished in the years between had nudged the world a bit further toward racial equality, and every bit helped.

Not that aiding the cause of racial equality was ever Althea's goal. From the beginning of her career on through to her dotage, Althea maintained that she played for herself alone, not as a representative of her race. In that sense, too, she was a precursor to the modern athlete who shrugs off any mandate to be a role model. "I tried to feel responsibilities to Negroes, but that was a burden on my shoulders," she said in a *Time* cover story written after her first Wimbledon singles title in

1957. "If I did this or that, would they like it? Perhaps it contributed to my troubles in tennis. Now I'm playing tennis to please me, not them." In an interview years later, she would add: "I did not change anybody. I played good tennis. Being a good athlete has nothing to do with race."

But her race couldn't help but resonate, making everything she did or said that much more important. Anyone with a degree of distance from her couldn't fail to realize this. In the November 1950 issue of *American Lawn Tennis*, Marble used her column space to compose an open letter to Althea. "You made history in your own right, which is quite a burden of honor for twenty-three-year-old shoulders to carry," she wrote. "You also played some remarkably good tennis, considering that you had only played on grass three times previous to Forest Hills."

Marble also criticized Althea for certain aspects of her behavior at Forest Hills. She noted the "amazing number of 'managers' and 'advisors' you suddenly acquired," referencing the retinue of bandwagon-hoppers from Harlem and beyond that Althea (who undoubtedly figured she'd take all the support she could get in her lonely pursuit) had seemed only too pleased to welcome. She exhorted Althea not to listen to anyone who claimed to know what was best for her now, unless they were there advising her before. "They weren't willing to go out on limbs to help you achieve what you've done," she wrote, "but now that you have become a national figure, they'd like to get in on the ground floor where a little of the glory might reflect on them."

Althea responded with a letter of her own that served as a sort of manifesto of independence. Never again, she vowed, would she allow outsiders to influence her during the course of a tennis tournament. "Believe me, Miss Marble, I have no manager," she wrote. "Some people think because they gave me some tennis balls eight years ago, they have a right to dictate my future." Characterizing herself as a poor girl from a family unable to support or help her, she stressed that she had relied on the kindness of others to get as far as she had. Now she asked to be invited to more USLTA events. "I don't mind getting beat," she wrote. "The more I am beaten, the more I will learn." In her mind, she had already set her sights on her next target, the most famous tennis tournament in the world.

Not long after losing to Brough, Althea met with Bertram Baker and Hollis Dann, an entrepreneur and USLTA member who planned the logistics for tennis trips, to discuss traveling to Wimbledon the following summer. No black of either gender had ever competed at the Championships there. It was agreed that the USLTA would support her entry, but it wouldn't fund her travels. Given what her entry at Wimbledon would represent, Althea sensed that money wouldn't be a problem, and it wasn't. While in Detroit training with Jean Hoxie that fall, she so impressed the black community there that it raised enough to cover her expenses in England, and local hero Joe Louis volunteered to buy a ticket to get her across the ocean.

Before Wimbledon, she traveled to the Fairfield Country Club in Montego Bay, Jamaica, for a tournament in February 1951. The tournament field included some of the better USLTA players, but on that predominantly black island, Althea was the main attraction. Each of her matches was covered on the front page of the local newspaper, complete with photos and bold headlines. A cocktail party was held in her honor, and she was the featured guest at a dance at the Casa Blanca Hotel. In the final against Betty Rosenquest, Althea rallied from a 7–5 defeat in the first set to win by 6–4, 6–4. Rosenquest played the steadier game but Althea simply hit the ball too hard for her.

She returned to New York for the U.S. Indoors. She survived several match points against her by forty-two-year-old Midge Buck, then in the third round came up against California's Nancy Chaffee for the third consecutive year. Again, the match was a disappointment. Althea looked listless and devoid of energy. She rarely advanced to net, preferring to flick her racket at Chaffee's forehand drives, looking for impossibly angled winners and—far more often—spraying the ball out of bounds. Chaffee won 6–1, 6–3, and went on to win the tournament.

A month later, Althea was on a plane again. She had been invited to the Good Neighbor Tournament in Miami Beach, her first foray into the American South to play a mixed-race event. Except for the fact that Althea was unable to stay at the same hotel as the rest of the competitors, the tournament came off without incident. On the court, she played perhaps her best tennis since the Brough match. As the fourth seed, she swept through the bracket to the finals, then overwhelmed Rosenquest again, 6–4, 6–2. These weren't the top players in the world, but they were creditable opposition, and Althea was winning matches against them.

In June of 1951, she touched down in London for the first time. A week later, she walked off the court at Queen's Club after winning her first-round match at the Wimbledon warm-up tournament there. She signed the autograph for young Angela Buxton dutifully enough, but her mind was elsewhere.

Over the course of a winter and a spring, Althea had come to understand what Wimbledon meant in the context of the white world of sports. Even for an American, it was the most important tennis tournament of each year, far more so than the U.S. Championships. You could lose every other tournament, she knew now, but winning Wimbledon would make it a successful season. "Wimbledon was the crowning glory," according to Billie Jean King. "There was no comparison with anything else."

Wimbledon is arguably the premier tournament in the world even today, but before the advent of open tennis in 1968, there could be no argument. Without those oversized checks for the winners, presented on center court by sweating sponsors in suits and ties, the importance of an event turned on its history and its ambience. Today you can manufacture a desirable tour stop with ready millions and a television deal, but in 1951 it was the weight of history and the allure of aesthetics that served to separate a few venues and their tournaments from all the others—and Wimbledon from that select few.

The Championships at Wimbledon's All England Lawn Tennis and Croquet Club dated from 1877. They had grown in prominence through the years. By 1951, Wimbledon had become one of those few sporting events that much of the world followed. They knew about Wimbledon in South America, in Communist Eastern Europe, even in Japan and China. The dish presented to the Gentlemen's and Ladies' Singles champions was as coveted a prize as the heavyweight championship belt. Winners became members of the All England Club for life.

Wimbledon was part of England's cultural heritage. The newsreel images of the stateliness of the event—the crowds impeccably dressed in jackets and ties, the members of the royal family applauding politely from their box—added to the worldwide perception of English elegance. Without Wimbledon, England simply wouldn't have seemed like England. The disruption to the sequence of championships during World War I and World War II was as debilitating to the country's collective psyche as the loss of several complete baseball seasons would have been to America's. Six Championships were canceled in the 1940s, and the damage inflicted by the war wasn't merely symbolic. On October 11, 1940, an explosion from a German bomb destroyed part of Centre Court. Even when the championships resumed in 1946, it remained unrepaired. Rationing was still enforced and provisions were scarce; many Americans brought their own steaks to England that year.

BY THEN, the cast of characters had changed. Bobby Riggs and Don Budge and Germany's Gottfried von Cramm (who had lost three consecutive Gentlemen's Singles finals in the 1930s without ever winning one) had given way to Americans like Jack Kramer, and a new set of Australians. Alice Marble, Helen Jacobs, and Helen Wills Moody, the best female players of the previous decade, had retired. Instead, Pauline Betz defeated Louise Brough to win the first postwar Ladies' Singles' tournament in 1946. Then Margaret Osborne, not yet a du Pont, defeated Doris Hart in the 1947 final.

These women would contest every final for the remainder of the decade. Betz was forced to retire after winning Wimbledon, because she'd considered touring as a professional (hadn't actually done it, mind you, just made the mistake of mulling it over in public: that's how strictly the USLTA interpreted the rules regarding amateur standing). Brough beat Hart to win her first Wimbledon in 1948, taking the Ladies' and Mixed Doubles titles, too. The next year, she won the singles final over her friend Osborne, who had married Will du Pont in the interim and appended his name to her own.

In those days, the same players would reappear again and again during the course of each fortnight. The top competitors, men and women, were expected to participate in all three brackets—singles, doubles, and mixed doubles. As the tournament winnowed out their lesser rivals, they'd be on this court for singles, on that court for doubles later in the day, and somewhere else on the grounds playing mixed doubles before nightfall. It was possible to watch a favorite player for hours on end, moving from court to court with a schedule of play in hand.

To be successful in all three events was to set yourself up for a difficult day of tennis on the final Saturday of the two-week tournament. In 1949, Brough spent more than five hours on Centre Court on finals day, at a time when sitting down to rest between games was forbidden. First she won the Ladies' Singles, beating du Pont 10–8, 1–6, 10–8. After a brief respite and a costume change, she and du Pont returned to Centre Court to play the Ladies' Doubles final against Gussy Moran and Pat Todd, winning in two difficult sets, 8–6, 7–5. Brough already had played sixty-nine games of tennis that day, but she staggered back to the court in her third outfit of the day, alongside partner John Bromwich of Australia, to contest what turned out to be an epic mixed-doubles final against South Africa's Eric Sturgess and Sheila Summers. Brough and Bromwich pushed the match deep into the third set before losing 9–7, 9–11, 7–5. That gave Brough a total of 117 games, singles and doubles, over the course of an afternoon.

She played so long and so late that the ceremonial first dance at the Wimbledon champions' ball was delayed until 11:30 P.M. Ted Schroeder, who won the singles title that year in his only appearance at Wimbledon, remembers sitting at the head table and drinking glass after glass of champagne with British prime minister Clement Attlee as the room waited for Brough to arrive. By the time she did, he was tipsy enough to be unsure on his feet, a perfect match for Brough's tired legs. The following day, Brough recalls, she was scarcely able to walk.

In 1950, only a few months before playing Althea at Forest Hills, Brough beat du Pont in the Ladies' Singles final, becoming the first woman to win at three consecutive Wimbledons since Helen Wills Moody two decades before. Then she teamed with du Pont to beat Fry and Hart in the doubles. This time, she'd chosen Sturgess as her own partner, and she completed the triple with him in straight sets.

As three-time defending champion in 1951, Brough was seeded first at Wimbledon. She advanced into the semifinal easily, losing just one set in four matches. Then she was unexpectedly beaten by Shirley Fry, a former badminton champion from Ohio who had won the French Championships for her first major championship the previous month and was playing the finest tennis of her life.

This was the Wimbledon at which Hart and Fry did everything together, including contest the Ladies' Singles final, which Hart won in a walk. Hart and Fry then teamed to outlast Brough and du Pont in a second set that went twenty-four games to take the Ladies' Doubles. When Hart successfully partnered with Frank Sedgman for a quick two-set Mixed Doubles victory, she had a finals-day triple of her own.

These were formidable players, memorable players, "nonpareils," as Ted Schroeder would call them, but at the time it was difficult to put their achievements into context. The sport, much like the world at large, was trying to rekindle the sense of continuity that had been shattered by the war. The performances of Brough, du Pont, and Hart unfolded in present tense, pencil-sketches of history. Looking back now, we can see the marvelously entertaining artistry they brought to the game, and appreciate their greatness.

And yet, these women—so well-mannered, so unthreatening, and in many ways so similar—are more easily perceived as a group than as individuals. Their traits blur together, their names intermingle, their numerous championships jostle for room in the record books, until the defining characteristics of each are all but lost. With the exception of Maureen Connolly, whose brief and stunning career will race across these pages, this clique of talented women dominated the sport for more than a decade without managing to produce one of the game's more memorable characters. Framed by Alice Marble and World War II on one side, and the emergence of Althea as a genuine champion on the other, they constitute a forgotten generation in the history of tennis. Few fans know them beyond their names.

BY THE TIME DORIS HART won those three titles on the second Saturday of the 1951 tournament, Althea was long gone. She'd walked onto the Wimbledon grass as the first black to compete in the Championships, one of the more prominent of the unseeded players, but there was no stirring confrontation like the Brough match to herald her arrival. As at Forest Hills, she won her first-round match, beating Britain's Pat Ward in three sets. She then played Californian Beverly Baker, who was beginning to emerge as a standout player.

Baker is a personality worth remembering. As a teenager, she had spent the 1940s somewhat less known for her tennis than for her romantic dalliances. She was not especially mature for her age, "a little girl, in all ways," according to Judge Robert Kelleher, who knew the family well. Her father, a Santa Monica recreational supervisor, watched over her with a hawkish eye. Nevertheless, she attracted the affections of the spirited Richard (Pancho) Gonzalez, who squired her to parties and to the informal nights on the town that inevitably resulted whenever men's and women's events intersected. "He had very strong feelings for her, though it was unclear even to me what exactly was happening between them," says Ralph Gonzalez, Pancho's brother. Years later, Pancho Gonzalez acknowledged that he considered Baker the love of his highly charged and exceedingly complicated life.

During a single week in April 1949, profiles of Baker appeared in *Sport* and *Sports Illustrated*, the latter written by former champion Helen Jacobs. (This *Sports Illustrated* was a short-lived precursor to the Time/Life publication that would debut several years later.) Her name appeared regularly in the gossip columns, overshadowing her formidable baseline game. That September, Baker became the teenage bride of child actor Scotty Beckett, Spanky McFarland's best friend in *Our Gang*. Beckett would later fall into drugs and dissolution, and commit suicide at the Royal Palms Hotel in Los Angeles in 1968. Even then, he was at least a little unhinged. Beckett and Baker traveled on their honeymoon to Mexico, where Beckett threatened to punch a bystander in the face for gazing a bit too covetously at his wife. He commanded her to stop playing tennis, stop visiting her parents, and to have no contact whatsoever with "males between the age of six and sixty." In all, the marriage lasted only six months, ending soon after she jumped out of a car while he was driving it. She received a cash settlement of $5,700 in lieu of alimony.

After that, she was Beverly Baker again, and dating in frenzied fashion. She got engaged, ended the engagement, continued to climb the U.S. rankings. On the June day in 1951 when she played against Althea, she was romantically linked with one player, American Hal Burrows, while fending off the advances of another, South Africa's Jean Norgarb. By year's end, she'd be married to yet another suitor, a University of Southern California student named John Fleitz. Somehow, she didn't let the ongoing soap opera affect her tennis. By then, she was the fourth-ranked player in the country, behind du Pont, Hart, and Brough.

Beyond the gossip about her romantic dalliances, the other fascination with Baker was her peculiar tennis technique. On the asphalt courts of Santa Monica, she'd been taught by her father to utilize two forehands. She'd reach wide to get a ball with the racket in her right hand, then flip it into her left for a forehand from the other side. She was small at the time, barely taller than the net, and the technique gave her an extra two feet of court coverage. She grew into full womanhood, but never bothered to develop a backhand. Conventional wisdom said to hit the ball directly at Baker, but she was nimble-footed and usually able to step in one direction or another and set up a powerful return. She'd traverse the baseline, gliding from one side of the court to the other, hitting with power from both sides. "The only time I came to net," she recalls, "was to shake hands at the end of a match."

With a talented net player like Althea, Baker knew she had to hit a winner off a passing shot, or she'd likely lose the point. Althea would come to net behind her serve, giving Fleitz one chance to power the ball past her. Too often for Althea, that's exactly what she did. Baker won the first set of their match by 6–1, and after that, Althea stuck to the baseline. She'd try to coerce Baker to the net with drop shots, but Baker refused the bait, played her own game, and ended Althea's first Wimbledon run in a straight-sets victory that lasted less than an hour.

In years to come, Althea would walk to the net after losing a match in Havana—a mere exhibition, at that—and horrify Baker, who was by then Mrs. Fleitz, by testily announcing that she was far superior and would surely emerge victorious the next time they played. For now, losing in forgettable fashion at her first Wimbledon, Althea hurried off the court without a word, disgusted with herself. She would not play another singles match at Wimbledon for five years.

In truth, Althea's loss had more to do with her own play than Baker's. Though she'd temporarily raised her game in the match against Brough, she wasn't ready to compete on a regular basis against the best players in the world. She lacked consistency, and would routinely make more mistakes than she'd hit winners. "She was a very confident person, but she made a lot of errors on the court," Beverly Fleitz says now. "No matter how well she might be playing, you were never out of a match with her." In an assessment of Althea's game in *Ebony* magazine, a prominent coach named Mercer Beasley agreed. "She is deficient in some strokes," he wrote. "On deep balls, she tries too hard. She needs the patience to pick her shots, and right now she plays too much of an attacking game."

Others felt even more strongly that Althea's game was flawed. One future Wimbledon champion remembers watching Althea from the stands during that tournament and being disgusted at what he saw. "She was a miserable player," he'd say later. "She stunk. Her ground strokes were awful. Her serve was pretty big for a woman and she could volley and move, she could run, but it was just athleticism, nothing more."

Brough felt Althea posed little threat to the top players, despite having teetered on the edge of defeat against her at Forest Hills. "I don't think she was even that great the year I played her," she says. "I always thought she was very vulnerable. She had a good serve and a nice overhead, but I figured she would make errors if I waited long enough. That day was unusual, with the trains going by and the wind blowing and all that noise coming from over on the stadium court. Still, she must have been a better player than I ever gave her credit for, because she kept on playing, and eventually she started to win."

Others realized her potential immediately. John Barrett, a British player of the day and a future broadcaster who would write the seminal reference work on Wimbledon, extrapolated a champion from a half-formed talent the first time he saw Althea play. He came upon her in the midst of her Wimbledon match with Baker in 1951. Watching a silhouette of a player serve with such power and advance to net, Barrett felt certain, as Angela had, that Althea was a man. It was only when he stepped closer that he understood. He saw her pushing the ball into the net too often, and slicing potential winners closer to the umpire's chair than the court, but she charged the net with an aggressiveness he had never seen from a female player.

"It wowed me," he says now. "She was a very good athlete at a time when there weren't many good athletes playing. She had her own shots, her own strokes, her own way of hitting the ball, but champions find a way of making those shots work for them. Given time, I felt certain that she, too, would find a way to make them work."

Angela with Groucho Marx and a rodeo cowboy

CHAPTER 6

Angela Goes to Hollywood

THAT WIMBLEDON OF 1951 was the first that Angela followed with
any intensity. Seeing Althea at Queen's Club had made Angela realize
that she wanted to not merely play tennis, but to be a tennis player. As
the tournament unfolded, she listened in on the BBC and became inti-
mately familiar with the best players in the world for the first time.

Of the eight seeded women in that 1951 bracket, the first seven were
Americans. The vanguard of the coming generation of British women
was competing that year, but neither the nineteen-year-old Angela Mortimer, who would emerge as the most talented of them, nor the twenty-
two-year-old Pat Ward won a match. Those two players, along with Pat
Hird, Anne Shilcock, and Shirley Bloomer, who would appear soon
after, were about as different from Angela as their American counter-
parts were from Althea. Nice girls from so-called nice families, they
shared a British sense of reserve and a distaste of unorthodox behavior.
There were some ways that people simply did not behave, they felt, and
things that were just not done—quite a long list of them, actually. It is
telling that the singles and doubles championships at the All England
Club are not titled "men's" and "women's," as they are for the other
major tournaments around the world, but Gentlemen's and Ladies'.

In Angela Buxton, Angela Mortimer saw a player of about the same
age with an utterly different approach and temperament. "We didn't
have a lot in common," Mortimer says now. "She was on her own and

she liked it that way. I don't know anyone who might say they were close to her. Perhaps she thought she would make it easier if people didn't like her." Mortimer remembers that Angela had more money than the rest of the teenage girls who traveled to tournaments. She also did little to hide her ambition, which Mortimer viewed with distaste. There was nothing wrong with ambition; Mortimer herself was "bloody-minded and refused to give up, and just went on and on and ground her opponents down," said John Barrett, who would marry her many years later, after she'd finally won a Wimbledon singles title in 1961. But those who were raised properly were taught never to let that ambition show, at least to the point where it would cause someone else discomfort. It was an elaborate charade, but it served to further the illusion that tennis was a sport played by the well-bred and well-schooled. "Tennis is a nice hobby for you," Mortimer's mother told her when she started competing. "I remember enjoying tennis parties myself when I was your age."

Angela Buxton didn't fit. "I think Angela [Buxton] puts people off because of her pushiness and pushing herself all the time," says Barrett. Such pushiness is a Jewish stereotype, and it was commonly ascribed to Jews in England just after the war. Though little was available in the way of material goods, proper Englishmen—that is, Anglican Englishmen— were trained to behave as though nothing was abnormal, even as queues for staples like meat and flour occasionally stretched around the block. Jews were perceived by many as prone to grabbing for their share and more, paying little regard to the common good. Angela had a willingness to do the unorthodox if it would get her where she wanted to go, and she did happen to be Jewish. It was easy to place those elements in juxtaposition.

Coincidentally, that same Wimbledon fortnight of 1951, a Jewish player won the Gentlemen's Singles championship for the first time. It was Dick Savitt, Betty Rosenquest's old hitting partner from New Jersey. Dark-haired and dark-eyed, he'd come off the campus of Cornell to parlay his sixth seed into a place against Ken McGregor of Adelaide, Australia, in the final. When he disposed of McGregor, he was celebrated as an American wunderkind at age twenty-four.

Angela remembers hearing the match on the radio and being aware that Savitt was Jewish. Strangely, she never made the connection to herself. She recognized that it was slightly odd that a Jewish player had won Wimbledon, but didn't delve beyond that. She refused to identify herself by her Jewishness, even in her own mind. Just as Althea didn't want the responsibility of playing for her race, Angela yearned to win for herself, not to prove anything to anyone about her religion. She was a tennis player, she liked to believe, not a Jewish tennis player.

As it happened, Savitt felt the same way. He downplayed his religious background and beliefs for fear of making a difficult road to the final any harder. "I played," he says simply. "Angela and I probably couldn't have joined the clubs in those days, but we played." He does recall making something of a stir in the Jewish areas of North London. "Nobody knew tennis there, but after I won, people started picking up rackets," he says.

Savitt's open-field run through the Wimbledon draw may have temporarily kindled interest in Jewish London, but it didn't create any champions. Just as more than forty years passed after Althea won Wimbledon and the U.S. Championships before another black woman, Serena Williams, won either one, Jews who follow tennis are still waiting for Savitt's successor.

NOBODY AWARE of the relative positions of Angela Buxton and Althea Gibson that summer of 1951, of autograph-seeker and autograph-signer, could have envisioned that Angela would be playing at Wimbledon the following June and Althea would not. But in 1952, their fortunes diverged in unexpected ways.

Following her loss to Beverly Baker, Althea began the darkest period of her tennis career. It was to last more than four years, until late in 1955. The improvement that had come so readily as she learned the game slowed and eventually stopped. Her strokes degenerated, and her serve-and-volley game narrowed to a single dimension. This can happen in tennis, a game in which improvement happens not at a steady pace but by fits and starts. Ted Schroeder, the 1949 Wimbledon champion, recalls not being able to win a match "for several years," at one point, before unexpectedly finding his game again and emerging better than before. Althea's fortunes never dipped to that extent; she would remain ranked among America's top players year after year and dutifully win the ATA championship each summer. But she made few inroads toward bettering her position against the first rank of female players.

During that time, Althea's personality never changed. She knew she was floundering, knew that her tennis needed to improve if she were to have a chance to win the major tournaments, yet somehow she managed to approach each match with the same absolute confidence she'd had since 143rd Street. "She always thought she was the greatest thing when she walked on the court," said former ATA champion Bob Ryland, who remembers winning an informal but hard-fought match against Althea, 6–3, 6–4, during that time. "She'd tell you, 'I'm the greatest.' Like Muhammad Ali later on. She'd say it all the time."

Even among her peers on the circuit, Althea continued to behave like the champion she hadn't yet become. In a sense, it saved her. She managed to intimidate many opponents by the sheer force of her personality. This didn't work against the more experienced players, but her self-assurance was usually enough to get her deep into every tournament.

Angela lacked confidence, but she had the same kind of determination. By June 1951, she had finished her schooling at Mrs. Jepson-Turner's. She then took a year's worth of domestic science courses at London Polytechnic on Regent Street, where the University of Westminster now stands. All along, she had been playing junior tournaments in London and around England, even managing to win a few. In June of 1952, she attempted to make the main draw at Wimbledon as a qualifier. In order to do so, she had to play in a preliminary tournament to gain one of the ten qualifier spots in the field of ninety-six. She won two rounds and then lost, which put her out of the picture. But when two places in the main draw opened up because of injuries, Angela's name was one of those pulled from a hat as replacements; in tennis parlance, she became a Lucky Loser. She was fortuitously slotted into a match against the one player of the other ninety-five whom she'd beaten before, an Englishwoman named Valerie Lewis. But after winning the first set against Lewis, she lost the next two and exited the tournament. It was her Wimbledon debut, and a forgettable one.

At just about that time, an idea arose from somewhere deep in Harry Buxton's psyche. He'd sent Angela to London to learn tennis, then marveled to see her actually playing at Wimbledon less than two years later. Now Angela was telling him that all the best players were coming out of California. Alice Marble was a Californian, and Louise Brough had learned to play there, and Margaret Osborne du Pont, and Nancy Chaffee, and Beverly Baker. The latest was the teenaged Maureen Connolly, who had emerged after Wimbledon in 1951 to win the U.S. Championships, then swept through Wimbledon in 1952, ousting both Fry and Brough without dropping a set. She had the tennis world in an uproar, yet she was a month and a day younger than Angela.

It was common in those days for wealthy families to send their daughters abroad so they could take advantage of cultural opportunities not available in England. Harry was rich and getting richer, and he wanted the world to know it. He thought it might be a clever idea for Angela to take a trip to California. She could meet all the movie people—just say you're Harry Buxton's daughter and it'll open every door in Tinseltown!—and she'd get the same instruction, presumably, that was transforming these American girls into champions.

An extended trip would also get her out from underneath the British tennis infrastructure, and give her a leg up on her domestic rivals, just as her time in South Africa had done. Harry turned to Violet in that demonstrative way he had, as though he were a character on stage. "You take her for six months, and I'll pay," he said.

Angela spent the weeks that followed in a frenzy. With no Internet or fax machines to help her then, she dug out telephone numbers at public libraries, made inquiries, wrote letters. From England, she managed to enter tournaments in Bakersfield and Riverside. She located an apartment to rent in Hancock Park, right beside the Los Angeles Tennis Club—the site of the annual Pacific Southwest Championships, and the haunt of many of the best players of the day—where she assumed she'd be getting instruction. She made contact with a friend of her mother's who was living in New York and could meet them when their ship arrived. She did a tremendous amount of preparation in a matter of months, laying the groundwork for the trip of a lifetime. And in November of 1952, full of hope, she and Violet set sail on the *Queen Mary*, bound for America.

THE LOS ANGELES TENNIS CLUB SITS, hacienda-style, on a slight swell of land south of Melrose Avenue, at the corner of Clinton and Cahuenga in Hollywood. Since 1920, it has served as a bastion of Southern California tennis, though it was built only as an afterthought.

When the oil wells in Hancock Park dried up and turned to tar in the early years of the century, another use was needed for the land. Twenty-three acres of it were apportioned to create the Wilshire Country Club complex, a golf course surrounded by homes. After that, another five and a half were allocated for tennis, almost by default. Over the years, the two original courts, abutting the sidewalk, grew to number sixteen. All were hard-surfaced, in the California fashion.

Each September beginning in 1927, the LATC erected temporary stands seating more than three thousand and staged the Pacific Southwest Championships. It was second in importance among North American tournaments only to Forest Hills—and, some claimed persuasively, even harder to win than Wimbledon. At a time when overseas travel was expensive and rare, those eager but overmatched British players who filled out the Wimbledon draws were absent at the Pacific Southwest, replaced by talented Californians who might log more outdoor court time in a calendar year than an Englishman could manage in a career. Locals pegged the tournament as the third or fourth most important in the world, depending on where they ranked the French Championships. Quips Pat Yeomans, a former U.S. junior champion and a longtime LATC member, "We never did care much about Australia."

Under the de facto leadership of the imposing Perry T. Jones, a future Davis Cup captain who ran the Southern California Tennis Association with imperiousness from his office on the grounds, the LATC became a gathering place for many of the best players in America. Nine of Jones's charges, including Ellsworth Vines, Bobby Riggs, Jack Kramer, Pancho Gonzalez, and Ted Schroeder, are enshrined in the

Tennis Hall of Fame. It wouldn't be uncommon to see Kramer and Schroeder on one court, Vines or even the incomparable Bill Tilden on another, and perhaps a visiting standout from the East Coast or beyond, a Tony Trabert or a Lew Hoad, on a third. Kramer's parents even arranged his schedule at Montebello High School so he could take his classes in the mornings and spend his afternoon time at the club: a mere teenager reveling in the opportunity to play with and against Tilden, Vines, Frank X. Shields, Riggs. "The L.A. Tennis Club was the one place to play the game in this country," Kramer wrote in his autobiography. "If you wanted competition, you had to play there." Alice Marble played there often, as did Connolly and Brough. Well into the 1960s, Gonzalez would haunt the LATC, holding court—literally—for the length of an afternoon, taking bets against all comers.

The paying members of the LATC were culled from the Los Angeles social register, and most of them had ready money. Elaborate social events were held, and the paneled bar did a thriving business, but the club existed for serious tennis. If you were a top player from anywhere in the world and you came to Los Angeles, you could find a suitable game at the LATC. "The members always wanted to see good players around," says Allen Fox, who played often there as a guest when he was a top junior in the 1950s and beat the reigning champions of all four majors in one magical week at the Pacific Southwest in 1966. "It was like watching an exhibition for free. You'd buy them a beer or two, talk to them after the match. And the players loved it. The courts were great, it was beautiful. It was nothing but positive for them."

Jones had thinning, slicked-back hair that he parted in the middle, and wore black-framed glasses. He looked not unlike J. Edgar Hoover, and he seemed to have similar ideas about power and its uses. He wasn't officially president of the club, but he ruled it with an iron hand. He decreed that anyone playing on its courts needed to be properly dressed, and that meant not merely tennis whites but pristine ones, with no objectionable additions such as headbands or towels. He controlled the membership rolls, bringing in many of the area's best juniors as associate members, no dues necessary, and he dominated the club's board of directors. Whether he set the club's exclusionary policies or merely sanctioned them is open to debate, but under Jones the club resolutely refused to allow Jewish members. That was in keeping with a social tradition in Los Angeles, which proved far more difficult to dismantle than those of America's major East Coast cities. As late as the 1980s, the Jonathan Club and California Club, where much of the city's business was transacted, still did not allow Jews. In the 1950s, it would have been taken for granted that Jews needn't even try to apply to the LATC. "The board was very much against having Jews as members," says Yeomans, who has authored a book about the history of the LATC. "They were worried about the motion-picture people, who would run up big bills and not pay them." That may have been true, yet Errol Flynn was a member, and Efrem Zimbalist, and Rudy Vallee, and Bing Crosby, gentiles all. Nobody seemed to worry about them.

Angela knew nothing of what she would encounter at the LATC when she left England for California. She knew she wanted to be in Los Angeles, knew the Pacific Southwest was played annually at the LATC, and knew that some of the best players in the world could be found there on almost any day of the week. As a teenager with a single Wimbledon match to her credit, it was something of a reach for her to assume that she'd be welcomed by such august company, but if she wasn't going to assert herself on the trip to America, to keep pushing until she met resistance and then push even harder, what was the point of going? Beyond that, she saw a bit of serendipity at work in the geography of the club. The nearest major north-south artery, two blocks east of Cahuenga, was called Rossmore Avenue, like her own Rossmore Court at home. The coincidence made her comfortable in the neighborhood from the day she arrived.

The small house that she'd rented, sight unseen, for herself and her mother was so close to the LATC that she could see courts from the window of the living room. The Monday after her arrival, Angela presented herself at the door of the Los Angeles Tennis Club, asking for a temporary membership—and was astonished to encounter the family of one Daniel Prenn, an acquaintance from London.

Prenn was a Polish Jew by birth, a German national, and a

renowned tennis player who had fled to England after being denied a place on the 1933 German Davis Cup team because of his religion. There he married a gentile named Charlotte, sublimated his faith, and joined Queen's Club, where he'd play tennis and socialize. By the time Charlotte and their son, Oliver, traveled to Los Angeles after the war, Prenn himself was no more Jewish than Perry T. Jones. He is remembered at the LATC as a stylish player, tall and graceful, and a perfect gentleman. "He had nice manners," the historian Yeomans recalls. "We liked him very much."

The LATC prided itself on being discreet when it told potential applicants that they weren't wanted for reasons of religion or color, but in truth the matter didn't arise very often. Nearly anyone who would trouble themselves to apply for membership would know in advance who was acceptable and who wasn't, and it wasn't merely a matter of the fifteen-hundred-dollar fee. Jews had their own clubs, such as Beverly Hills and Hillcrest, and blacks had—well, they had the public courts and some of the more progressive private clubs if they really wanted to play tennis, though relatively few of them did. Angela wouldn't think to hide her Jewishness, but her name didn't sound Jewish and her fair hair wouldn't have given her away. After seeing the Prenns, however, she knew her fate was sealed.

Shortly thereafter, she was informed ever so tactfully that she would not be allowed to play matches at the club. For a moment, she wondered why she'd bothered to leave London for what was supposed to be a new world, open and unencumbered, but ultimately she took the news in stride. She turned her attention elsewhere. "Never mind," she told a fuming Violet. "Where are the public courts?"

As it happened, a short distance away from the LATC were public courts with a quality of play unmatched by most others in the country. The La Cienega courts boasted none of the accoutrements of a posh private club. There was no wood paneling, no annual fete. But Kramer and Gonzalez had played there, among others. Angela took a job stringing rackets and working behind the counter at Arzy's, a racket shop run out of a Quonset hut. She'd go each morning, get in some tennis, put in her shift, then head to Fairfax High School for a shorthand course. Violet would sit on the roof of the house, soaking up the winter sun, smoking her cigarettes, gazing off at the mountains in the distance, dreaming of love. It reminded her of South Africa.

FROM DECEMBER 1952 through March 1953, Angela played in tournaments throughout Southern California. She played at Griffith Park in the citywide championships in January, losing early. She played in Riverside, and as far away as Bakersfield. She was gaining experience, but seldom advanced beyond the first few rounds of tournaments. The Californians of the same age were a level above her in ability, and two levels above in experience. "But it was wonderful," she recalls. "I lapped it up. I enjoyed every second of it."

Rejected by the LATC, Angela delved into the challenge of finding an alternative with her customary vigor. "I was a busybody," she says, "and I asked plenty of questions." All roads led to former champion Bill Tilden, who was as desperate as she was enthusiastic. Tilden was a legendary talent, regarded by many at the time—and even some today—as the greatest tennis player of the century. He played eighteen years as an amateur, from 1912 to 1930, and won almost ninety-four percent of his matches, an astonishing statistic. He won ten major singles titles, a record that would stand for thirty-seven years. Beginning in 1931, he toured as a professional, at one point beating Ellsworth Vines in an unforgettable match at Madison Square Garden before a sellout crowd of more than sixteen thousand. He continued to earn a good living as a touring pro well into his forties.

But Tilden was a complicated man, and a closet homosexual who favored teenaged boys. He had spent his formative years at home with an overprotective mother, who treated him as frail and sickly, though he showed not the slightest symptom. Later, after his tennis success, he lost much of his sizeable inheritance backing Broadway plays. By then, he was loitering near school playgrounds, looking for potential partners. In 1946, he was stopped by a policeman because of his erratic driving. As it happened, Tilden was actually a passenger in the car; the driver was a fourteen-year-old male Tilden had picked up at the LATC. Tilden had his arm around the boy, whose trousers were unbuttoned, and a hand in his lap. Imprisoned for six months for contributing to the delinquency of a minor, he never really recovered. He was ostracized by the tennis community and barred from the clubs that had reveled in his presence, most notably the LATC. At Philadelphia's Germantown Cricket Club, where he was a life member, his picture was removed from the wall and his name stricken from the club's rolls. He was arrested again, for molesting a hitchhiker, at about the same time that a poll of sportswriters conducted by the Associated Press judged him the greatest athlete of the first half of the twentieth century, ahead of Babe Ruth, Red Grange, and Jack Dempsey.

Barely able to make a living, Tilden pawned his trophies. By 1953, he was living in a rented room. He trolled the public courts of Los Angeles, offering lessons to anyone who would pay for them. He would die of coronary thrombosis in his bed later that year, at the age of sixty. Angela was among his last pupils.

She knew of Tilden purely from his tennis success. She had no idea he was a homosexual. Hard as it may be to believe now, she swears that, at seventeen, she had no idea what a homosexual was. Not that it would have mattered if she had; she was focused on improving her tennis. She found Tilden and made an appointment for a lesson. Tilden picked her up in a rattling old car, the same Packard Clipper he'd been driving for years, and drove high into Beverly Hills. At some point, he mentioned that they were headed for a house belonging to Charlie Chaplin, whom he'd known since the 1920s, when they both competed in matches on a court at Douglas Fairbanks's studio. A true tennis aficionado who would go as far as to leave his cross-country train on the way to New York in order to play a match in Chicago or St. Louis, then continue on his way, Chaplin had taken pity on Tilden. He paid him exorbitantly to give lessons to his wife, Oona, and allowed him to use the court as necessary for other lessons he might drum up.

The house was on Summit Drive, and many of the top players of the day had competed there, as well as actors, producers, writers, and politicians. The Welsh poet Dylan Thomas had once driven Shelley Winters's car on the court and directly into the net, but usually the competition was far more sedate and ended with tea taken at the teahouse above the court. By that time, Chaplin was gone from America. Pursued as a possible Communist and a potential tax evader by an array of government agencies, he was spending the winter in Lausanne under a cloud. Eventually, the Chaplins would settle in a fifteen-room estate near the Swiss lakefront town of Vevey, in permanent exile. In November, just as Angela was arriving in the United States, Oona Chaplin had closed up the Summit Drive house and shipped out the furniture. By the time Angela saw it, it was all but abandoned. The door to the tennis court was locked, but Tilden had a key.

Tilden taught Angela to vary her shots; to hit deep to the forehand, then shallow to the backhand, varying speed, distance, and placement. They'd hit for a while, and he'd give pointers. Once she hit a shot off the wrong foot: a backhand sliced with a relaxed wrist. That's not how you'd do it according to the textbook, nor how Angela had intended it, but it slid down the line for a winner. Tilden stopped the proceedings and walked to the net. "That's the best shot you've played today," he said, truly impressed. "How often can you do that?"

"Not often," Angela replied.

Angela began to see Tilden once a week for lessons. They were expensive—by one account, Tilden was earning more at Chaplin's each week than nearly all the tennis coaches in Southern California—but they were bankrolled by Harry, who was as thrilled as might be imagined by the Hollywood connection Angela was establishing. Beyond that, all she'd done was tour a studio and have a photo taken with Doris Day. Harry Buxton's name, it turned out, meant little at the studios.

Tilden took a liking to Angela that transcended the weekly paycheck. He'd take her to the Beverly Hills Tennis Club and introduce her to the occasional minor celebrity. He urged her to enter mixed-doubles tournaments with a strapping twenty-one-year-old named Art Anderson, who had just returned from military duty in Japan. He'd let them rally together, but he was loathe to leave them alone for fear that a romantic attachment might develop. She'd notice him peeping out from behind the hedges, spying on them. "She had aspirations of being one of the better women tennis players, but she wasn't at that time," Anderson says now. "Her game improved radically with Bill." It is intriguing that Anderson was never aware that Angela was Jewish, leaving it an open question as to whether Tilden knew, not that it would have mattered to him.

Intercontinental travel was still relatively rare in those days, and word spread among some of the Hollywood elite that a young woman from London who had actually played at Wimbledon was taking lessons on Chaplin's court. "People were fascinated," Angela recalls. "I was the flavor du jour." One day she arrived to find several of Chaplin's neighbors, including Walter Pidgeon and Katharine Hepburn, milling about the court. As Tilden gave Angela her lesson, these famous actors scampered around the edges of the court, fetching balls. It was a surreal scene. Angela couldn't help but think of her peers in London, waiting out another dreary winter, putting in their time on the few indoor courts that had survived the war. She was playing with the famous Bill Tilden, the sun was shining, and movie stars were running down the balls.

At some point, her mother picked up a Hollywood agent lolling at a pool. The agent told Angela that he could make her a television star. "You're already a star*let*," he said. "You've played at Wimbledon, and that's worth something." One day he arrived with the announcement that he'd booked her on the nationwide program *You Bet Your Life*, hosted by Groucho Marx. Angela was dubious, but he insisted they'd film it before she left for London.

That time was approaching. In mid-March, Angela played her final tournament in California, losing to Maureen Connolly, who was already close to unstoppable, 6–3, 6–0, in the first round of the La Jolla Invitational. Nevertheless, her lessons with Tilden had advanced her game considerably. Looking back, she may have done better with him than she would have if the LATC had deigned to admit her. "You didn't go to the LATC for coaching," Anderson says. "If Perry T. Jones took a liking to someone, he would make sure that the player had matches to play that he had arranged, and that was about it. And whether he would have done that for Angela Buxton under any circumstances, I sincerely doubt. She probably did a hundred percent better with Bill than she would have done there."

Before she left, she arrived at the Palace Theater in Hollywood on

the appointed date to find that Groucho's bookers were, indeed, expecting her. She was billed as a "British tennis starlet," the description the
agent had concocted, and paired with a rodeo cowboy. Together, they
were given trivia questions to answer. Between the two of them, they
knew all the answers, right up to the end. For his final question, Groucho asked them to identify the name of the dried meat that American
Indians took on long journeys. They had bet all their accumulated winnings; this was for the jackpot. They now had a few seconds to huddle
and come up with an answer.

Angela had lived in South Africa and knew dried meat as biltong.
The rodeo cowboy had traveled the American West and called it pemmican. Neither wanted to impose his or her will on the other on
national television. They couldn't decide which to say. Angela thought
fast. "Let's say both at once, and if they hear the right answer, they'll
give it to us," she whispered.

They turned toward Groucho and spoke simultaneously. "Pemmican," said the cowboy. "Biltong," said Angela.

"Pemmican!" Groucho echoed, with Angela nodding fiercely. The
tennis starlet and the rodeo cowboy had won. They walked away with a
total of $1,980 in 1953 dollars, a formidable sum. Angela salted her
share away in an American bank and promptly forgot about it, an over-
sight that would cause her much agitation years later, when the Inland
Revenue came calling.

CHAPTER 7

Patterned Dresses and Pattern Tennis

ANGELA'S TRIP TO CALIFORNIA was hardly a secret in England. She'd been overseas for specialized tennis training, and that was beyond uncommon: it was unprecedented. All of a sudden, by virtue of that trip alone, she had emerged as England's hope, the local girl who would help win the annual Wightman Cup against the Americans, following decades of disappointment.

By 1953, the British tennis community was getting desperate. The sport had been a British invention, the product of a patent by Major Walter C. Wingfield in 1874, though its origins date from the Middle Ages. The British had retained proprietary feelings about it despite overwhelming evidence that they no longer held dominance. They had convinced themselves that the lengthy era of success by former colonies America and Australia was an aberration. They looked forward to a time when British players would again dominate the sport. Any ray of hope was significant news.

As a consequence, Angela stepped off the boat that April and directly into the pages of the London papers. Reporters wanted to know whom she'd played, what she'd seen, how much she'd improved, and what her prospects were. She was thrilled by the attention. It raised her level of confidence, even as it raised her profile. One inquiry came from Teddy Tinling, also a Queen's Club member, who had made a name for himself by outfitting tennis players. Gussy Moran's lace panties were his, and, later, avant-garde outfits worn by Maureen Connolly, Brazil's Maria

Bueno, and Billie Jean King would be, too. "You're going to be big news when you hit that tennis court," Tinling told Angela. "Everyone wants to see how well you're playing. As a matter of fact, I've already designed two dresses for you, one for Bournemouth and one for Wimbledon."

The first, made from Sudan cotton, was reverse-scalloped and trimmed in white satin. It had a fitted bodice, like a belly dancer's, and a skirt gathered in at the waist. It wasn't Angela's style, a bit too pretty in a girlish way—but she did look glamorous, she had to admit. Something like a ballerina crossed with a movie star.

Bournemouth was a shale-court tournament held each year in late April, the climax of the English spring season that led up to the French Championships. All the top British players were there, and the better Americans who had crossed the ocean for the European tournaments. Angela drew the best of them in the first round, Doris Hart. She stepped out on the court in her Tinling creation and felt as if everyone in the grandstand was staring at her, probably because they were. "I remember she had been saying that she was ready to play Doris Hart, was ready to beat Doris Hart," recalled Pat Hird, who was entered in that tournament. "I think it might have spurred Doris on a little bit."

Hart won the match in an astoundingly rapid twenty-two minutes, and she needed that long only because the mortified Angela stalled near the end, grasping for any way to make her performance seem respectable. She showed all the signs of schoolgirl nervousness. She sprayed balls to the left, to the right, even behind her once or twice. The final score was 6–0, 6–0. Angela walked off the court and ripped the bodice from the skirt. She was sure she was finished as a tennis player. All the expense and the effort of traveling to Los Angeles had been wasted, and far more than that. All the time invested, from South Africa onward. The weeks in Southport, the time at the Cumberland Club, the struggle to get a place at Wimbledon—and she couldn't even last half an hour on the court with a serious player! Angela was as prepared as she'd ever be for a match, yet she didn't win a game against Hart. What business did she have getting on the court with a Wimbledon champion?

She walked away from the grounds and down a road to a bus stop.

She was heading back to her room at the Ambassador, the hotel in Bournemouth where Jews routinely stayed. She'd pack up her things and then go back to London on the next train. She already had resolved to quit tennis and finish her education as a seamstress. An old Jaguar pulled up: at least secondhand, possibly third. Inside was a journalist who had just come from the match. He rolled down the window and informed her that she'd be pilloried in the newspapers the next day. That's how it worked, he said. The papers built you up as something, and then if you couldn't live up to the billing they'd given you, they'd tear you down.

But don't be too upset, he told her. I can tell you've got something by the way you play. Angela looked at him, incredulous. She'd barely been on the court long enough to wrinkle her Teddy Tinling dress. She hadn't won a single game, and he had something positive to say about her play? It didn't ring true.

He invited her into the car, offering a ride to her hotel. When they arrived, he handed her his card. He was Clarence Medlycott Jones, but asked to be called Jimmy. He had represented England in the Davis Cup years before. He might be able to help her, he said. But Angela shook her head vigorously. "You don't understand. I'm giving up tennis."

"If you ever change your mind, my office is in Fleet Street," he said. "I'm not a coach, I'm a writer. But I've got ideas. This was just an unfortunate day for you today, from every point of view. I'm convinced of that."

She thanked him and tucked the card away, returned to London, and promptly forgot about it. She spent the months that followed at school, learning to design dresses. She didn't quit tennis, not officially, but she subordinated her fantasies to reality. Without pressing, she had a measure of success. She landed a spot in Wimbledon, was handed a first-round bye, won a match against Thelma Lister in three sets, and then won another against Anne Goldsworthy, which put her into the Round of 16.

Even during Wimbledon, tennis hardly filled her day. She attended her classes at the Katinka School of Dress Design on Gloucester Road each morning, then headed out to the All England Club for matches, which began at two in the afternoon. In her mind, Wimbledon was more a showcase for her nascent dress designs than for her tennis. She wore her own creation, a pantsuit with her initials stitched on the breast and the shorts. She ran into Doris Hart in the next round and lost 6–3, 6–1, but this time she hardly noticed. Tennis was an avocation now, not an obsession.

In July, she applied for a place in the Maccabiah Games as a lark. Held in Israel, they were open to Jews around the world. Angela hadn't seen the inside of a synagogue in years, but that hardly disqualified her, and she wanted to see the Holy Land. She tried out at the Chandos Lawn Tennis Club in Golders Green and was accepted, then traveled to Israel that September. In singles competition there, she advanced to the women's final against the formidable Anita Kanter of Santa Monica, California, who had won matches against some of the world's best players and was ranked No. 9 in America that fall. With much of the English Maccabiah Games soccer team rooting her on, she beat Kanter in straight sets, 6–3, 6–1. It might have been the best match she had played in her life.

Angela had barely returned to England when she came across Jones's card in a drawer. She'd paid little attention to the journalist when they'd met in Bournemouth, but now her mindset was markedly different. After beating Kanter, she was again sanguine about her tennis career. She had no affinity for the Lawn Tennis Association, had heard no encouragement from private coaches, had no school program to participate in. This Jones had at least extended a hand, and he seemed to believe in her ability.

He was overjoyed to hear from her. He'd noted her success in Tel Aviv and wanted to commission a first-person article for *Lawn Tennis and Badminton* magazine, which he owned. "Terrific," Angela said. "But is the other offer still open?" It was. Jones reminded her that he wasn't a proper coach, but reiterated that he had novel ideas. He didn't have much time, so they'd have to meet near his office. He warned that the locker room facilities at the court were almost nonexistent, little more than a peg in a wall and a space barely large enough to turn around in. Still, if she wanted to come see him at Fleet Street the following week, they could play a little and talk. Angela made a date, recording the information in her handsome script. Her tennis career, and her life, were about to be transformed.

OVER THE SPREAD of her seventy years, Jimmy Jones stands as the most important person in Angela Buxton's life. Jones was her teacher and collaborator and, much later, her companion and lover. His sensibilities shaped her own, far more than those of her erstwhile husband, Donald Silk, or any blood relation. By extension, they also altered Althea's way of looking at the world. The success she enjoyed following her exposure to him was, to a not insignificant extent, a product of his innovative mind.

Jones was born in the Norwood area of South London in 1912, the son of a man who assisted Marconi in his experiments to perfect radio. His father was also a gambler and an occasional drunk. Throughout Jones's youth the family had little money, at times dispatching him to the butcher to beg for food. Jones did not have a university education, but he had a keen intellect; he spent World War II devising ways to jam German radar transmissions for the Royal Air Force. He later designed and constructed an early model of a combined radio receiver and record player. Near the end of his life, he was probably the first to use computers to chart the shot selections of tennis players.

Jones's father had roots in the Indian subcontinent and did not look classically English, though Jones himself did. In combination with the family's periodic tumbles into poverty, and his own lack of formal education, that sense of not quite being the same as his childhood peers helped form Jones's character. "He was an exceptionally fair-minded person," says his son, Simon Jones, now an editor for *The Independent*, the London-based newspaper. Though gentle and genial, Jones wouldn't hesitate to speak up to right a perceived wrong, especially in support of someone downtrodden or otherwise disadvantaged. He couldn't understand the passiveness with which many Englishmen watched injustice happen. If a newcomer appeared in a press box, Jones would be among the first to greet him, especially if he was visiting from a distant country.

"He wanted everyone to feel welcome, to feel at home, because he hadn't always been welcomed," Simon Jones says.

He was a talented tennis player. He played at Wimbledon each year from 1932 to 1951, except for the six years during which the Championships weren't held. In 1938, he represented England in the Davis Cup. In 1939, he founded *British Lawn Tennis* magazine, which he ran from his Fleet Street office. He later added a second magazine to his stable, *World Bowls*. But it was as a daily journalist for many of England's national papers that Jones gained a measure of renown. He was quite possibly the most prolific English-language sportswriter of his day. Nominally employed by the *Daily Mirror* as chief tennis correspondent, he would range far afield, to Europe and beyond, in the service of anyone who would hire him. Writing under a variety of aliases, as well as his own C. M. Jones, he covered tennis, lawn bowling, soccer, snooker, and a range of other sports for broadsheets and tabloids throughout England, as well as South African, Indian, and Australian publications. He would report the same match for four or five different newspapers, writing each in an appropriate style for the publication. Such aggressive freelancing was not unknown among journalists of the day, but nobody carried the multiple bylines to such lengths as Jones. (One British writer, David Gray, filed dispatches under the name of Henry Raven, a famous murderer. On the day that Gray, inundated by assignments at Forest Hills, was unable to produce Raven's column for the *Sunday Telegraph*, he had his imaginary alter ego killed off. A death notice went in the paper, furthering the charade.)

In such a way, Jones made a dependable living, though he wasn't driven by money. Frequently, he'd neglect to negotiate specific terms with the different papers, but would file stories in the hope that they would be used. He was always pleasantly surprised when a check would arrive. Part of that was a British middle-class bias against preoccupation with money, which exists to this day. "To be constantly thinking about money is seen to be very vulgar," Simon Jones says. "My father didn't put a particularly high value on money."

Instead, he was motivated by his passions, and foremost among those was tennis. He'd write about most any sport in which a score was kept, and a few in which a score wasn't, and he excelled at pursuits as varied as snooker, cricket, and table tennis, but lawn tennis was his avocation as well as his vocation. His tennis magazine barely stayed solvent, but it gave Jones entry to all the important tournaments. He saw the magazine as a shop window for himself, leading him to other things.

Coaching was among them. He never trained to be a coach, as he stressed to Angela, but then, few tennis coaches do. Jones was an original thinker, perhaps because of his lack of formal education. During the course of his career he came to see aspects of tennis in innovative ways. Some were tactical insights, like his belief that holding the racket with a slight bias toward your backhand side when you stood at net greatly aided your chances of making a successful volley, the theory being that one can naturally get the racket into forehand position much more quickly than to backhand. Others involved training. At a time when standout players such as Pancho Gonzalez and Alice Marble were heavy smokers, Jones never smoked, rarely drank so much as a glass of wine, and kept trim throughout his career.

By the time he encountered Angela at the bus stop in Bournemouth, he was in the process of constructing a methodology for shot selection that extended to its logical extreme Bill Tilden's premise of varying lengths and angles. He called it Pattern Tennis, and in Angela he found the perfect instrument for its implementation. "A person's tennis game begins with his nature and background and comes out through his motor mechanisms into shot patterns and characteristics of play," John McPhee has written. "If he is deliberate, he is a deliberate tennis player; and if he is flamboyant, his game probably is, too." Angela was a dutiful shotmaker with a steady, if unexciting, game. She was smart enough to understand the theory behind Jones's dictums, and talented enough to carry them through. But she wasn't so naturally talented that she'd be tempted to stray from the prescribed strategy. She was also willing to do the unorthodox, such as picking up stones in the street and running wind sprints with them to increase quickness and coordination, if it meant that she would improve. In a sport that relied on convention, this was a decided asset.

"So much of what people call talent is actually mental ability," says Shirley Bloomer, now Shirley Brasher, who was a highly ranked British player from 1955 to 1958. "For the game that Jimmy taught her, Angela would score rather highly. If you'd given the game that Jimmy was trying to teach to Angela Mortimer or myself or Ann Jones or Christine [Truman], we would have done awfully. But it suited Angela Buxton."

DURING NOVEMBER AND DECEMBER OF 1953, Jones taught Angela the rudiments of Pattern Tennis. On an all-weather tarmac in Lincoln's Inn Fields, they'd play during Jones's lunch hour. Jones had theories he'd been working on for years, and he was eager to impart them to a serious pupil. Hit the ball here, and then there, Jones would tell Angela, detailing a series of strategic moves in sequence. "It was like chess, not tennis," Angela remembers. "It was a way to move the ball around, stay in control, and not choke. You could let memory take over."

The barristers and law court officials who worked at the high court nearby would sit in the sun eating their brown-bagged sandwiches, and watch dumbfounded as the peculiar drills unfolded. They had never seen tennis played in such a fashion. Jones would ask Angela to hit the ball up the line twice in succession, then follow with a backhand across the court to the other side, then back up the sideline again. If she failed to execute the pattern correctly, the lesson would stop and Jones would show it to her again until she had it. "Commit it to memory," he would say, and they'd move on to the next sequence.

Jones was a journalist who wrote about many of the tournaments Angela participated in, so he tried to minimize his public relationship with her. But in the small and somewhat incestuous universe of London tennis in the 1950s, it quickly became an open secret. What this passionate forty-year-old saw in a game but not exactly gifted teenager was a source of spirited, and occasionally ribald, debate. "He had a very strange relationship with Angela that none of us could quite understand," John Barrett says. "I think he was infatuated with her.

And he wanted to make her into something. He became a Svengali figure for her."

On reflection, Barrett wonders if fascinated isn't a better description of Jones's feelings than infatuated. "Was there more than teacher-pupil? I don't know," he says. "But here at last was someone to try out all the theories. And he was a terrific theorist."

Barrett is quick to admit that many of Jones's theories were sound. Jones preached flexibility, bending, and stretching, at a time when few competitive players from anywhere, let alone traditionalist England, utilized such a regimen. Instead, athletes were routinely told to take salt pills during a match, and not to drink anything, for fear of cramping. It's a wonder, Barrett notes, that no one died of dehydration. He and the others did token training, the occasional jog, but nothing consistently except play tennis. Meanwhile, Jones had Angela racing against the cars in Regent's Park to improve her footspeed.

Their need for each other was symbiotic. She could put his theoretical strategies into living motion, as if she were a "robot," as Maureen Connolly later called her. He was the tennis extremist she had been searching for since she couldn't get in more than half an hour a week in South Africa. "She was almost a fanatic," Barrett says. "Work, work, work. She was on the borderline of fanatic. That was a good word to use in the context of Angela Buxton: fanatical. Still is."

IN JANUARY 1954, Jones and Angela put Pattern Tennis to its first test. She had entered a post-Christmas under-twenty-one at tournament Roehampton, in southwest London. Perversely, the tournament was played outdoors, and the uncertainty of the elements was supposed to add flavor to the proceedings. It certainly didn't help attendance, as few fans wanted to huddle in the January chill, the wind whipping in off the English Channel.

Before the tournament, Angela's father took her shopping at Simpson's. Stepping off the elevator, she saw a bottle-green jacket with lamb's-wool lining on a stand, and Harry bought it for her to wear at Roehampton. The jacket proved a sensation with the local fashion photographers, especially when Angela unexpectedly won the tournament.

It wasn't much of a field, and it didn't mean that the patterns Jones was drilling into her head would work against the likes of Hart and Brough, but it affirmed that she was advancing. She had been working with Jones for six weeks.

Angela parlayed her interest in fashion into a job at Lillywhites, on Regent Street off Piccadilly Circus. At the time, and even today, Lilly-whites was the finest store in the city for fashionable sportswear, although the glamorous designs of the 1950s have been all but sup-planted by soccer and rugby jerseys from around the world, and sport-ing goods of every description. She had written a letter to the store telling them she was a tennis player who wished to become a cham-pion. She was seeking a job that would give her time off to play and practice. Such relationships between athletes and employers are rou-tine now, but in London in those days this was revolutionary. Tennis was something you fit in when you were able to, not something to bend your life around.

Lillywhites accepted, perhaps understanding that the store had something to gain from the affiliation if she succeeded. But because of her uncertain schedule, it was willing to pay her just five pounds a week. She took the job and kept it for four years, through the rest of her tennis career. Later, when she started to make the newspapers more fre-quently, she was given an annual clothing allowance of 150 pounds, but she never received a raise. She started as a secretary to the shoe man-ager on the fourth floor, Mr. Greatrex. She'd sit behind the stock and use the shorthand she'd learned in Los Angeles to take notes. You couldn't even see her behind all the shoes.

DURING THE FIRST FEW MONTHS OF 1954, women's tennis found itself in one of its periodic epochs of absolute dominance by a single individ-ual. Like Helen Wills Moody before her, like Martina Navratilova and Steffi Graf who followed, Maureen Connolly played the game at a higher level than her peers. She didn't look like much of an athlete, but she rarely lost a tennis match. She was a natural, a tennis prodigy. As a nineteen-year-old from New Jersey, Betty Rosenquest had spent much of 1947 in California, trying to catch the eye of Eleanor "Teach" Ten-

nant, Alice Marble's former coach. At one point, Tennant asked Rosenquest to accompany her to San Diego, where she had a young pupil. It
was Connolly, slight and skinny and all of thirteen years old. Tennant
had Rosenquest, who was ranked in the top twenty nationally, play a set
against her, to gauge Connolly's level of ability. Rosenquest eked out an
8–6 victory and returned to Los Angeles reeling. She could see the
future in this pocket-sized girl.

Once Connolly, who was quickly nicknamed "Little Mo," hit her
stride in the middle of 1952, she wasn't beaten in a major tournament.
She rarely dropped as much as a set. In three seasons, she won nine
straight majors, an accomplishment that has never been equaled. During that time, her record at Wimbledon, the French Championships,
Forest Hills, and the Australian Championships was an incomparable
50–0. She also won everything else there was to win, including her
Wightman Cup matches.

She had perfect footwork, and she hit the ball hard. She rarely came
to net, because she didn't have to, preferring to stay at the baseline and
blast ground strokes with her forehand and backhand. She seemed to
be in perfect position no matter where you hit the ball, and had a
knowledge of the geometries of the game that seemed preternatural in
someone so young. Across the net from Connolly, time would almost
seem to stop. You'd hit a winner, but somehow she'd be there—not so
much *get* there as already *be* there. She'd send it back your way harder
than it came. It was demoralizing, and the best players of the day
folded up one after another. She had uncanny powers of concentration
and a deadly consistency. Rosenquest remembers playing doubles with
her in several tournaments early on and never seeing her miss a service
return. Not once. "Just watching her made the rest of us better," Rosenquest says.

Connolly never questioned a linesman's call, just kept on playing.
Any point she lost, she figured, she could make up for later. If she was
down 0–40 in a game, it still felt like she was up 40–0. "She conveyed it
with her manner," Doris Hart says. Hart was a decade older than Connolly. They were both Catholic, and when they played the same tournaments, they'd go to church together on Sundays. Connolly would talk to

her like an older sister, but on the court she played Hart the same way she played everyone else. She was, says Ted Schroeder, the most competitive athlete he or anyone else ever encountered, and Schroeder knew Kramer and Gonzalez and McEnroe and the rest. Scared to death of failure, she hit each ball fueled by an unquenchable fury.

After becoming the first woman (and one of only three to date) to win all four major championships in a single season, Connolly had skipped Australia in 1954, not willing to brave the extended journey. Then she won the French Championships and glided through another Wimbledon, beating Louise Brough in the final. With an injured Shirley Fry absent from the U.S. Clay Courts in River Forest, Illinois, that July, Connolly teamed with Hart in the doubles. They were unstoppable. Connolly made up for Hart's lack of mobility, and then some. Connolly and Hart beat Althea and Nancy Norton with little difficulty, and as they were at the umpire stand, Althea turned to Connolly with a hardness in her eyes. "You guys aren't that good," she said. "We should be able to beat you."

Connolly didn't know what to do. Nobody had ever been impudent enough to say such a thing to her, much less someone on the level of Althea, little more than a footnote in women's tennis at the time. She looked at Hart, seeking intervention. Hart was livid, her sense of propriety offended. Instantly, she proposed a bet: "You and Nancy, you'll be here tomorrow, won't you? You know what we'll do? You get your friends and collect as much money as you can. Maureen and I will do the same. And we'll have a rematch."

Althea demurred. "I'm entitled to my opinion," she said.

"That's right, you are entitled to it," Hart said, staring hard into Althea's face. "But until the day comes when you beat me or Maureen, you don't say anything. If you ever manage to beat us, you can say whatever you want about us."

After that tournament, Connolly returned home to San Diego for two weeks of relaxation prior to the U.S. Championships, while Hart stayed on in Chicago. The plan was for Connolly to fly back to the Midwest, and then they'd drive to New York together in Hart's car. "She couldn't wait to get home," Hart remembers. "She told me she planned to ride her horse every day." It appeared that Connolly would continue to go on winning for many years to come. She was not yet twenty-one years old.

On July 20, 1954, Connolly went out riding on her horse, Merryboy, near her home. She strayed from a bridle path toward a construction site. A cement mixer rumbled into view and startled the horse. The horse shied toward it, caught its leg, and fell. Pinned against the cement mixer, Connolly broke her right leg and severed the muscles in her calf. She needed four hours of emergency surgery.

Eventually, Connolly sued the Pro-Mix Concrete Company. She hired top San Diego trial lawyer John Butler, later the city's mayor, who brought Jack Kramer to the witness stand. Kramer had been running professional tours of two and four male players barnstorming around America, and he testified that he'd had conversations with Connolly about her possibly turning pro after Forest Hills that summer. Harry Hopman, the Australian coach, offered the opinion that a tour featuring Connolly could have earned her $75,000 a year for two years. Connolly was awarded $95,000. She never played competitive tennis again.

In Hart's mind, Connolly was already ready to retire, even at twenty. "She'd won everything there was to win," she says. "I seriously doubt that she would have played another year after 1954." Even after the operation, Hart insists, Connolly could have picked up where she'd left off, as the best female tennis player in the world, but she didn't have the inclination. Her husband, Norman Brinker, used the money from the lawsuit to open the first Steak & Ale restaurant. Later, plastic surgery covered Connolly's scar and she played recreational tennis. She died of cancer in 1969, at thirty-four.

Whether the accident altered the course of tennis history or not, Connolly was gone. And Hart would soon be gone, too, as one generation gradually ceded ground to the next. She played at the U.S. Championships that year, and finally managed to win it after having lost the final five times. In 1955, she would defend her title at Forest Hills. Then she retired to teach tennis at Miami's Flamingo Hotel.

There was no professional women's tour to join, no other way to make a living with your tennis beyond teaching. When you were finished, you were finished, and you set out to do whatever else you could.

Hart taught tennis at the Flamingo and the Bath & Tennis Club in Spring Lake, New Jersey, and then for nearly three decades at the Hillsborough Club in Pompano Beach. There you'd find her, into the 1980s, one of the finest tennis players of her era, teaching footwork to anyone who might book a lesson. It was a cautionary tale for the likes of Althea, and anyone else who would wish to make a living from an amateur game.

With Sydney Llewellyn

CHAPTER 8

She Didn't Have
a Name

As Doris Hart had so pointedly told her, Althea was in no position to behave like a champion. She had never beaten Hart, never beaten Maureen Connolly, never beaten Louise Brough, never won anything of consequence. Since losing to Brough at Forest Hills in 1950, she had been playing tennis as though she were treading water. She was showing little improvement, and seldom upset a better player. "For a year, Althea's name has been missing from the headlines of the sports pages," *One World* magazine wrote in June 1953. "Does that mean she has slipped?"

She hadn't exactly slipped, but she hadn't made the progress that had been expected of her in light of her strong showing against Brough. Althea returned from Wimbledon in the summer of 1951 and lost to Connolly at Forest Hills. She reported to Tallahassee for the fall semester, then resumed playing USLTA tournaments in 1952. She journeyed downstate to Miami Beach for the Good Neighbor tournament that she'd won the previous year, but this time lost in three sets to the underwhelming Magda Rurac. In May, she played a well-promoted exhibition in Chicago against Connolly and lost again. In August, she lost in the first round of the Eastern Grass Courts at Orange to Anita Kanter, whom Angela would later beat in Israel, prompting Hamilton Chambers to write in *Racquet* magazine: "Time is running out on Miss Gibson."

That week in Orange, she roomed with the Darbens of nearby Montclair, New Jersey. She'd met Rosemary Darben while playing an ATA event at the Shady Rest Country Club in Scotch Plains, New Jersey. A passable player on the Negro circuit, Rosemary invited Althea to stay at her family's home during the Easterns, and she did for the next seven years. Althea's friendship with Rosemary would outlast the century, and Rosemary's brother, William, soon felt like a brother to Althea, too—though he clearly longed to be more than that.

Althea had few if any true friends on the tour, nobody to confide her hopes and passions to, so she welcomed the Darbens' support. It didn't seem to improve her tennis, however. At Forest Hills the following month, Althea had a 5–3 lead on Doris Hart in the first set. Then Hart took all but five points over the next four games and all but a handful the rest of the way, winning 7–5, 6–1. Hart never moved well, but it seemed as if wherever Althea hit the ball, she was ready for it. It was the benefit of having played so many competitive matches, Hart would say later. She'd needed half a set to figure out what Althea was going to do, and after that she knew exactly how she had to position herself to take advantage. Althea couldn't understand what had happened; she finished the match angry and frustrated.

Because she was caught between youth and experience, such frustration was all too common for her. After graduating from Florida A&M in the spring of 1953, Althea played tournaments all summer. The results can be read as a litany of lost opportunities. She dropped the final of the Western Championships in Milwaukee to Australia's Thelma Long. At River Forest on July 26, she reached the final of the National Clay Courts, then earned the distinction of losing to Connolly 6–4, 6–4, in one of Connolly's rare appearances on that playing surface. At the Merion Cricket Club the following week, she played a highly competitive match with Brough, their first meeting since Forest Hills three summers before. She lost 7–5, 6–1, but it was a high point. In August, she lost at Orange to Hart, winning just five games. Then she ran up against Connolly again at Forest Hills, found she had left her vaunted serve somewhere along the way, and was through in two brief sets.

Immediately after Forest Hills, Althea set out for Lincoln University, in Jefferson City, Missouri, where she'd been offered a job coaching the men's tennis team. She spent the academic years of 1953–54 and

1954–55 coaching there, far from the mainstream. She still competed in ATA and USLTA tournaments, though she didn't leave North America. She'd play Lancaster and Orange each summer, and she'd dutifully win the ATA championship and then go on to compete in Forest Hills, but the competitive lapses in her game were frequent. In the month of July 1954, for example, she lost in straight sets in the quarterfinals at Orange to England's Helen Fletcher, hardly an immortal, then lost in the second round at Merion to unknown Janet Hopps. At the U.S. Clay Courts in River Forest that month, she played one of the worst matches of her life, losing 6–0, 6–1 in the first round to Lois Felix, who will never be confused with Alice Marble. At Forest Hills at the end of the summer, she dropped a first-round match to Helen Perez. Clearly, Althea had lost her way.

Earlier that year, she'd made an appearance on the television show *This Is Your Life,* honoring Marble. Marble aside, many in the viewing audience probably wondered what had happened to Althea Gibson. She was ranked ninth in the United States following the 1952 season, seventh in 1953, thirteenth in 1954. "You can't call that progress," she wrote.

Beyond that, she felt as if she'd taken two steps backward regarding race. She had integrated Forest Hills, integrated Wimbledon, yet she was still being denied service at many of the hotels that white players were billeted at during tournaments. Gardnar Mulloy, who would occasionally team with her in mixed doubles, remembers the difficulty Althea had finding a hotel that would admit her in his hometown of Miami. It wasn't just the South, either. Private homes at the top Eastern tournaments were no better.

There were exceptions. When Althea came to Merion for the Pennsylvania Lawn Tennis Championships, Bill Clothier had her housed at the home of social-register members such as Radnor's A. Willing Patterson, on the theory that if she deserved to be in the draw, she deserved a comfortable place in which to stay. That was enlightened, especially for a staunch conservative like Clothier, but such thinking was rare. Usually her lodging was a tumbledown motel on the far side of town, with no transportation to get her to and from the courts. One year at the Colorado State Championships in Denver, a regular stop on the post–Forest Hills circuit, Mulloy attended the Tennis Ball with both his wife and Althea, his mixed-doubles partner. The whispers started when the three of them walked in the room together, and they didn't stop until Mulloy pressed Althea into service singing two songs with the band. Her voice was borderline professional in quality, and it won her the room. Or perhaps the assembled socialites were more comfortable considering her part of the night's entertainment, as opposed to an honored guest.

Betty Rosenquest remembers noticing Althea in the locker rooms in those days. She couldn't help but stand out. "What you have to remember was, we hadn't had a black person with us," she says. "It was all new to us." Few of the players had more than a glancing acquaintance with "coloreds," as they were called, "Negro" being seen as a rebellious term. And though she often showed her wry sense of humor and a willingness to take part in the card games and gossip sessions that larded life on the amateur circuit, Althea's personality wasn't suited to making her one of the girls. Each week, someone would tack up little stories on a bulletin board wherever they happened to be playing, using nicknames for everyone. Rosenquest was "The Trainer," probably because she did the occasional situp. By dint of both her surname and her brainpower, Dottie Head Knode was "The Head." It was like a private club, a sorority with pet names used only by those on the inside. Althea would walk past such notices, uncomprehending and uninterested. She wasn't in the club. She didn't have a name.

That summer of 1955, a fourteen-year-old Negro named Emmett Till, visiting Mississippi from Chicago, was brutally beaten, shot in the head, and tossed into the Tallahatchee River. The killing was a visceral reaction to the enforced integration set out in the *Brown v. Board of Education* decision of the previous year, and it resonated across America, and around the world. In 1955, too, Althea still faced segregation in Jefferson City. She was barred from the local bowling alley because of her color, barred from renting a house in the neighborhood around the college, which was limited to whites only. She had graduated from Florida A&M; she was a nationally ranked tennis player. Yet in many ways her life held less hope than it had when she was playing basketball with Gloria Nightingale and the Mysterious Five, in the days when her tennis career and the grand adventure of the world beyond Harlem was still ahead.

WHILE AT LINCOLN, Althea started dating the army captain who ran the school's ROTC program. He was a man in his early forties, nearly two decades older than she was, and unlike anyone Althea had ever considered for a romantic partner. It was an experiment of sorts. She was getting little joy from her tennis, and ready to think about a radical turn. She'd sing in a five-piece jazz combo that performed in a Jefferson City nightclub, stay out late, concern herself even less about her fitness than she previously had. "Tennis no longer seemed like everything in the world to me," she wrote. "I was much more interested in going out on dates and having a good time."

She was getting paid only three thousand dollars a year at Lincoln, renting her own apartment, diligently paying off her car. Weary of not having money, her confidence at an ebb, she began thinking about joining the Women's Auxiliary Army Corps. The army seemed almost egalitarian, at least from how this captain she was dating described it. The money was comparatively good, expenses were low, and with America no longer at war, the lifestyle appeared to be a lot more enjoyable than playing cards night after night in sleepy Jefferson City. She submitted an application, made plans to get a physical. It bothered her that she'd be abandoning tennis, something she'd worked so hard at, but ensconced in the suffocating world of small-town Missouri, she saw few options for herself.

While waiting for her application to be processed that summer of 1955, she entered several tournaments. She won the ATA singles title, her perennial. In July, she played in Lancaster, Pennsylvania, at the USLTA's Red Rose Championships, another of her favorite events. There, Althea won the singles for the second year in succession, and she won the mixed doubles with her old friend Billie Davis, whom she'd known since the Cosmopolitan Club. Davis was coached by Sydney Llewellyn, a Jamaican-born New Yorker who taught tennis in Harlem when he wasn't scraping together a living by driving a taxi. Llewellyn was a highly visible figure in black tennis, and Althea knew him well. They'd met in 1946, played mixed doubles together at some tournaments in 1950, spent time at various events through the years. Occasionally, he'd offer her advice on her game, though she wasn't someone who took casual instruction to heart. If Llewellyn knew so much, she couldn't help but wonder, why hadn't he been more successful as a player? Success was Althea's currency, the only bona fide that mattered to her.

Not long before he saw her in Lancaster, Llewellyn had read a magazine article criticizing Althea. Now he approached her and said he believed he could help her, if she'd let him. Her sights already set on the army, Althea agreed, though she wasn't convinced she had anything to learn from him. He began by convincing her to abandon the Continental grip. Fred Johnson had taught it to her when she was new to the sport and she was still using it, all those years later. To replace it, Llewellyn introduced her to the Eastern grip, in which the racket is grasped as in a handshake and the wrist is rotated slightly from backhand to forehand. This required her to learn a new technique, which is seldom easy, but it added both power and touch to her strokes.

Over the weeks that followed, Llewellyn spent hours breaking down her game and building it up again. They'd meet at his house on 161st Street in Harlem and talk tennis. For the first time, Althea began to understand the theory of the game, why certain shots worked in some situations but not in others. She'd known intuitively that there was a time to come to net and a time to stay back at the baseline, but Llewellyn gave her a primer in court movement, teaching her where she should be at any given time, and why. Llewellyn believed in mastering the geometry of tennis. He was convinced that angles and positioning would win a player more points than simply slugging the ball. He felt that every shot had one, and only one, proper response. That response, taken in conjunction with a player's skills, dictated his or her positioning and movement. "You don't play one person," he once said. "You just play the board as if you were a machine." His philosophies didn't require the same sort of memorization as the Pattern Tennis that Angela was learning from Jimmy Jones, but the principles were nearly identical.

Beyond that, Althea's game had started evolving of its own accord. That's how it happens in tennis, as in many pursuits. You work, you struggle, you feel despair—and then, all at once, you make a leap. In Althea's case, part of it had to do with the competition she was facing. As the older players who were not intimidated by her moved on, she was able to assert her dominance over those who remained. "When Althea came in, the Broughs and Frys and Harts were a very dominant part of women's tennis," England's Shirley Bloomer says. "It was quite difficult for her to break in, mentally and physically. Against my generation, it was different. Her demeanor on court was a huge advantage to her."

The week of July 24, Althea upset second-seeded Darlene Hard in the quarterfinals at Merion in straight sets. In the twenty-game second set, Althea and Hard stayed within a game of each other from 3–3 to 7–6, when Hard held set point on Althea's serve. Althea unleashed a ferocious serve to Hard's backhand to save the game and the match, then won it several games later on an overhead. She'd played smart, tenacious tennis. That Saturday, she sprinted to a 6–1, 2–0 lead over Brough, but then proceeded to lose all but fifteen points over the next eleven games. Llewellyn urged her to walk away heartened by the first half of the match, rather than discouraged by the outcome. Unseeded at Orange, Althea advanced to the semifinals, but lost to Barbara Breit after repeated foot-fault calls flustered her. For every stride forward, she'd take a small step back. Still, Llewellyn saw progress.

And yet, even as she began to experience tangible improvement, Althea felt tired of tennis. The confidence that had sustained her since she'd taken up the game was getting harder and harder to rationalize. "If I was any good, I'd be the champ now," she writes in her autobiography. In a contemplative moment, she told Llewellyn, "But I'm just not good enough. I'm probably never going to be."

Llewellyn believed in her ability. To his dismay, she passed her physical and was awaiting her acceptance into the WAC when she played at Forest Hills that September. She beat Sara Mae Turber in the first round and Nell Hopman in the second. Then she ran into the resounding left- and right-handed strokes of Beverly Baker Fleitz, lost in straight sets, and was gone from the tournament again.

IT WAS A TYPICAL TOURNAMENT RUN for the Althea of those years, with one vital exception. Along the way, she received an invitation from Ren McMann, the president of Forest Hills' West Side Tennis Club and a USLTA potentate, that would end up altering the history of the sport.

McMann told Althea that the United States State Department was sponsoring a goodwill tour of tennis players to Southeast Asia over the coming holiday season. Two American men and two women would play in tournaments in India, Ceylon, Pakistan, and Burma. They'd give clinics, visit troops, and act as ambassadors of the so-called free world. All expenses would be covered by the government. Karol Fageros of Miami, an above-average player who had gained some fame for the golden panties she wore under her tennis skirts, was likely to be one of the American women. She'd had an eight-page spread in *Cosmopolitan* and was frequently referred to as the sport's "glamour girl." Years later, designer Ted Tinling would rank Fageros with Helen Wills Moody as the most beautiful woman he had seen in decades of watching championship tennis. She had light hair, dark eyebrows, clear blue eyes, and an exotic, triangular-shaped face. On the Indian subcontinent, she would draw crowds and attention, and that mattered to the State Department.

Ham Richardson and Bob Perry already were penciled in as the American men. McMann didn't put it quite so bluntly, but in the wake of the Till murder, which was both energizing a restive civil rights movement at home and sending an unfortunate message about America overseas, having a black woman travel under the State Department's banner and talk up the American lifestyle had strong symbolic resonance. This was no isolated instance, as Amy Bass recounts in *Not the Triumph But the Struggle,* her book about the coming of age of the African-American athlete. Congress had passed a five-million-dollar Emergency Fund for International Affairs appropriation in 1954, in large measure to fund black athletes on tours designed to spread goodwill and make the American society inclusionary. Olympic hero Jesse Owens was dispatched to India, high jumper Gilbert Cruter to West Africa, and the entire Harlem Globetrotters team to Germany, Indonesia, Burma, and Italy.

Althea was well aware that she was being chosen for her skin color. Her public relations value to the U.S. government, not the strength of her net game, would be getting her on that plane to Asia. But she also appreciated that this was a better offer than anything else that had

come along. Standing there, listening to McMann try to sell her on letting the government send her to Asia, she saw that the moment was
analogous to Doctors Eaton and Johnson introducing themselves at
Wilberforce a decade before and proposing their grand scheme for
making her a champion. "Who would turn that down?" she thought then,
and she had a similar reaction to McMann's proposal. Representing her
country would give her an official standing in the tennis world that she'd
never had, and allow her to continue playing tennis for a few more
months without worrying about money. It would also get her to a part
of the world she'd be unlikely to see in any other fashion. She accepted
the offer on the spot. The Women's Auxiliary Corps could wait.

WHILE ALTHEA HAD BEEN STALLED in the doldrums, Angela's tennis
had continued to improve. On May 5, 1954, a year after being humiliated in Bournemouth at the British Hard Courts, she managed to win a
set from Doris Hart on a rainy day at Shirley Park in London. After
that, she nearly won another.

The first pattern she'd worked up with Jones began with a short ball
to Hart's forehand side, followed by a deep backhand, then a sprint to
net. The second, a variation on that, was short to the forehand, long to
the forehand, long to the backhand, and then to net. And so it went. It
wasn't so much befuddling as soothing. It removed the element of shot
selection from the sport, so you didn't have to think, just hit the ball.
Angela could have won the match, onlookers agree, but she didn't have
it in her head that she could actually beat Doris Hart. She lost 5–7, 8–6,
6–2. Nevertheless, it was a significant accomplishment.

The previous week, Angela had lost in the quarterfinals of the
Bournemouth tournament. The week before that, she'd beaten Pat Hird
in Surrey, then extended Shirley Bloomer to three sets in an entertaining final. And earlier in April, she'd returned to the Cumberland Club in
Hampstead and won the tournament. Her confidence was building.

Following the event at Shirley Park, Angela advanced all the way to
the fourth round at Stade Roland Garros in Paris before running into
the maelstrom that was Connolly, and winning only one game in a two-
set drubbing. So when one English player came down with the mumps

and another fell ill with a sinus infection, Wightman Cup captain Mary Halford turned to Angela as a substitute selection.

The Wightman Cup had been created in 1923 by Boston's Hazel Hotchkiss Wightman, a four-time U.S. champion, as a counterpart to the men's Davis Cup. It set the best female players of Britain against those of America in an annual seven-match team competition, held over a three-day weekend in England one year and then America the next. The 1954 Wightman Cup was played at Wimbledon in the middle of June. The American team, perhaps the strongest ever assembled, consisted of Connolly, Hart, and Brough, all multiple winners of the Grand Slam events, with Shirley Fry tacked on to play doubles with Hart. The rather less distinguished Helen Fletcher, Anne Shilcock, and Angela played singles for Britain, accompanied by the doubles pairings of Fletcher with Shilcock and Angela with Pat Hird.

Britain hadn't won a single match in Wightman Cup competition since 1951, let alone the competition itself, and had won only two matches since play was resumed after the war. This June was no different. The Americans swept, 7–0, though Angela extended Louise Brough to an 8–6 first set in their singles match. After that, at the Queen's Club tournament that always preceded Wimbledon, she lost in three sets in the quarterfinals to Betty Rosenquest, who had married, moved to Jamaica, and was playing as Betty Pratt. It was another match Angela believed she could have won.

Still, she entered Wimbledon a week later as a recognized Wightman Cup player. She was expected to make at least some kind of showing, and she did, advancing to the Round of 16 in the strongest performance of her young career. When her nerves started to manifest themselves, as they often did, she had the lulling repetition of Pattern Tennis to fall back on and gain her composure. That, more than anything else, helped her against the weaker opponents, who could only beat Angela if Angela beat herself.

That she didn't manage a game against Connolly in the Round of 16 is hardly an embarrassment. "Angela was simply outplayed in every department and had no answer for Maureen's superior stroke equipment and power," was how *World Tennis* reviewed the match, but it had far less to do with Angela than the historic level of tennis that Connolly was playing. In what would be her last appearance in a Grand Slam event before her accident, Connolly raced through the draw. A 7–5 second set in the final against Brough was the only one in the tournament that extended her in the slightest. In all, she won seventy-three games and lost nineteen.

Jimmy Jones was there, writing about it all for the *Mirror*. He hadn't seen Angela in several weeks. He greeted her as though he were Spencer Tracy in the 1952 film *Pat and Mike,* about a young female golf and tennis standout and her older male coach. He'd narrow his eyes and pointedly wonder if she'd partaken of too many cream pies in his absence. He was jesting, but he also wanted to get a message across. He knew that Angela would never succeed in tennis on talent alone. She had to be fitter physically and stronger mentally. Pattern Tennis could help with the latter, but her training regimen was equally important. While other players wilted in the heat, she had to learn to make the second and third sets her own.

BY THEN, Angela had found a better place to practice. A doctor she knew from Rossmore Court informed her one day that a few successful businessmen typically played tennis on Sunday mornings at the private indoor court of department store magnate Sir Simon Marks in Maida Vale, between Paddington and St. John's Wood. The court existed for use by the directors of Marks & Spencer, but Marks's friends also had access by appointment. If Angela liked, he proposed, she could join them on the occasional Sunday when they needed a fourth player to round out two doubles teams. She did one Sunday and discovered a court that would have been deemed luxurious by any standard. Made from soft red shale, it had an upstairs changing room for the women and a separate facility downstairs for the men. It was kept by a resident housekeeper and his wife, who lived on the premises. Angela played in the Sunday game several times, but she wanted more than that. The only proper indoor courts in all of England at that time were at Queen's Club, and they were in the process of being renovated. Playing at Marks's would give her regular access to an indoor facility, something none of her English rivals had.

So she picked up her pen and composed her customary letter, with one significant departure. "I am a young Jewish girl and I've got ideas to become a tennis champion," she wrote to Marks. "I will not get in anyone's way, and I will leave the court clean." This was something of a gamble. She'd heard Marks was Jewish, though that wasn't generally known. She figured she had little chance of persuading him unless she let him know that she was Jewish, too, and by inference didn't have access to the best clubs. Marks wrote back immediately, telling her to use it with pleasure, any time she wanted.

From then on, throughout the rest of 1954 and 1955, she and Jones practiced there every Tuesday morning. They'd invite a third player to join them. Jones would feed the first ball to get the pattern going, then step out. Angela and the third player would then finish the point. The patterns were both a training mechanism and a strategy. It didn't take long before everyone in tennis knew what Angela was doing, but it hardly mattered. "We had so many patterns by then," she says. "They didn't know which one to expect."

The months of training on Marks's court were to prove invaluable. It was about the only time that Angela can recall her religion actually aiding her tennis, rather than hindering it. Judaism opened few doors for a burgeoning English athlete, and kept all too many tightly closed. Few Jews became top-class athletes in England in those days, in large measure because they had limited or no access to the private clubs and the schools and universities where golf, tennis, rugby, and cricket were played at their highest level. Alan Jay was a top fencer of the time. Sheila Van Damm had won the European women's diving championship in both 1954 and 1955. Sprinter Harold Abrahams, a distant memory, had won a gold medal in the one-hundred-meter dash at the 1924 Olympics. Boxer Kid Berg was a junior welterweight champion in the 1930s, and Kid Lewis was twice world welterweight champion before him. But these were anomalies and eccentricities; with the exception of Abrahams, they were standouts in sports that few Englishmen considered important. Asked to name the country's most successful Jewish athlete circa 1955, a typical Londoner would have scratched his head and looked lost.

Derek Dutton, a journalist and business executive who was at one time a director of British Gas, was a member of the Argyle Club in Southport, which promoted a women's tournament each year around Easter. When he'd attempted to join the club at age twenty-three, he'd been blackballed because of his working-class upbringing, but the chairman of the club, Leonard Grossmith, pushed him through. And yet the club would not allow the admission of any Jewish members. That was seen as typical, not unreasonable. If they wanted to congregate, let them build their own clubs. They certainly had the money, didn't they?

In March of 1955, Angela entered the tournament at the Argyle Club. (As with London's Cumberland Club, Jews were allowed in for the odd appearance.) It was Easter weekend, and her luggage had gone astray. She arrived in Southport wearing a gorgeous ensemble purchased from Lillywhites with her annual clothing allowance—a camel's-hair jumper and an overcoat to match—but nothing to use on a tennis court, so she went to Woolworth's and bought a pair of men's gray pants, a T-shirt, gym shoes, and socks. She looked like a student taking physical education class, but that's how she played her first round.

She also found herself without a hitting partner, so she asked the club if it could provide one. This wasn't exactly standard procedure— but then, most of the better players traveled in pairs, and Angela was on her own, as usual. Dutton, a journalist for the *Southport Guardian* at the time, was a reasonable club player, but he was hardly the person you'd have chosen to hit with the fourth-ranked woman in Britain. Yet Grossmith called him and asked him to do exactly that. Many years later, Dutton learned that he'd been asked only because none of the other club members would step on a court with a Jew.

The following year, when Dutton noted that Angela had started playing doubles with Althea, he figured the pairing made perfect sense. "Blacks and Jews were made to feel like they were apart from the rest of us," he says.

Class was still a matter of great importance in English society in the 1950s, according to Dutton, and blacks had recently replaced the Irish at the lower end. He remembers seeing Angela and Althea being ostracized, ever so discreetly, by other players. "I always figured that playing doubles together gave each of them someone to hit with," he says now, "but it also gave each of them someone else to talk to."

CHAPTER 9

Rendezvous in Asia

IN 1955, CAPTAIN Mary Halford again chose Angela for her Wightman Cup team. That July, while Althea was contemplating abandoning tennis for the WAC, Angela and the rest of the British women sailed to New York on the *Queen Elizabeth*. It wasn't as luxurious as the name implies, not in steerage class, merely the easiest way to cross the ocean.

Shirley Bloomer stepped into her tiny stateroom to find Angela, her designated roommate, standing there with six large suitcases—four or five more than anyone else carried. Even then, barely out of her teens, Angela cultivated a sense of style. She hoped she looked smart, in the British sense, and glamorous whenever possible. It was one more manifestation of the difference between her and the rest of the English playing on the tennis circuit: sturdy, solid women who may have been attractive enough but would hardly have considered glamour a positive attribute.

Bloomer had never traveled with Angela before, hardly traded words with her. They got along perfectly well on the trip, yet Bloomer came away with the sense that Angela was determined to get ahead in tennis, and in life generally. "She knew what she wanted, and she was going to get it," Bloomer says, "and if you got in the way, bad luck to you." Angela recognizes herself in that characterization. "All I wanted to do was go straight ahead, the shortest way possible," she admits. "If anyone or anything stood in my way, I went right over them."

By then, Angela had earned a reputation as a loner. Even the magazines picked up on it. "Although the girls on the English Wightman Cup team deny it, rumor is that there is a certain amount of coolness between one of the players and the rest of the team," *World Tennis* wrote at one point, and there wasn't a member of the Lawn Tennis Association who needed to be told which player the reference meant. At the end of the summer, Angela, Bloomer, and Angela Mortimer would be invited to play in tournaments in Colorado, California, and Mexico. Bloomer and Mortimer were hardly the closest of friends, but they drove to Denver as teammates, flew together to Los Angeles for the Pacific Southwest tournament, then flew on to Mexico, rooming together along the way. Angela traveled alone. Mortimer and Bloomer ate dinner together every night in several states and two countries; it never occurred to them to ask Angela to join them.

Long before, Jimmy Jones had noticed that Angela was kept at a distance by the other players. From his own experience as a tradesman's son, he understood the ramifications of being on the outside. In his mind, it could work to Angela's competitive advantage. If she seldom had feelings for the player across the net, she could approach each match the way Connolly did, with a cold heart and an assassin's eye. "Don't have your friends in tennis," he advised her. "You're not going to be popular, anyway—to begin with, you're Jewish. So don't play the popularity stakes. Keep to yourself. Do what's best for *you*."

That was easy enough. It was Angela's predilection to begin with. Yet her conduct on and off the court had to be impeccable. She couldn't question calls, or give anyone in an official position reason to discriminate against her. At one point, Jones admonished her by saying, "You have to win twice as much as anyone else. That way, they can't help but send you places."

ANGELA HAD PAID HER OWN WAY to one tournament earlier in 1955— or, rather, her father had. She'd been left off the British team for a minor competition called the Pierre Gillou Cup that January, in favor of lesser-ranked players. Harry was laid up in the hospital following a kidney operation when she visited him with the news. Looking for something cheerful to engage himself with while he recuperated, he asked her if she truly believed she had a chance to win the tournament. When she said that she did, he footed the bill for the trip to Paris, then followed her march to the championship in the papers.

She built on that success by winning two local tournaments, both in May: at Shirley Park in Croydon and the Paddington Hard Courts. She advanced into the third round at the French Championships, then won three matches at Queen's Club before drawing Brough in a semifinal and losing in straight sets. By then, Angela seemed to rank just outside the upper echelon of women's players. She was having little trouble beating inferior talent, but couldn't break through against the likes of Hart, Brough, or Mortimer. But that was the first step for a young player, Jones told her. Win the matches you're supposed to win, and then learn to step up and start winning some that you aren't expected to win.

At Wimbledon, she reached the quarterfinals for the first time, the only British woman to do so. But if that showed how far she'd come, her quarterfinal match revealed how far she needed to go. She was powerless against Beverly Baker Fleitz, who not only looked like a movie star in a sleeveless ruffled dress and with dyed-blond hair, but needed just half an hour to advance by 6–2, 6–2. Angela stubbornly stuck to her patterns, most often playing a short cross-court ball to Fleitz's forehand, then hitting deep to the backhand corner and coming to net. But Fleitz was hitting the ball too hard, and she'd routinely whack it past the advancing Angela for a winner. Angela had no Plan B: "Scrambling," as one journalist wrote, "is not within her capacity."

That match was used as an example of how poor Britain's 1955 Wightman Cup prospects were. Here was Angela, the surviving English-woman at Wimbledon, and she couldn't stay on the court more than thirty minutes against the American Fleitz, who was ranked behind two other Americans, Hart and Brough, at the time. Even Maureen Connolly, writing a column for a British paper during the first Wimbledon since her retirement, felt compelled to weigh in with a verdict that seems needlessly harsh, though probably accurate. "Angela's problem is that she has no talent whatsoever," Connolly wrote. ". . . Mrs. Fleitz, on the other hand, is loaded with natural ability. What a difference it makes!"

Lance Tingay, writing in the *Daily Telegraph,* was only slightly more forgiving. "Naturally slow of foot and deliberate in her stroke . . . it was a wonder she withstood the lambasting Mrs. Fleitz dealt as well as she did."

THOSE WHO SAW EVIDENCE of coming British futility in Angela's hopeless effort against Fleitz were proven prescient by the Wightman Cup that August. Matches were delayed a day following the torrential rains of a storm that was being called "Capricious Connie," but the delay couldn't forestall the inevitable. Britain did manage to avoid utter embarrassment and win one of the seven matches. Angela Mortimer, who had captured the French Championships that summer (the first major title by an Englishwoman in years), defeated Doris Hart in three stirring sets, but that was all. Angela lost a singles match and, paired with Mortimer, a doubles match.

Absent again was Althea. Through 1955, she still hadn't represented the U.S. in Wightman Cup play. Much of the reason was inherent in the rankings: Hart and Brough had been first and second in the U.S. the previous year, and Fry was fourth. But Dottie Knode, like Althea, was unranked in the top ten, and Margaret Osborne du Pont, who captained the team, had all but retired from competitive play. Althea wasn't troubled by her omission; she never expected to be chosen. She hadn't played overseas in the French and Italian Championships or at Wimbledon that summer, nor the summer before, nor the summer before that. She remained a curiosity, a talented athlete with a distinctive style and skin color, but as late as 1955, she was hardly considered a player of the first rank, even in her own country.

She did travel to Mexico City for a tournament there, held in October with Hurricane Katie fast approaching. Karol Fageros, effervescent and eager as always, bounded up to Althea when she spotted her during a dinner at the Chapultepec Club, kissed her on the cheek, and expressed her excitement about traveling with her on their impending Asia trip. Angela, who happened to be sharing a room with Fageros, was standing nearby, yet somehow she and Althea never managed to have a conversation.

Angela lost in the first round in Mexico, but she and Mortimer beat Althea and Fageros in a doubles semifinal. It was the first time Angela and Althea stepped on a court together. Later, Angela saw Althea lose an astonishing 16–14 first set to Mortimer in the semifinals, with Mortimer getting by game after game on pure tenacity. Emotionally spent, Althea dissolved in the second set and lost 6–1.

Angela's tennis remained a cut below both Mortimer's and Althea's. At Forest Hills a month before, she'd squandered a service break against Nancy Chaffee and lost in two sets. We can catch a glimpse of her playing the role of the seasoned starlet at the swank Beverly Hills Hotel, shouting a hello to Fred MacMurray and Rosemary Clooney on the other side of the pool in her first trip back to Los Angeles. But on the court there at the Pacific Southwest championships, she lost in the quarterfinals, as she would again a week later at Berkeley.

She was speaking to Jones by overseas telephone occasionally, no cheap endeavor, and he would place tidbits into his tennis column. At one point, he floated the idea that the Angelas, Buxton and Mortimer, would be an ongoing doubles team in 1956. They'd played together several times that summer and fall, actually beating Hart and Fry at the Essex Women's Invitational in Manchester, Massachusetts, in late August. (In the singles competition of that tournament, Angela extended Brough to 7–5, 6–4: a straight-sets loss but her finest match of the summer nonetheless.)

In truth, a permanent partnership of the Angelas was never going to happen. Mortimer and Anne Shilcock had won Wimbledon the year before and felt obligated to defend their title. Beyond that, Mortimer sounds aghast even today at the idea of teaming with Angela. But by initiating the idea in the pages of a London newspaper, Jones provides evidence that he was looking for a more formidable doubles partner for Angela. Pat Hird, her occasional partner at Wimbledon and Wightman Cup matches, was a fine player, but she wasn't in a position to push Angela to improve, nor to help her win. And that, Jones believed, was what Angela needed now. Victories begat victories, he knew, and after a year of Pattern Tennis, it was time for Angela to not simply play well, but to win matches more regularly and start winning tournaments. If she couldn't find a doubles partner to help her win, she would opt out of playing doubles.

He also seemed to sense that Angela wasn't a marathoner, but a sprinter. She didn't have the physical constitution to be a top-ranked player for years and years, and she probably didn't have the talent, either. He felt that she had a brief window of opportunity, beginning in 1956, to stake a claim as one of the best players in the world. Doubles with Pat Hird would squander her energy in a futile cause. Accordingly, Jones set out a plan that he believed would have her among the first rank of players within six months. The first step was convincing Angela that she could get there. Upon her return to England after the North American swing, he told her that she now was capable of a level of play that could win a match against anyone. "With a bit of luck, you could win Wimbledon next year, or one of the majors," he said. "With the right partner, you could certainly win the doubles."

Angela was stunned to hear it, which was proof of the problem. What she needed now, he said, was a change in attitude. She had to become more aggressive on the court, less willing to let her opponent determine the course of play. That was one of the prerequisites of Pattern Tennis, that you take charge of each point, and it was also a reason that the strategy actually worked. It forced a player to establish dominance. "I want to make you mentally tougher," he told her. "When you're on the tennis court, I want people to almost revere you, like the Queen of England."

Toward that end, Jones devised an exercise. He was always coming up with exercises, whether physical or mental, one reason much of the British tennis world considered him something of a crank. At one point, he had sent out a questionnaire on tennis psychology to many of the top players through his *British Lawn Tennis and Squash* magazine, and some of the questions had provoked much merriment in the locker rooms. "Are you always equally keen to win?" one asked, and "Are you ruthless in the elimination of weaknesses, or do you let them slide and think perhaps they are not serious?" The players were accustomed to simply arriving at the tournament and playing their matches. Thinking of the sport in such an oblique way, they felt, was preposterous.

This time, Angela was to walk into a Fleet Street restaurant, order a meal, then send it back. "If it's cooked rare, tell them it's undercooked," Jones instructed. "It's medium, tell them it's overcooked. Whatever it is, complain that it isn't how you want it." He wanted her to demand attention, take charge of the situation.

Angela was horrified. Complaints about food you'd been served were rare in 1950s London; they aren't so common even today. If a dish arrived that wasn't to your liking, you ate it or you didn't, but in either case you kept your mouth shut, and you paid the bill. If you wanted to protest, you didn't return to the establishment. To complain was inevitably to make a scene, and that was contrary to the English character. Jones knew it. He was compelling Angela to assert herself—and, after a few false starts, she did. It thrilled her to feel such control. "It was the making of me as I am today," she says now.

This newfound attitude polarized people even further. "They either accepted me as different, looked up to me, even," she says, "or else they thought, 'Who in the world does this woman think she is?'" The mindset helped her stake a claim as a formidable player. That December, the French newspaper *L'Equipe* published its world rankings for 1955. In a judgment that must have irked Mortimer for weeks, she and Shirley Fry were each rated below Angela, who had somehow earned the No. 9 position. Althea remained unranked.

IN EARLY DECEMBER, the American contingent heading for Asia met in England, where Ham Richardson was attending Oxford. They flew from there, via several stopping points, to Rangoon, Burma. In a nod toward self-improvement, perhaps, Althea was reading Robert Ruark's best-selling *Something of Value* on the trip, a novel about the Mau Mau crisis in Kenya. The book served as a kind of handbook for the situation they would stumble across in Burma, which was in the throes of its own political crisis.

In Rangoon, amidst gunfire in the streets, Richardson, Perry, Fageros, and Althea gave clinics and held exhibitions. They traveled to Thailand for more of the same, then to Calcutta and Delhi for the two tournaments on the itinerary, the Indian and Asian Championships. In

Calcutta, everyone was ill, to varying degrees. Richardson, the captain of the team, had a ten-thousand-dollar discretionary fund to dole out over the seven weeks, and he used about nine thousand dollars in medical expenses. Then someone broke into their hotel rooms and stole valuables, and the psychological damage loomed larger than the actual loss. They were a long way from home, and they felt it.

But the sense of disorientation pulled the quartet closer together. Richardson, a Rhodes scholar, had grown up relatively affluent in Baton Rouge, Louisiana. As a teenager, he regularly visited the campus of Southern University, the all-Negro school in the shadow of Louisiana State, because two of the best tennis players in town were studying there. He'd play matches with them during evenings, after his own tennis practice had ended. His family had employed a black maid growing up, but this was different; he came to know these two older blacks as peers, and as people. Still, in mid-century Louisiana, such friendships had limits. "As a practical matter, we didn't invite them to our house for dinner," he says. "My parents were very open about race, but it was something that would have caused them trouble."

To Richardson, developing a friendship with Althea felt easy and natural. Before long, he was helping her game. He recognized at once that she had formidable athletic skills. What she clearly didn't comprehend, even after working with Llewellyn, was how to use them to win a match. Richardson taught her the importance of certain points, that the first point in a game was not nearly as vital as 30–40 or 40–30. "Before that, she had played every point the same," he says. "She just hit the ball as hard as she could, and went for her shots. And some went in, and people clapped—but too many of them didn't go in, and her opponents eventually beat her."

Richardson taught her what to consider when she angled a volley, and when to use her ground strokes to attack. Amplifying on what Llewellyn had been teaching her, he helped her to identify when it made sense to attempt an ambitious shot, when to try to wrest control of a point from her opponent, and when to concentrate on merely keeping the ball in play. She was a quick study; she'd just never thought that way before. In truth, not too many coaches, black or white, would have understood the nuances that Richardson, a seasoned international player, was imparting. Althea was faster than most of the women tennis players of the day, she had a better serve, she was stronger, and she had better hands. "She just had to learn how to win," he says.

Arriving in New Delhi for the Indian Championships, the Americans encountered a quartet of Englishmen who had been sent by their own tennis federation to play there and in Delhi. The men were John Barrett and Roger Becker; the women Pat Ward—and Angela. To her surprise and delight, she'd been chosen to make the two-week trip. The Americans and the English were staying in the same hotel, and Angela spotted Althea for the first time in the lobby. Though they'd seen each other on the court in Mexico that previous October, it seemed as though Althea didn't know Angela's name.

EVEN IN SUCH EXOTIC SURROUNDINGS, Angela struck the rest of the English contingent as unusual. Jones had exhorted her to take care of her body, and as with everything he said, she responded with the devotion of a zealot. She'd go to formal dinners and refuse to eat a bite. Her compatriots felt that was extraordinarily rude, but Angela didn't care. Later they learned that she was having steak and a salad in her room early each evening so she could avoid eating anything unfamiliar. It worked. Unlike everyone else on the trip, she didn't miss a day of tennis because of illness.

Angela was intrigued by India's culture, but she remained immersed in her tennis to an almost comical extent. On one particularly hot afternoon in Calcutta, Barrett and Becker were languishing in the hotel lobby, which was only slightly less stifling than their rooms. Great ceiling fans beat slowly in the heavy air. It was the picture of a colonial outpost. Ward had taken to her bed with a fever that would last the better part of a week, and the others were being indolent, waiting for the midday heat to subside, as the locals had suggested they should. Angela strode past them in tennis whites, off to hit with some Indian army officer. She was so intent on improving her game that she hardly realized how obsessed it made her seem. Barrett simultaneously admired and disdained such dedication.

The British weren't exactly taken with Althea, either. She seemed arrogant in her conversations with other players, tight-lipped and suspicious with interviewers, and quick to take offense. Barrett believes it was a defense mechanism she'd subconsciously adopted as a black in a white man's world. With each passing year that she didn't attain her goals, she seemed to exude even more confidence that she eventually would. Precisely the quality that Jones was trying to instill in Angela came naturally to Althea. "She had a very cocky walk, despite the fact that she'd never really won any important tournaments," Richardson remembers. "She had a tremendous ego, as all champions do."

After Althea, Angela was the best and most accomplished player on the tour, a two-time Wightman Cup selection with several years of Wimbledon experience. Neither Angela nor Althea was particularly interested in forming a friendship with a potential rival. But as the tournament gained momentum, Fageros started inviting Angela to practice with herself and Althea. Ward was ill, and Fageros knew that Angela had no other options.

They'd hit on the court together, the three of them, taking turns teaming with each other and manning a side alone. Angela was struck by the purposefulness with which Althea hit each shot. Althea would come to net with the confidence that she was *meant* to be there, or stay back and slug balls from the baseline. Her game was becoming a better fit for her athleticism. She had improved noticeably from when Angela had seen her in Mexico less than three months before.

Against the backdrop of these spectacularly beautiful colonial clubs, some more English than England itself, Althea and Angela's friendship eventually flourished. Each recognized in the other a kindred soul, though not exactly an equal in tennis terms. In New Delhi, Althea was clearly superior to Angela when they met in a semifinal, beating her 6–3, 6–4. In the doubles tournament, too, Althea and Fageros swept past Angela and a weakened Ward in two quick sets. In Calcutta, Angela fared better. She played three close sets with Althea in a semifinal, while the women's doubles event was canceled because both Ward and Fageros were too ill to compete. Except for her net game, Althea wasn't playing especially well on the trip, though she won both tournaments.

"Possessing poorish ground strokes, she prevailed over all comers by her mere presence in the forecourt," wrote a local correspondent, covering the match for *World Tennis*.

The Americans and British parted in Calcutta, but not before Angela had convinced Althea to travel to Europe following the end of her trip. Althea had a return ticket home that could be cashed in and repurchased at a later date. More important, there were tournaments from Scandinavia to Egypt that would be thrilled to have Althea Gibson to promote—and after that, she could play the various clay-court events leading up to the French Championships. Althea could survive from week to week on expense money, Angela told her, augmented by the occasional under-the-table appearance fee. Althea listened. She had nowhere else to go, nothing else to do. She had left her job in Jefferson City, parted with the army captain at least temporarily, put the WAC on hold. She was as free of obligations as she'd ever been in her life.

In East Pakistan, where the Americans headed next, Fageros developed a bad case of rheumatic fever and couldn't play, so Althea was matched against the champion of the locals, a man named Mohamed Ali. She beat him handily, striking a blow for her race, gender, and nationality simultaneously. Later, the Americans repaired to the poolroom, where she cleaned up on Richardson and Perry. She was winning now, and winning led to more winning.

ON JANUARY 28, 1956, Althea played Angela Mortimer in the final of the Scandinavian Championships in Stockholm. Mortimer had been the fourth-best player in the world the previous year, according to the rankings published by Lance Tingay. She had won the Stockholm tournament three years in succession. Althea took the first set 6–4, but Mortimer kept pushing, wouldn't let Althea stay on the offensive, and won the next two.

Mortimer was by nature fragile and sickly. At one point, she would be hospitalized for excessive nervousness. Once on the court, though, she was nearly as tough as Maureen Connolly. "She refused to give up and just went on and on and ground her opponents down," said Barrett, her future husband. Mortimer had played Dorothy Knode in the final of the French Championships the previous year, and the match seemed to go on forever. Mortimer came off the court with bleeding feet, but she won, taking the deciding set 10–8.

Mortimer had grown up in a working-class family in Torquay. She couldn't afford tennis lessons, but volunteered to fetch balls for the esteemed English coach Arthur Roberts. On the court day after day, she soaked up the instruction Roberts gave to his pupils. When Roberts saw her hitting against a backboard one afternoon, putting his precepts into practice as best she could, he understood in an instant that she'd heard and remembered every word he'd said. Realizing that she had the makings of a champion, he offered to coach her for nothing.

Mortimer thrived whenever she sensed that she had more grit than her opponent. Seeing Althea, by any measure a superior athlete, across the net brought out the best in her. From the time Althea set out for Rangoon before Christmas through Wimbledon, more than six months later, Mortimer was the only player who managed to beat her. She did it in Sweden, in Cairo in March, and again that month in Alexandria. Mortimer was stubborn enough to disregard the aggressiveness in Althea's manner that intimidated so many other players. "It gave me more reason to want to show her that I could beat her," Mortimer says, the determination in her voice showing through almost half a century later.

Losing to Mortimer was good for Althea. It forced her to keep improving. From January to May, when she finally solved Mortimer and won at Roland Garros in Paris with a memorable second set that lasted twenty-two games, Althea became a far more consistent player. She had to, in order to beat this woman who was emerging as her first genuine rival. Playing week after week, one city to the next throughout Europe and beyond, Althea synthesized what she'd been taught by Llewellyn and what she'd culled from Richardson's instruction into the natural attributes of her tennis. She forged a new game on the anvil of more regular play than she'd ever experienced. Entered in singles, doubles, and mixed-doubles tournaments most weeks, she averaged more than a match a day for six months against many of the top players in Europe. By the end, she had come to accept that she didn't have to prove herself with each swing of the racket. She could dump a short forehand to the service line to get a less mobile player scrambling toward the net, come to net herself, then dare her opponent to pass her. On some points, she might indeed be passed. But the odds, she came to see, were on her side. If she made the proper shot point after point, she'd win the match. And winning matches, not necessarily playing spectacular tennis, was the goal.

She was also having fun. In Stockholm, she strummed the guitar in a rudimentary four-person band with tennis cohorts Anne Shilcock, Sven Davidson, and Michael Davies. In Solvalla, Sweden, she bundled up in a coat and scarf and tried her hand at harness racing in the snow. Traveling the world was new to Althea. She liked being the center of attention, and not having to worry about the racial protocol like she still did at too many of the private clubs across America. It was a fine life, flying from India to Sweden on somebody else's money. But if she wanted it to continue, she knew, she would have to win tournaments. Her novelty couldn't carry her forever.

With Jimmy Jones

CHAPTER 10

Doubles Partners

After Stockholm, Althea traveled to Cologne, West Germany, for the German Indoor Championships. It was a lesser tournament that didn't attract many of the sport's big names, but Althea couldn't afford a week off even if she'd wanted one. She needed to be lodged in a hotel room somewhere on somebody's account; needed to collect per diem in order to eat; needed travel expenses to get her to the next place. She carried only a few dollars in her purse, and that unused ticket home from Ceylon that she'd saved and would eventually cash in for another. If she sprained her ankle, if she caught the flu, if she found herself unable to play for whatever reason, the ride would end and she'd have to leave. She had no margin for error. So she showed up somewhere each week, ready for singles and doubles in whichever tournament would have her.

The smaller events buttressed her confidence. At Cologne, she won the singles championship in three sets over the Belgian national champion. She paired with a local player to win the women's doubles. Against that level of competition, she was clearly the class of the field. Then she took the train to Paris for the international indoor tournament there. As planned, she met up with Angela, who had been following Althea's exploits in the British papers, hoping that her money and her luck would hold out so they could see each other again. Angela felt she had a proprietary interest in Althea's success. She had urged Althea to stay abroad following the State Department trip. From what she could glean from the newspaper accounts, at least, the idea had been a propitious one.

Angela had been training hard and felt determined to make 1956 her year. After returning home from India, she had forced herself through a difficult conversation with Mary Halford. Still the British Wightman Cup captain, Halford had called as expected to inform her that Pat Hird would be her doubles partner again in 1956. Angela, in accordance with Jones's wishes, told her she didn't want to play with Hird.

Jones had talked her through the script in advance because he figured Halford's call was coming. "You've got to say, firmly but politely, what I'm going to tell you to say now," he said. "You've got to practice it, and you've got to say it." When the time came, Angela had half a mind to keep her mouth shut and accept the status quo. But she feared Jones's disapproval more than Halford's, so she spoke her lines as rehearsed. "I'm awfully sorry, Mary, and thanks very much for asking me, but I will be unable to play with Pat Hird this year." And then, after Halford inevitably asked why: "Because I think that with the right player, not Pat Hird, I can win Wimbledon. If I don't find the right partner, I'm not going to be playing Ladies' Doubles." Halford responded with a long silence. Whether it was Angela's impudence that upset her, or the ruination of her plans, the conversation ended badly.

The idea that Angela might not play doubles—not even in the Wightman Cup, though she'd been asked—would have been shocking to a staunch member of the English establishment such as Halford. Though she'd been something of a rebel in her youth, wearing shorts on a British grass court when most other women wouldn't be seen in anything but a skirt, by 1956 Halford held a deeply rooted place in the tennis community. Entering a tournament and only playing singles just wasn't done, in Halford's mind. Doubles was an integral part of the sport. Players were identified far less by their coach, if they happened to have one, than by their doubles partner. It was Hart and Fry, Brough and du Pont, Shilcock and Mortimer. A doubles partner was a friend, a traveling companion, someone to practice with, a roommate, all in one.

Winning a doubles title at a major tournament wasn't as important as winning the singles, but it was far more important than it is today. Among aficionados, arguments would rage about which form of the game, singles or doubles, was aesthetically superior. Some would come to tournaments and watch nothing but doubles, getting great joy out of the impromptu ballet that would unfold on virtually every point. To remove yourself from doubles competitions as a matter of principle, or—even worse—to save energy for playing singles, was to set yourself up for ridicule from the tennis establishment. Angela hoped it wouldn't come to that, but she was steeled to handle it if it did. Jones had fortified her well.

WITH NO FANFARE, Althea and Angela stepped on the court together for the first time as a doubles team in a first-round match at the French indoors. Since neither had a regular partner, it seemed natural. They were spending much of their time together in Paris, anyway, eating lunch and sampling the nightlife. They were friends now. They didn't correspond during the weeks away, but, like so many other players on the women's tour, they looked forward to seeing each other when the occasion arose.

Playing doubles with Althea was a singular experience. She was so fast, so athletic, she seemed to be all over the court at once, seeking angles from which she could hit devastating winners. It was difficult to know where to move so you'd be out of her way. Angela and Althea didn't have a rhythm down, but it hardly mattered. They romped through the doubles' bracket together, and individually worked their way through the women's singles. They were each playing the best tennis of their lives.

On February 10, each won semifinal matches. On February 11, a rest day for women's singles competition, they defeated Anne Shilcock and Susan Chatrier to win the doubles, their first title together in their first attempt. The next day, in the women's singles final, Althea needed fourteen games in the second set to subdue Angela in one of the more competitive matches they'd played. Althea "amazed and delighted the French with her repertoire of booming serves, savagely hit ground strokes, decisive volleys, and man-like smashes," *World Tennis* reported. The magazine's verdict on Angela wasn't as kind. She had no real weaknesses, it wrote, "but no outstanding strengths, unless it be her doggedness."

Later, Angela gained a measure of revenge when she and Torsten Johansson won a three-set battle with Althea and Hugh Stewart to win the mixed doubles. They all went out to celebrate, Angela treating Althea to a dinner. It was Angela and Althea, Althea and Angela, everywhere you looked. They were pictured dining together in a magazine snapshot, a white and a black sitting at table in the clubhouse at De Coubertin Stadium, laughing as if they were in on a joke that the rest of the world didn't understand. It caused comment.

Then they parted. Angela returned to England, which was in the throes of another damp winter. Althea's one-woman tour embarked for the South of France. She rolled through the Coupe Georges Lozon in Lyon, then caught the train for Nice and what was actually the annual Cannes tournament, pushed inside a gymnasium by ten inches of snow. Althea sailed through a draw that didn't include Angela Mortimer for the second tournament in a row, and stopped an overmatched Shirley Bloomer in the final, 6–2, 6–2.

Cologne, Paris, Lyon, Cannes: Althea looked up and realized that she hadn't lost a match in a month. After years of uneven play, she was suddenly thriving. Traveling to a new city each week, alone and undoubtedly lonely except the one week she had Angela to pal around with, she was winning every match she played. In plain sight, with nobody watching, this twenty-eight-year-old veteran was recasting herself as a star.

There were tangible reasons. Sydney Llewellyn's instruction the previous summer had altered her technique, and the practice sessions with Ham Richardson on the Indian subcontinent had opened her mind to the intricacies of tennis strategies. Unquestionably, the quality of the opposition at these European tournaments wasn't nearly as high as it was during the summer season on America's East Coast. Yet none of that quite explains Althea's transformation from a talented athlete to a tennis champion that was beginning to play out over the courts of Europe. To the untrained eye, Althea still looked like the same player, with the exception of the grip that Llewellyn had altered the previous summer. She still strolled through life with an insouciance that masked whatever fears and insecurities were hidden inside. She still stepped on the court as if she expected to win every match she played, just as she always had—but now, suddenly, she was winning them.

Not every week was a success. After Cannes, the setting was Cairo, where she and an Egyptian woman, Betty Abbas, won the doubles. But in the women's singles final, it was the same story as it was in Stockholm, even more briskly written: Mortimer sailed past a befuddled Althea, 6–0, 6–1. After the match, Althea could barely look Mortimer in the eye to congratulate her. The following week, in Alexandria, was much the same. Althea won the doubles with Abbas, but lost in the final of the singles to Mortimer. This match was closer—6–3, 6–4—yet Althea never threatened to win it. Reverting to her old approach, she seemed to be trying for winners on nearly every shot. "The American, who has all the shots in the game, lost many points because of her impetuosity," wrote John Clarke in *World Tennis*. Had she forgotten so quickly all that Richardson had taught her?

She hadn't. She didn't lose again until the summer. After Cairo, she landed back on the Riviera at Monte Carlo. At the end of an enjoyable week in one of the world's prettiest places, she swept past Bloomer in a perfunctory final. Then came five weeks in Italy: five tournaments and five singles titles for Althea. At Palermo, and again the following week in Naples, she beat a Bermuda-based American named Heather Brewer in one-sided finals.

Along the way, she disposed of an Australian player named Daphne Seeney, who had the pluck but not quite the talent to succeed playing singles at the highest level. The tour was filled with players such as Seeney. They were the underpinning on which championship runs were constructed, first- and second-round opponents usually dispatched in an hour or so, good for a sad smile and a handshake at the net, a few laudatory words, and a wave good-bye until another match in another town. They might occasionally upset a seeded player and maybe even two in the same week, yet they rarely won tournaments, and almost never any of the important ones. Every era of tennis history is stocked with these players, and their careers are usually forgotten as soon as their names cease to appear in the agate type in the world's newspapers. Yet the story of how each of them happened to emerge from whichever village or country club or urban center spawned them is often a compelling one, lacking only the sanction of a championship to make it resonate.

Exactly one year before, Seeney had arrived in Naples on the boat from Brisbane with a wild shock of short, wavy hair, looking a bit like the old aviatrix Amelia Earhart. She'd never played on a clay court before, never even seen clay. She'd spent six weeks on the water, playing the occasional match in port in Adelaide or Perth or Colombo but otherwise jogging around the decks to stay fit, which is hardly the way to keep your game sharp. She lost her first match to a fearsome-looking woman who had a drop-shot serve that seemed to screw itself into the brick-colored dirt. Seeney stayed up all night crying, wondering what she'd gotten herself into. Later she learned that the woman was the French champion.

Seeney had learned to play the sport in the most rudimentary fashion, utterly devoid of formal instruction. Where she'd grown up in the Australian bush, 350 miles northwest of Brisbane, there was no television, no movie theaters, only tennis. Her school had fourteen students, a tennis court, and a tennis team. They'd load everyone into a truck, drive as much as an hour to another school, play a match. She was the youngest of nine children, and emerged as the most talented. Her brothers and sisters worked to get her a chance to succeed. She felt the pressure of their sacrifices every day of her tennis career.

When she left home early in 1955, her father had handed her the family savings of 75 British pounds, the equivalent of perhaps 750 dollars today. "You've got no money and you don't know anybody," he'd said. "But you've been brought up with good principles and good manners, you've got a good personality, you look whomever you're talking to in the eye, and you're well-mannered. Just remember to smile whenever you can. A smile will cost you nothing in the world."

So she smiled at the tournament officials, she smiled at their wives, she smiled at her opponents, she smiled at everyone she saw. It didn't hurt that she was "reasonably good to look at," as she puts it. That's what got her from one tournament to the next, playing and learning and getting by. She wasn't getting any appearance money; unlike Althea, she was a nobody, and wouldn't add a single ticket to the gate receipt. She paid for her own travel. Breakfast was usually a hard roll, and if you ate enough of the lunch they fed you at the venue, you weren't too hungry for dinner. She learned to make her own arrangements in city after city and country after country, where nobody understood English—especially not the twangy Aussie bushman's English she spoke. "We had to be problem-solvers," she says. "And that carried over to solving problems on the court."

Seeney spent much of her time with her doubles partner, Fay Muller, and a pair of emerging South African players, one of whom, Trevor Fancutt, she later married. (Their three sons, Charlie, Michael, and Christopher Fancutt, would each play at Wimbledon; the five Wimbledon players in one family constitutes an All England record.) By 9:30 each night, wherever she happened to be in the world, she tucked herself into bed. She well remembered that her siblings' toil was offering her this chance, and felt it wasn't right to squander it at a party or a nightclub.

Walking into the dressing room in Naples her second year on the circuit, just back from her Christmas break at home, Seeney fancied herself a veteran. Then she saw Althea in the dressing room putting on a pair of men's shorts, zipping them right up the front. "My eyes nearly fell out of my head," she says. "She looked so fantastic, so tall. I was a young, impressionable Aussie girl. I'd never seen anyone but my brothers zip pants up the front." Not only had Althea been winning tournaments, Seeney remembers thinking, but she looked and carried herself like a goddess. "It was intimidating," Seeney says. "She was halfway home before we started."

While Althea was busy beating Seeney and winning the tournament at Naples, America's 1956 Wightman Cup team was announced. It consisted of Louise Brough, who was a playing captain, Shirley Fry, Beverly Fleitz, and Dorothy Knode, the second-, third-, fourth-, and fifth-ranked Americans from 1955. Doris Hart, ranked No.1, had taken the position as a teaching professional, and was therefore ineligible. That Althea was arguably playing better tennis than any woman in the world at the time, and certainly better than any American, was given no consideration.

If it bothered her, Althea didn't show it. From Naples she went to Genoa, where, on April 22, she defeated Thelma Long in straight sets to win her fourth consecutive tournament. Florence was next, and even the American newspapers were beginning to take notice of what she was accomplishing. On the day that Rocky Marciano's retirement as the undefeated heavyweight champion dominated the headlines, Althea swept into the semifinals and onto the front page of the *New York Times* sports section with a 6–1, 6–1 lashing of local favorite Anelisa Bellani. Three days later, she'd beaten Long again for her fifth tournament title in a row.

THAT SPRING, something was happening to Angela, too, though she still had the trappings of a local player. She busied herself working at Lillywhites, playing in nearby tournaments, training with Jones on and off the court. She'd run wind sprints in Kent's Passage, the alleyway leading to Regent's Park across the street from Rossmore Court. Jones had devised intricate drills for her. (As usual, he called them experiments, as though it were proper science.) She'd wait until the alley was clear, then place potatoes at specific intervals. Then she'd run from one to the next and pick them up as a stopwatch charted her progress. It was supposed to help make her nimble.

She did distance work in the park itself, running on the sidewalk past Wingfield House, where the American ambassador lived. She'd wait for a car to pass, then sprint beside it for as long as she could, as if she were a barking dog. Bypassers would gawk with a mixture of incredulity and fear, hoping it was some sort of prank. (Weeks later, after the tour had alighted in London for the Queen's Club tournament and Wimbledon, she'd bring Althea out for an aborted sunrise run that lasted all of a quarter-hour. "Don't you ever do that to me again," Althea would say, then slip back into bed.)

On April 1, Angela won the Southport tournament, where she'd practiced with Derek Dutton the year before. The next week, she again returned to the Cumberland Club, where she'd taken lessons while attending school at Mrs. Jepson-Turner's, and won the clay-court championships in straight sets. Later that month, American Darlene Hard arrived in Bournemouth without a doubles partner. "She'll do," Jones said, and asked Hard if she'd team with Angela for the week. Such machinations by coaches were rarely seen then; it was almost as though he were her agent. Hard accepted, but remarked that she was committed to playing the French Championships with someone else. Jones didn't mind. He figured that playing with Hard for a week would give Angela the experience of sharing the court with one of the world's top players. She might glean something useful along the way.

Angela and Hard pulled off an upset to win the doubles at Bournemouth, beating the carefully calibrated Mortimer and Shilcock, the English tennis establishment's favored doubles pairing, in three sets. Even the skeptical Mortimer could see in Bournemouth that Angela was no longer merely the wishful striver they'd snickered at in previous years. "By this time, she didn't ever make stupid mistakes," Mortimer says. "She had become a formidable player."

The next week, Angela and Althea's paths again converged. They met in Rome for the Italian Championships, though they didn't play doubles together. Angela was again teamed with Hard, while Althea had signed up to play with a German named Totta Zehden, whom she'd met along the way. In the quarterfinals, Althea and Zehden defeated Seeney, the plucky Australian, and her stylish partner, Fay Muller. But in the semifinals, they ran up against the suddenly formidable team of Angela and Hard, who disposed of them easily. Althea was surprised, but pleased for Angela.

And Althea had the singles competition to assuage her ego. Seeded first, she brushed aside all opposition, losing only a single set on the way to her fifth title in Italy in a single month, and sixth in a row overall. The surprise was that Angela, playing better with each tournament, came within a set of meeting her in another final. Angela lost the first set of her semifinal with Hungary's Suzi Kormoczi, but pushed her way to a 9–7 equalizer in the second. By then, though, Angela was exhausted. Kormoczi was a veteran player who knew enough to keep some energy in reserve for a deciding set. She won it, 6–1, to advance into the final against Althea.

Althea's two-set victory over Kormoczi that followed in the final stands as a sharply etched example of the player she'd become. She won the first set without incident, 6–3. In the second, Kormoczi gained a service break and held her own serve to take a 5–3 lead. The match seemed headed for a deciding set, but the woman who had "seemed to give up," in Mortimer's words, at Cairo only a few months before now raised her game at the right time. She won four consecutive points off her serve to narrow the gap to 5–4. Kormoczi then went up 40–30 and set point, but Althea saved the set by rushing forward behind her return and forcing the Hungarian to hurry a passing shot, which she netted. Althea eventually won the game to recoup the break, then delivered two aces in her service game to take a 6–5 lead.

In the twelfth game, with Kormoczi serving, Althea fell behind, 40–30, but again rallied. She brought herself back to deuce with an overhead smash, then won the final two points of the game after long baseline rallies, breaking Kormoczi's serve and winning the match. She'd used net play, her serve, her overhead, and her ground strokes to erase a two-game deficit and win the final against a smart and resourceful veteran player. It was an impressive performance.

Still, it was against Suzi Kormoczi, not Brough or Fleitz or Fry. Throughout her long winning streak, Althea still hadn't faced any of the world's top players, the women she'd have to defeat to win Wimbledon.

Ever the outsider, she was the expatriate champion of early 1956, an American gathering trophies throughout the capitals of Europe, but now the rest of the Americans would start to arrive for the French Championships and Wimbledon, and the world would be able to better gauge what it all meant. "She is unquestionably very talented," *World Tennis* wrote of Althea in its account of the Italian Championships, "and it will be interesting to see what happens when the top American contingent arrives, and whether she will have it quite as much her own way as she hopes."

DESPITE HER SUCCESS in Bournemouth and Rome, Angela arrived at the French Championships without a doubles partner. Hard was committed, and nobody else had stepped forward to ask her. Instead, she had convinced herself that playing all three events in Paris would not necessarily be a smart idea. She was fully prepared to find a strong male player to team with in mixed doubles, skip women's doubles, and channel her energy into singles play.

Then she ran into Althea in a hallway and they hugged each other— "You're looking good, Angie," Althea said, examining her in sisterly fashion—and Jones's eyes widened. He hadn't appreciated what close friends they'd become since the previous Christmas. "Now, there's a partner," he said. With the deadline for the doubles draw only hours away, they invited Althea to dinner. When Angela lost her courage between the starter and the main course, Jones jumped in and asked Althea if she would agree to play doubles with Angela. He could see what a team they'd be. He also understood that the two of them were, in a certain sense, kindred souls. Althea, who had been traveling by herself since leaving Southeast Asia five months earlier, was homesick and lonely. Pleased to be wanted and impressed by the way Angela and Hard had beaten her and Totta Zehden in Rome, she readily agreed.

In 1956, as today, the four tennis tournaments that comprise the Grand Slam were reflective of the places in which they were held. Wimbledon was the most staid and conservative, while the Australian

Championships, an itinerant event that wouldn't settle in Melbourne until 1972, was the friendliest and least formal. By contrast, the U.S. Championships, as held at the West Side Tennis Club in leafy Forest Hills, bears scant relation to the raucous atmosphere of today's Flushing Meadow facility, hard by La Guardia Airport. Forest Hills was America at its most genteel, and the New Yorkers who made the journey out to what was then the equivalent of a suburb were on their best behavior.

In those days, the most atmospheric of the four events was the French Championships, held at Stade Roland Garros (named for a World War I airman) in the center of Paris. French tennis fans were emotional, at times bordering on rude. They made their affections and disaffections known. A favorite at Roland Garros, particularly if he was a Frenchman, would gain substantial support from the crowd.

Harry Buxton had come to Paris to see his daughter play. He was staying at the swank George V and eating dinners on the town. Like most everyone else, Harry was intrigued by Althea. He understood that she'd been raised practically as an orphan on the streets of Harlem. She filled the room with a superstar's presence, and, of course, she was an American Negro at a time when American Negros were in the news. She was also fast emerging as one of the two or three favorites to win Wimbledon. "Bring her along, bring her along," he'd say when Angela inquired about Althea accompanying them to dinner.

Twice that fortnight, they ate at Le Fouquet's on the Champs Elysées: as exalted—and expensive—a restaurant as Paris offered. Althea loved it. She had been doing the tennis equivalent of backpacking through Europe on an undergraduate's budget; now here was someone's rich parent showing her a glimpse of the most sophisticated lifestyle in the world. "That was really living for her," Angela says. "The best food, drinking good wine." More than once, Althea vowed that more of such meals would be in her future.

Slotted into the same half of the singles bracket, Althea and Angela each advanced through the first week. On May 22, Angela needed a fourteen-game first set to defeat Edda Buding, the steadier of Germany's two Buding sisters, in her quarterfinal match. The same afternoon, Althea lost just three games in a two-set quarterfinal with Bloomer, who still hadn't found an answer for Althea's power. That meant Althea and Angela would be playing each other in a semifinal on May 24.

The impending match—for a place in the final of one of the four majors, which neither had reached before—didn't impinge on their friendship. Not unlike Doris Hart and Shirley Fry, or the mutually adoring Williams sisters of half a century later, Althea and Angela kept their competitive instincts on the court. Angela realized what Althea was on the verge of accomplishing in Paris, and she reveled in her roles as confidante, adviser, and friend.

Althea lived life in a way that Angela never would have dared. She was a gypsy, carrying her world in her suitcase, always aware that the carousel she was riding might stop at any time and she'd be left without money, without a job, without a real home. She was attempting to make a living as an adult at a pursuit that barely offered shelter, let alone actual remuneration. She was acutely aware of her poverty, yet chose to act as though it didn't matter. She'd spend money she didn't have, splurge on an extravagance like a rented car when she could barely pay her bills. Together, they were like a couple of movie characters, stumbling in and out of fun and harmless trouble. Althea would goad Angela into accompanying her on some jaunt, some nightclubbing escapade, and Angela would figure out how to extricate them at the end of the adventure.

In some ways, Angela was like a younger sister to Althea. "She was the only person who would talk about sex with me," says Angela. It was a taboo subject in those days; even Angela's mother, Violet, who'd had a string of boyfriends following her divorce from Harry, was loathe to mention the virtues of contraception to her daughter, let alone the pleasure to be gained from loving relations with a sexual partner. Althea had no such inhibitions. Though she was far from promiscuous, she'd had her sexual adventures and could counsel the bewildered Angela. "It wasn't so much advice about relationships," Angela says, "as the enjoyment a woman could have together with a man. She had done things that I hadn't."

For her part, Angela understood how the world worked—or, at least, she thought she did. While Althea butted her head against bureaucracy, trying to break through, Angela usually found a clever way to avoid it. She used their burgeoning celebrity to best advantage. "We never paid anywhere," Angela says. "My father was big news, Althea was big news, and I was big news. So why bother to pay when they'll give it to you for nothing?"

One night in London, a few weeks after the French Championships, they would find themselves at a private club in Berkeley Square. Angela would talk their way in, and by the time the night ended, Althea had replaced the on-stage entertainment, belting out jazz standards until well past midnight. It was all a lark, and such a difference for two young women who had been nobody's darlings such a short time before. It was amazing, Angela often thought, what winning a few matches could do.

UNQUESTIONABLY, Angela wanted to win the French Championships herself, almost as much as she wanted to win Wimbledon. By winning any of the major tournaments, she would embarrass the skeptical British tennis establishment that had written her off as bothersome and pushy, those charged attributes that so often were meant to signify "Jewish." She would justify the belief she'd had in herself, despite Maureen Connolly and others offering the opinion that she had no talent for tennis, and all the work she'd put in since childhood.

Almost as important to her by then, winning a major championship would validate the unorthodox approach of Jimmy Jones. Increasingly, he was being seen as a crackpot, a journalist moonlighting as mad scientist, conducting his various experiments with Angela as guinea pig. Her winning would gain him a cachet with his peers that he'd never had.

But Angela also sensed that, if she'd come a long way, Althea had come much farther. Angela had a good home, parents who'd taken an interest in her success, a fine coach, all the money she needed—and it would all be there in the months or years to come whether she won or lost. Althea had none of that. Angela longed to beat Althea at least once, just to prove that she could, but she realized it was a tall order. As Angela saw it, "She was just stronger and more experienced. Her strokes had more penetration than mine in getting to the net. That was the difference. But I always felt it was within my reach. I came close several times, and I felt I was on the verge of doing it."

As it turned out, the French Championships would be her last chance.

With Barney Goodman

CHAPTER 11

Making History

ALTHEA HAD PLAYED THROUGH the entire draw of the 1956 French Championships to the semifinals without ever appearing on Center Court inside Stade Roland Garros. Her drive to win a major title was the most fascinating story in tennis, yet it was unfolding in the cramped quarters of the various satellite courts, witnessed by pockets of spectators on wooden bleachers.

Part of it had to do with the European attitude toward women's tennis. Only in England and the United States was the sport regarded as a pursuit of some importance. The rest of the world, especially the Latin countries of France, Italy, and Spain, considered it little more than a curiosity. This was the case despite the success of stylish Suzanne Lenglen of Paris, arguably the most compelling female player up to that time, who won at Wimbledon every year but one from 1919 to 1925.

By 1956, the entire top ten of newspaperman Tingay's ranking of the world's female players was either American- or British-born, with the exception of Hungary's Suzi Kormoczi, number five. Germany's Cilly Aussem won the Ladies' Singles title at Wimbledon in 1931, and for forty-seven years, until Czechoslovakia's Martina Navratilova in 1978, no Continental European succeeded her. Even at Roland Garros, Kormoczi's 1958 title at age thirty-three was the only one for a European woman between 1940, when the championships adjourned for the war, and 1967, when Francoise Durr of France won it. Not for nothing did only American and British women contest the prestigious Wightman Cup; with the exception of the occasional Australian, they were the only ones taking women's tennis seriously.

So Althea didn't play on Center Court at the French Championships, because few women ever did before the semifinals. But that was only part of it. Paris, which had embraced the African-American dancer Josephine Baker three decades before, was decidedly lukewarm about Althea, who was in some ways her tennis equivalent. Despite her entertaining play at the French indoors in February, she was perceived as too sure of herself for the success she had achieved, and not yet deserving of the showcase that Center Court would provide. In addition, her muscular style of play was the antithesis of the graceful baseline game the Roland Garros faithful so admired.

When she reached the semifinals, she could no longer be denied. But it was made clear to her from the moment she walked out of the tunnel and onto the court that she was no favorite of the crowd. Even before the start of her match with Angela, she was jeered by many of the eight thousand fans in attendance. It rattled her. Angela was wise enough to remain at the baseline for stroke after stroke, perform her memorized patterns, and let the jittery Althea make the mistakes. Angela won the first set, 6–2—the most successful set she had ever played against Althea.

But Althea won the first three games of the second set, quieting the crowd. Sensing she had little hope of a comeback from three games down, Angela seemed to play out the rest of the set expending as little energy as possible. She didn't win a game. She was saving her strength in expectation of a rousing battle for the match in the deciding set.

And then, several points into the first game of the third set, Althea took a mighty swing and snapped the right shoulder strap on her brassiere. (The newspapers of the day, more prurient, called it a dress strap.) The crowd might have been sympathetic to the plight of a more favored player, but to Althea they reacted like drunks at a fraternity party. Hoots and whistles cascaded down on the court. Althea, who took pride in being too cool a customer to often feel embarrassment, stood motionless, too mortified to do anything else. Without thinking, Angela raced from her side of the net and shielded Althea in an embrace, then escorted her toward the dressing room. "She was in a mess," Angela says now. "I had to help her." Yet at that moment, as Angela freely acknowledges, there was not a single player in tennis other than Althea whose plight would have stirred her into action. Had it been anyone else in such agony across the net, Angela might have felt sympathetic, she says, but she would have "sat down and waited for the situation to resolve itself. It wouldn't have been my business."

This, on the other hand, *was* her business. Althea was her opponent, but also her doubles partner and her friend. They'd known each other just a matter of months, yet they had developed a bond that, in the moment that mattered, transcended even Angela's fanatical drive to succeed.

Althea and Angela were drawn together for reasons they might not even have been aware of. Not once in all their time together can Angela recall them discussing their positions as relative outsiders in the locker room; they were too absorbed in what movies were showing, what exhibits were on, and where they might like to have dinner. But the covert hostility toward each of them from many of the established players was never far from the surface at every tournament they entered, and it linked them to each other as much as any common interest or goal. "I felt for Althea," Angela says now. "I wanted her to do well nearly as badly as I wanted to do well myself." Consequently, when Angela walked to the dressing room beside Althea and watched her fish a spare brassiere from her bag and put her outfit back into working order, she was motivated by pure empathy. By doing so, she altered the chemistry of her relationship with Althea to one that had the depth to last a lifetime.

THEY RETURNED to the court together and found it in an uproar. Nobody was certain how to proceed. As the minutes passed, Angela was pressured by tournament officials to charge Althea with a code violation and force her disqualification. It was a clear-cut case, they explained: Althea had received aid from another individual during the course of play, and had left the court before the completion of a match, both of which are strictly forbidden. Never mind that Angela also had walked off the court, stride for stride with Althea. To lose both competitors would have meant awarding the championship without playing a final, and that couldn't be allowed to happen—not with so many tickets already sold for the Saturday session. Althea may have been the victim, but a player is deemed responsible for her own clothes and accoutrements. Clearly, she would have to be the one to go.

Though it would have put her in the final of the French Championships, Angela argued with the officials that Althea's disqualification was precisely what she didn't want. It was, one contemporary later said, "the lone magnanimous gesture in Angela's entire career."

With Angela refusing to claim a violation, the officials had little choice but to allow the match to continue. The debate finally subsided, though the crowd continued to roar. "All the little men went away at last, and we finished the match," Althea later wrote. She quickly took a 4–1 lead, but a newly resourceful Angela changed her tactics. Instead of trying to win points from the baseline, which had been her strategy entering the match, she started employing shot sequences designed to send her to net. Althea was able to pass her occasionally, especially when Angela couldn't get the ball deep enough, but she also became flustered, hitting several potential winners long or into the net. She double-faulted, and when Angela held service to pull within 5–4 and the crowd cheered, a dejected Althea flipped away her racket in disgust. That sent the assembled crowd off on another round of catcalls, and brought a disapproving look from the umpire's chair.

Despite her frustration, Althea managed two match points in the tenth game, but Angela rallied again to pull to deuce. That moment was as close as she ever came to beating Althea in her tennis career. Instead, Althea won the next two points in rapid succession, finishing off the match, 6–4, with a crisp forehand volley that nearly drove the racket from Angela's grasp. At the advanced tennis age of twenty-eight, almost six years after her debut in one of the four major tournaments, Althea finally had reached a final. Her opponent would be Mortimer, who had dispatched Hungary's Kormoczi in two sets despite digestive problems—"gypsy stomach," she called it—that would land her in the hospital later in the year.

ALTHEA STARTED THE MATCH against Mortimer as if she'd booked an early dinner. She raced through the first set, winning every game. She was an entirely different player from the one who had lost all three finals to Mortimer earlier in the year. Then Mortimer, the defending French champion, dug in—as Althea knew she would.

The first game of the second set went to deuce seven times before Mortimer won it to hold her serve. Althea held serve easily to equalize, a pattern that would continue. On her service games, Mortimer would scrap out each point, and manage to win after at least one deuce and often two. Then Althea would get the ball and the tone of play would be utterly transformed. Her serve never better, she'd cruise through another game virtually untouched. By 6–6, each player had won a game on the other's service once, but neither could manage a service break again until 9–9, when Althea's net play finally undid Mortimer. But then, with Althea serving for the match at 10–9, Mortimer somehow managed to break her back.

Just when it seemed that the match might continue indefinitely, Mortimer followed her serve to net on break point in the twenty-first game, and Althea swept a forehand past her to complete the break. Up 11–10 now, she needed four points off her own serve to become the first black of either gender to win one of the four major tennis championships. It had been a long road from the Police Athletic League play street to the clay of Roland Garros and this moment, Althea must have been thinking. For her part, Mortimer was determined not to allow Althea's breakthrough to take place on her watch. It wasn't so much the historical import that bothered her, serving as a footnote in Althea's triumph, or even that she would be losing to a player whose behavior she didn't respect. It was the naked fact of losing, especially with twelve thousand spectators looking on. "I dreaded failure," she would say.

Now Mortimer stared hard across the net and bent into a crouch to receive Althea's serve, but will and resolve could take her only so far.

Althea raced through each point, unleashing a cadenced serve, then coming to net with machine-like precision. It was 15–0, 30–0, 40–0— and then, as an exclamation point to the tournament, she flung a serve down the middle of the court and past Mortimer to win the game, the set, the match, and the championship. She came to net with such jubilation that she'd leapt over it before she realized it. Then Althea startled her crestfallen opponent by wrapping her long arms around her in an embrace.

The French Championship was a level below Wimbledon and Forest Hills at that time, as many believe it is even today. "You could skip France," said Louise Brough, who often did; neither she nor Shirley Fry had been entered in the draw that year. But the French did fit New York sportswriter Allison Danzig's definition of one of the four major tournaments that comprise the Grand Slam, so the historic import of the moment should have been readily apparent. It wasn't. With no staffer at the event, the *New York Times* ran three paragraphs of an Associated Press story in a box on the front of its May 27, 1956, Sunday sports section, and jumped the rest inside, below the crew and fencing news. The story made no mention of Althea's race; perhaps the *Times,* ever scrupulous to keep politics off the sports pages, had edited it out.

Regardless, Althea had become the first black to rank as a true champion in tennis history. She also had established herself, along with Brough and perhaps returning finalist Beverly Baker Fleitz, as the woman to beat at Wimbledon. Following the conclusion of the Mortimer match, in fact, British bookmakers established Althea as the Wimbledon favorite.

Althea had looked almost as impressive over the course of the two weeks playing doubles. Angela had settled in as her steady partner, keeping the rallies alive for Althea to position herself for an easy volley, an overhead, or a deftly placed winner from the net. They had beaten a pairing of Argentinians, a pairing of Frenchwomen, and a pairing of Italians. In the final, they met Americans Darlene Hard, who had teamed so successfully with Angela earlier in the season, and her partner, the Wightman Cup player Dorothy Knode. Angela and Althea lost a listless first set, 8–6, but by the second set they had figured out how to exploit the weaknesses of Hard, who seemed off her game. They won the second set, also by 8–6, and cruised through the third, 6–1. Althea punctuated the victory with a smash at Knode's feet on match point. Now she was twice a French champion. Even more startlingly, Angela, who had begun the year by telling Mary Halford that she was prepared to sit out the Ladies' Doubles at Wimbledon rather than team with an inferior partner, would now return to England as the holder of the French doubles title, as well as a singles semifinalist.

"A DOUBLES TEAM is as good as its weakest link," five-time U.S. Championships doubles winner George Lott once wrote. Doubles tennis isn't merely two fine singles players standing side by side, but a different game that requires a different mindset. Many of the best doubles players have been singles standouts—Jack Kramer and Louise Brough, John McEnroe and Martina Hingis—but others have games that happen to be particularly suited for doubles. They usually had partners to match. Margaret Osborne du Pont won the U.S. women's doubles thirteen times, and could claim thirty-one major doubles titles in all, nearly all of them while paired with Brough. Each had strong serves, good overheads, good volleys, and good returns of serve. Brough had the best backhand in the game, du Pont a stronger forehand. Most important, perhaps, they felt comfortable with each other. In a decade and a half, Brough and du Pont never had a single argument on the court. "Or off it," du Pont remarks today. In doubles, personalities and how they interact always matter.

"The greatest doubles pairs have owed their success to mutual understanding and teamwork. Only on rare occasions have two individualists made a good team," wrote G. P. Hughes, a British doubles player of the 1930s and the editor of the *Dunlop Tennis Annuals* for many years. Most points in doubles are won by finding the space on the court not being adequately covered by the two opposing players, and the easiest way to create that space is to force your opponents to move. A disorganized or otherwise uncommunicative team is at a vast disadvantage to one that responds to the ball's movements with practiced choreography.

As a doubles player, Althea was an anomaly. She had the skills to be one of the very best in the sport, but her mindset was that of the sole practitioner. She knew her own strengths, and that was enough. They'd spin the racket and win the toss, and before her partner could speak, the words were already out of Althea's mouth. "I'll serve," she'd say. It happened that way in the mixed-doubles final against Vic Seixas and Shirley Fry at Wimbledon in 1956, though to open a match with the woman serving was as unthinkable then as having a woman hold a door open for a man. "It was difficult to play with her," her partner, Gardnar Mulloy, says now.

"Many top tennis players are loners, individualists," wrote Bill Talbert in his book *Weekend Tennis*. "They're much more successful at singles than doubles." He described doubles as postgraduate tennis, a more sophisticated version of the singles game. It favored players with maturity, willing to accept the strengths and weaknesses of their partners, and to work long and hard together to create a winning team. "[Doubles] isn't just two players on the same side of the net pooling their talents in a makeshift alliance," he wrote. ". . . It has to be a genuine partnership, a true union in a common cause . . . Squabbling doubles partners seldom win."

It is an indication of how talented she was that, despite it all, Althea managed to win at least one doubles title at each of the four majors over a two-year span. She won the women's doubles at the Australian Championships in 1957, at the French in 1956, and at Wimbledon from 1956 through 1958; and won the mixed doubles at Forest Hills in 1957. She did so without establishing friendly relationships with her partners, other than Angela. She'd arrive at a tournament and, ten minutes later, be walking on the court in that mannish stride. In all the time they played, Althea and Brazil's Maria Bueno, her partner at Wimbledon in 1958, and one of the finest female players of the early 1960s, did not hit a single ball together in practice. Beyond that, they barely spoke.

Her relationship with Angela was unique. After the French Championships, Althea partnered with Angela only three times. They played together at Surbiton, England; at London's Queen's Club that June; and at Wimbledon. Yet their friendship, which began on the Indian subcontinent, blossomed as doubles partners. For those few short months, it was Althea and Angela, just as it was always Shirley and Doris or Margaret and Louise. For the only time in their tennis careers, Angela and Althea found someone who made them feel as if they belonged, if only to their exclusive club of two.

EVEN AFTER WINNING HER FIRST MAJOR, Althea had no rest. Two days later, she surfaced at the Surrey Grass Court Tennis Championships in Surbiton. There, on June 2, she beat Anne Shilcock, Mortimer's doubles partner, to win her eighth tournament in succession, though she needed an extended second set to do it. She was up 5–0 and in absolute command of the match when her tennis collapsed. Seven months of constant play caught up with her in the time it takes to change ends of the court. All at once, the angled volleys that had been winning her points now sailed over the sideline; the drop shots bounced high enough to enable Shilcock to scramble toward the net and put them away. Shilcock won six consecutive games before Althea stopped her run. She finally won 12–10 on a Shilcock double-fault.

Althea was exhausted, but she still wasn't through. Later in the day, she and Angela lost to Betty Pratt and Thelma Long in the doubles final. Althea didn't know whether to be concerned about her precipitous second-set decline, or pleased that she was somehow able to win and keep her streak intact. Either way, she didn't have much time to ponder the thought. For better or worse, she was due in Manchester by June 5 for the Northern England Lawn Tennis Championships. As a bow to fatigue, she decided not to enter the doubles tournament there.

Angela was in Manchester, and so were Harry's movie theaters. One day rain canceled play, as it frequently does at English tournaments. Angela's brother, Gordon, who was serving as manager of Harry's cinematic empire, accompanied Althea to three movies, one after the next. He took her by the hand into the office of each theater and offered a terse introduction to whichever of his employees was stationed behind the desk. "This is Althea Gibson, she's playing in the tennis," he'd say. "I'll pick her up in three hours' time." Althea was delighted. Since Harlem, the movies had been her favorite source of recreation. No matter how precarious her fiscal situation, she'd happily spend money on movies.

Shirley Fry was also in Manchester, having made a late decision to travel to England to play the Wightman Cup and Wimbledon. Born the same summer of 1927 as Althea, Fry was almost twenty-nine. But unlike Althea, she had been playing competitive tennis for most of her life. She'd started as a little girl in Akron, Ohio, in 1936, barred by her parents from stepping on a court until she could hit a hundred balls in succession against a backboard with both forehand and backhand. That year, at nine, she'd won her first tennis trophy. By then, her father had started a scrapbook with a photo of Wimbledon's Centre Court as the first page. "My goal for 1945," it read. A year later, after she'd turned ten, he put her on a bus alone, bound for Philadelphia and the Junior Nationals. She first met Doris Hart there, and their lifelong friendship began. Independent-minded at a very young age, she traveled to Forest Hills to watch Davis Cup matches that summer of 1937, stayed alone at the Forest Hills Inn, negotiated her way through the crowd all week-end—but wasn't allowed into a movie theater because she didn't meet the minimum age requirement of twelve. By fourteen, she was playing in the U.S. Championships, the youngest competitor to that time. A year later, unseeded, she was a fifteen-year-old quarterfinalist.

In 1948, three years later than she'd planned for as a child, Fry made the Wimbledon singles bracket. Seeded eighth, she advanced all the way to a quarterfinal loss to Brough. By 1955, she had been ranked in the top ten in America for twelve consecutive years, had beaten Hart at the French Championships in 1951 for a major title, but hadn't managed to win a title at Wimbledon or Forest Hills. By then, she figured she never would.

Following the 1955 U.S. Championships, she'd returned home to St. Petersburg, Florida, where she'd moved several years before, and retired. She'd accepted a job as a copy girl at the *St. Petersburg Times*. She'd turned twenty-eight and was tired of living out of a suitcase. Her doubles partner, Hart, was retiring. It seemed like a fitting time to start living the rest of her life.

The days turned into weeks at the newspaper, one much like the next. Fry soon missed the camaraderie of the tennis tour. She began to realize how good she'd had it, visiting the capitals of the world with her friends, getting feted at the parties, having the chance to compete at something she did very well. In January, she played in local tournaments in Tampa and St. Petersburg, winning both. She journeyed to the other side of the state in February to breeze through a tournament in West Palm Beach, then took a month off work in March to travel in Latin America. She won a tournament in Panama, another at Barranquilla, Colombia, and a third at the Caribe Hilton in Puerto Rico. In April, she traveled to Jamaica and won two tournaments there, beating Darlene Hard in Kingston. For a retiree, she was playing rather well. Then Wightman Cup captain Margaret du Pont, who had already lost Hart off last year's team, called to try to convince her to return. Fry decided to make one last European trip.

With Hart's retirement, Fry had advanced to the top ranking among Americans. Nevertheless, few handicappers considered her as much of a threat to win Wimbledon as the apparently ageless Brough, or Althea, or even Beverly Fleitz, whose tennis had steadily improved throughout the decade. Fry hadn't won there before, in her prime; why would she win now, as a part-time player? Yet Fry remained a formidable competitor. Her effortless backhand hadn't gathered too much rust during the layoff, and she still moved as well as she ever had.

Like Hart, Fry always relished her matches against Althea, because she relished beating her. "It was fun beating her in Chicago, beating her in Australia," Fry said. There were no hard feelings; Fry would later tour with Althea in Australia following the 1956 season, and together they'd win the women's doubles at the Australian Championships the following January. "I enjoyed traveling with Althea," she says now. "I just didn't like her on the tennis court."

Fry didn't appreciate Althea's characterization of herself as too talented a player to be beaten, meaning that when it did happen it must be some kind of mistake. Fry was six inches shorter than Althea and hardly in her class as an athlete, but she clung to the belief that tennis was a game of skill, not pure athleticism. Steady but unspectacular, she'd watched Hart, whose legs had been weakened by disease as a

child, succeed with a combination of brains, shot placement, and carefully perfected technique, and she'd gained inspiration from it. "Babe
Didricksen tried tennis, and she lasted about a year and a half," Fry
liked to say of the Olympic track-and-field standout who is considered
the most talented female athlete of the twentieth century. "It's a hard
game." Until 1956, Althea had never beaten Fry in any tournament that
mattered. Records are incomplete from that murky era, and memories
have faded, but it may well be that she hadn't beaten her at all.

When they met in a semifinal at Manchester, Althea had been playing too much tennis; Fry hadn't played enough. Althea badly needed a
rest, but she was as resolute as she'd ever been. She won the first set,
lost the second, then won the deciding set, 7–5. It was a sloppy affair of
unforced errors, mis-hits, and double-faults, easy enough for Fry to disregard, but the outcome was significant. "The most important triumph
of [Althea's] brilliant foreign tour," wrote the *New York Times*. Then
Althea beat Brough in the final, 2–6, 6–4, 6–4, in the first match the two
had played since 1950 at Forest Hills, to win her ninth tournament in
succession on the European continent in 1956, and the fifteenth of
eighteen over three continents. "Many of the titles were won in tournaments where tennis nobodies and second-raters filled out the field,"
noted the Associated Press in a dispatch from Manchester. "But yesterday Miss Gibson downed Shirley Fry of St. Petersburg, Fla., No. 2 in the
world, and today she conquered Miss Brough, four-time Wimbledon
queen and defending champion . . . With her triumph, Miss Gibson
becomes one of the top candidates for Miss Brough's Wimbledon title."

Yet on another level, little had changed for Althea, as she well understood. London's *Daily Mail* caught her in a moment of hard-eyed candor, and she came as close to making a political statement as she would
during her career. "I am still a poor Negress, as poor as when I was
picked off the back streets of Harlem," she said. "I have traveled to
many countries . . . in comfort. I have stayed in the best hotels and met
many rich people. I am much richer in knowledge and experience. But I
have no money."

She had been unable to help her parents, who were still "poor, very
poor," she said, and she felt a responsibility to do so as the eldest of five

children. She was feeling sorry for herself, she'd say later, but at the heart of what she told the newspaper was the truth that, despite her remarkable rise from the pavement of Harlem to beating the best female players in the world on the pristine lawns of England, tennis wasn't able to sustain her. There was little money in it, even for a professional, and almost none if you were black. The best private clubs would hardly hire a black as a teaching pro, and few companies would contract a black woman to endorse their products. The realization that she would never be compensated for her efforts to the degree she believed she deserved shortened Althea's tennis career, and it hardened into bitterness as the years passed.

FOR NOW, the reigning French champion arrived in Bristol for the West of England Lawn Championships on June 11 and found herself a celebrity. After all these years, Althea had become an overnight success. "The world's greatest feminine tennis player, on current form," hailed newspaperman Tingay, and most of Greater Bristol must have read it. When a thunderstorm prevented her from practicing that first afternoon, a huge crowd of fans that had gathered to see her went away disappointed.

Althea sailed through the week against light opposition and beat Daphne Seeney in two sets in the final, though she needed eighteen games to win the second set. It was her sixteenth tournament championship of the season, and her tenth in succession. For years, *Ebony* magazine wrote in an article that had appeared earlier that month, Althea had lacked a "general plan of battle" and self-control. She had an unreliable backhand, and her feet sometimes would get tangled beneath her. Her talent was always latent, but now it was showing itself.

Yet Althea was competing in Bristol only because she hadn't been chosen for America's Wightman Cup team. While she was beating Seeney, Britain was once again challenging the United States, holders of the Cup since 1930, on the grass at Wimbledon. Among Americans and Englishmen, only Wimbledon and Forest Hills were deemed as important as the annual Wightman Cup tie—and some competitors, such as Margaret du Pont, might gauge the Wightman Cup the equal of any women's tennis competition in the world. As with the Davis Cup for the men, the Wightman Cup offered the only opportunity a tennis player had to compete as part of a team. That it also meant representing your country only added to its esteem.

As Britain's No. 2 singles player in the best-of-seven competition, Angela was scheduled to play both Fry and Brough, the American captain. (Coincidentally, each was coming off the loss to Althea at Manchester.) On the opening afternoon, June 15, Brough needed three sets to shake off the rust and struggle past Angela Mortimer, taking the third set by 7–5. Though she didn't get a victory, Mortimer's inspired play against the top woman in the world seemed a good omen for a British team that had been starved for success for decades.

Then Fry took the court against Angela. Fry won the first set easily, 6–2, but Angela matched her, service game for service game, in the second. Building on her baseline game with approach shots and then coming to net behind them, she held on to win it, 8–6. At that point, Fry's lack of match readiness began to show. Fry's serve—never a strength—faltered, and Angela took control of the third set. She went up a break. Up 5–3, and leading that ninth game by 40–15, she suddenly found herself with two match points.

This was momentous. Angela had never beaten Fry, or anyone of her stature. She'd taken a set off of Hart, played a few good sets against Maureen Connolly, and lately dominated lesser opposition, but a victory in this match would stand as a turning point in her career. More than that, Britain had won only three individual Wightman Cup matches, two singles and one doubles, of the sixty-six that had been played since the war.

On Angela's first match point, she slapped a forehand into the net. But at 40–30, she angled a perfectly placed volley that sent Fry scrambling off the court. On the run, Fry looped a half-lob down the right sideline, clearly in the alley. It hit the back stripe and sent a puff of chalk dust into the air, but the ball had landed several inches wide. Fry dropped the ball she'd been holding and advanced to the net, preparing to shake Angela's hand. Then both players realized that the line judge, who likely had seen the chalk rise and evidently lost perspective on the ball, hadn't called it out. The umpire called, "Deuce." Fry had won the point.

More than forty years later, Angela swears she remembers looking over at the chair and seeing the judge sitting with her eyes closed, fast asleep. Fry's recollection of the match for all these years was that she had actually lost it on that point. In reality, it was still 5–3 in the third set, and the score stood at deuce. Her will broken, Angela was barely able to finish. Fry won the game, held serve to even the score at 5–5, broke Angela for 6–5. Then she served out the victory in a matter of minutes.

In the newspapers the following day, British but also American, the line call wasn't even controversial, just blatantly wrong. "A lucky line decision was all that saved Shirley Fry," the *New York Times* wrote. Angela could take solace that she played the top-ranked American player even over an entire match, and lost certain victory because of a circumstance beyond her control. Yet Angela was always coming just so close and walking away a loser. In her contemplative moments, she couldn't help but think that the pattern had its roots somewhere in her psyche.

ON MONDAY, after two days of rain, the same theme played out again for Angela. By virtue of the closely fought victories by Brough and Fry, the United States held a 2–0 lead. Now the first- and second-ranked singles players for each country would switch opponents, and another singles match would be played between the third-ranked women, with two doubles matches to follow.

When Shirley Bloomer beat America's Dottie Knode to begin Monday's schedule, Angela's match against Brough took on added importance. And when Angela captured the first set 6–3, Britain's Wightman Cup fortunes seemed brighter than at any time in years. The hum in the crowd meant that five thousand versions of the same conversation were taking place concurrently. "If Angela can hold on to beat Brough, the

score will be tied at two matches apiece," every Englishman in attendance was thinking. Not since the war had Britain won as many as two
matches in a Wightman Cup.

As the second set began, the excitement in the air at Centre Court
was as palpable as at most Wimbledon finals. Spectators were tallying
up possible combinations of British victories, striving to find a way for
Britain to attain the magic number of four that would give it its first
Wightman Cup since 1930. But for that chain of events to unfold,
Angela had to win her second set against Brough, and the aging champion wasn't ready to fall so easily. She broke Angela's serve to go ahead,
4–2, in the next set, then served it out to win 6–3. The two traded service
breaks in the third set and found themselves tied at four games. Until
then, Angela actually had looked like the better player. She was stepping up on the ball with confidence, hitting it hard, dominating points.
She was ahead 40–15 and serving for 5–4 when Brough placed a backhand winner down the sideline. "It was the first ball I'd really hit perfectly all day," Brough would say later.

Instead of shrugging it off as a shot that was simply too good to handle, Angela panicked. She saw the Fry match playing out all over
again—and the semifinal against Althea in the French, and her loss
against Nancy Chaffee at Forest Hills the previous summer, and so
many of the other matches in her brief career that she'd played well
enough to win, yet hadn't. At deuce, she fed Brough consecutive volleys
that the Californian converted into easy points. As easy as that, Brough
had a break and a 5–4 lead. She won the match on a fierce overhead
moments later.

Later, Mortimer beat Fry, who still hadn't rounded into form, but the
United States won both doubles matches. By winning two of the seven
matches, Great Britain had equaled its best Wightman Cup showing
since a 4–3 defeat in 1936, but it could have been far better. Had Fry's
lob into the alley been called correctly, Britain would have had three
victories, meaning the outcome of the cup tie would have ultimately
hinged on the relatively small difference of both Angelas being unable
to hold one-set leads over Brough.

Perhaps, the English tennis fans mused in the days that followed,

America's dominance was beginning to wane. That was some consolation in defeat. On the other hand, the best female player for the first five months of 1956 was sitting in the stands on the second day of the Wightman Cup, with the championship of the Bristol tournament in her pocket. Had Althea been named to that Wightman Cup team in place of Fry, or even Knode, Britain's chances would have been diminished, even given Mortimer's record of success against her. At that moment, she was the most feared woman in tennis.

CHAPTER 12

Flatmates

As the London Grass Court Championships were beginning at Queen's Club, the Wimbledon seedings were announced. They were based on a combination of past performance, current form, success at previous Wimbledons, and the intuition of the seeding committee. Most of the attention was focused on the men's bracket, for which Australia's Lew Hoad had been seeded first, ahead of countryman Ken Rosewall. But the women also generated plenty of comment, especially since the eight seeded players included three Englishwomen for the first time in more than two decades.

All the Ladies' Singles seeds were American or English. All had played in the previous week's Wightman Cup tie except Althea and Beverly Fleitz, who was still recovering from an unexplained fainting spell she'd suffered at a tournament in Lugano in early June. With Doris Hart, Margaret du Pont, and Maureen Connolly—winners of five Wimbledons among them—now all inactive, the sport seemed primed for a generational shift. Of the entire field, only Louise Brough, a four-time winner, had taken the championship previously.

America's Brough was seeded first, followed by Beverly Baker Fleitz, Angela Mortimer, Althea, Shirley Fry, Angela, Dorothy Knode, and Shirley Bloomer. Doubles pairs were seeded, too. Angela and Althea, a confirmed entry for Wimbledon, were third, following Brough and Fry and Mortimer and Shilcock—and ahead of Fleitz and Darlene Hard.

News of the seedings circulated throughout Queen's Club, where play was under way. Brough had earned the top seed, it was assumed, on the basis of her four Wimbledon titles, and the pair of matches she won from a set down during the Wightman Cup tie the previous week. Fleitz had reached the final the year before, losing in a close two-set match to Brough, 7–5, 8–6. She was a natural for the second seed. Mortimer ahead of Althea at No.3 was something of a surprise, but she had beaten Althea in Stockholm, Cairo, and Alexandria earlier in the year. She was British, which meant she would be helped by the home crowd, and she had a track record at Wimbledon, which Althea didn't. Fry hadn't played well since arriving in Europe, but she was a formidable player with years of experience in major tournaments. As the current American No. 1, she could hardly be seeded any lower than fifth. Angela might have found a place higher than sixth, based on recent form, but she'd still won very few significant matches in what had been a very short career. Tellingly, she hadn't ever beaten any of the five players ranked above her.

Althea was the year's novelty. She hadn't played in England since 1951, and only had that one Wimbledon behind her, when she was still somewhat overwhelmed by the idea of competing against the best players in the world. She'd lost in the third round to Fleitz that year, onlookers recalled, and looked rather amateurish in the process. Five years later, though inarguably a better player, she was still something of an unknown quantity, despite her remarkable string of tournament successes. And the idea of a black player actually winning at Wimbledon was a difficult one for many observers to take seriously. Althea had only integrated the event five years before, and no black woman had played there since.

For all those reasons, Althea was the most compelling story entering the Championships. Two weeks before play started, she already was getting the full treatment from the dozen or so daily newspapers that were published in London at the time. She relished it and played to the cameras. She'd arrived in London in a floor-length coat, buttoned up against the June chill, and stepped from the car she was driving with a huge grin. She felt she finally was getting the recognition she deserved.

She had convinced Angela that they each needed to rent cars during their monthlong stay in London, though they'd be spending nearly all their time together and could get rides to Wimbledon from official transport vehicles if necessary. It was a substantial expense that Althea could ill afford, but she insisted on it—to the alarm of both Violet and Harry, who couldn't fathom the idea of their Angela actually driving around the bustling city. "Don't shed responsibility for yourself," Althea had said, and Angela never forgot it. If you could make do without relying on anyone else, that was clearly preferable.

It was the opposite of the way doubles partners are supposed to think, but Althea had made her way in the world for almost thirty years with that guiding principle. She'd received plenty of help, but always remained in control of her own destiny. If she wanted to arrive late to an event because she was taking a bath, she arrived late. She wouldn't deign to walk faster down a sidewalk if it meant the difference between getting to a movie on time or after the theater had darkened. She was determined that nobody would tell her what she could or couldn't do.

The newspapers portrayed her as independent, a bit of a loner: a proud woman who continued to believe that she was destined for success. As might be expected, the topic of race was never far from the surface. In every article written about Althea in the English papers, her skin color is used as an identifier. She is "the American Negro," or "the dusky American," or "the first of her race to . . ." or "the colored girl from Harlem." She is never merely Althea Gibson, the fourth seed, winner of eleven European and British tournaments in succession.

She faced the queries about race with politeness, but an undercurrent of resentment can be noted in her newspaper quotes. She believed the topic was irrelevant. She was playing tennis not for the cause of black Americans, or for minorities everywhere, but for herself. She tried to make that clear, subtly or in plain language, in most every interview she gave. "I am just another tennis player," she liked to say, "not a Negro tennis player. Of course, I am a Negro—everybody knows that—but you don't say somebody is a white tennis player. Do you?"

ALTHEA DIDN'T PLAY SINGLES at Queen's Club for reasons that are lost to posterity. In all likelihood, she was weary from competing in a tour-

nament nearly every week from January to June. She badly needed a
rest. Both Brough and Fry, who'd barely played at all that spring, chose
to skip the singles tournament, too, and concentrate on doubles. Althea
played women's doubles with Angela and mixed doubles, too, and otherwise drove around London in her rented car, spending as much time
as possible at the movies.

Back home, she was profiled for the first time in the *New York Times*
that Sunday, atop an article measuring Mickey Mantle's chances of
breaking Babe Ruth's home-run record of sixty in a season. "Home, for
Althea Gibson, is where a tennis court is," wrote Kennett Love of the
newspaper's London bureau. "She is as much in her element on a fast
lawn court as a panther is on an Arizona mesa." She has little time on
tour for anything but tennis, he reported, and reads the Bible, autobiographies, and detective novels. "She has no thoughts at present about
marriage. Her goal now is the Wimbledon championship."

First she had a doubles tournament to win at Queen's Club. Late in the
week, in their first real test, Althea and Angela needed three sets to beat
Mortimer and Shilcock. They advanced to the semifinal against Brough
and Fry, who had beaten the Australians Seeney and Muller. Without
Althea casting a shadow over the singles' bracket, Angela was concurrently enjoying the finest run of her career. She met Darlene Hard in a
semifinal for the right to advance against Pat Ward. Angela fell behind,
3–1, in the first set, but stormed back to win, 6–4, in a hail of ground
strokes. She was stepping up on the ball, taking it before it reached the
apex of its bounce, and hitting with authority. She won four of the first
five games of the second set and appeared on the way to her most important final yet. Then something happened, as it often did to Angela. She
became tentative, sat back on her heels, stopped taking the ball early.
Her level stroke became a flail. Hard rallied to tie the set at 5–5, and then
Angela forced herself to return in her head to the patterns she and
Jones had worked on. She won the next two games and the match.

She expected to feel nervous in the final, but Ward was a slow-
moving, deliberate player whom Angela *knew* she could beat. She gained
a service break in the first set to win it, and then Ward fell apart. It was
almost too easy to be believed. Angela cruised through the second set

with few errors, beating Ward 6–0. Without having time to think about it, she was the London Grass Court champion.

But Angela hadn't played nearly as well in the doubles semifinal against Brough and Fry. Her strokes, which had become so steady in recent weeks, reverted to their old, erratic ways. She missed one shot entirely, then missed another, looked over to Althea for reassurance, but found none. Althea was staring daggers at her. Althea considered herself the lead player in any doubles pairing, but she hardly wanted to carry her partner. The unspoken words in Althea's glance were, "How could you miss such a shot? Aren't you worthy of playing doubles with me?"

That look was all Angela needed to collapse entirely. Even though she was on her way to the Queen's Club championship and already had been anointed as a Wimbledon seed, her psyche was nonetheless that fragile, or perhaps Althea's approval meant that much to her. Althea made a miraculous effort to win the match by herself, but it wasn't enough. It seemed that every time she put Brough or Fry on the defensive with a well-placed ground stroke, Angela—now utterly devoid of confidence—would muff the easy followup at net. Brough and Fry, the aging remnants of two of the best women's doubles teams of that era or any era, advanced to the final together, winning 6–2, 7–5. Althea and Angela walked off the court not speaking to each other.

Angela all but ran to see Jimmy Jones, who was covering the tournament for several newspapers. Jones had seen the match and understood the situation. Before it had ended, he already was constructing a strategy. When he saw Angela, he told her they had to see Althea immediately, and that he would do the talking. Once again, he was playing a role that would become common in later years, that of the coach-as-manager. With a few exceptions—such as Teach Tennant, who guided the early careers of both Alice Marble and Maureen Connolly—such a job description didn't exist in the mid-1950s. Players were expected to fight their own battles, just as they booked their own travel and made their own way through the world.

With Angela in tow, Jones approached Althea in the Queen's Club cafeteria. When he wanted to, he could have a commanding presence. He couldn't intimidate Althea, but he could—and did—immediately capture her attention. The three of them sat down to talk. Althea denied that anything had happened on the court beyond a manifestation of her will to win, but Jones knew otherwise. He explained to her that doubles was more than singles with two players. She and Angela had had success at Roland Garros, but that didn't mean they could win Wimbledon while pulling against each other.

Jones was well aware of Angela's weaknesses as a player. His aim wasn't to convince Althea that Angela was the perfect partner—but rather, that nobody was. Two players, no matter how talented, had to work together to win. Mistakes were a part of the game, and how you treated your partner when she made them might well dictate how far you advanced in the tournament. "You must be conscious at all times of what the other player is thinking," he said.

Althea nodded politely, but Jones wasn't certain that she accepted what he was saying. She wasn't usually open to criticism. She had been so accustomed to going it alone that Jones feared she'd become constitutionally incapable of being a teammate, though she'd played basketball and softball at Florida A&M only a few years before. To find out, Jones asked Althea to meet him and Angela the following morning at one of the Queen's Club back courts, not far from the entrance gate. He'd round up a partner and they'd play a practice match. She agreed. When she arrived, she found them waiting with a journeyman player from Jones's era: Howard Walton, a thirty-nine-year-old former Davis Cupper (total experience: one match for Britain against India in 1948) who had a baseline game not unlike Shirley Fry's.

They played two sets, Jones and Walton against Angela and Althea. Jones asked Althea and Angela to pay less attention to the score of the match than to how the other was doing. "Be encouraging, not discouraging," was his mantra. He framed it as advice for both members of the team, but both Althea and Angela well knew that it was meant for Althea; Angela could hardly have said or done anything to puncture Althea's self-confidence on the court if she'd wanted to. The exercise worked. Althea was solicitous, Angela played almost flawlessly, and the partnership clicked as before. At the end of the practice match, Althea stepped over to Angela and embraced her. Something seemed to have

changed inside her; she was close to tears, and had a look in her eyes
that Angela had never seen. "I'm sorry, Angie," she said. "I didn't mean
to do it."

THE CONTRETEMPS, and the deft way in which Jones handled it, left
Angela and Althea feeling closer than ever. In the three days between
the end of the Queen's Club tournament and the start of Wimbledon,
they spent almost every waking moment together. Althea had moved
into the apartment on Rossmore Court for the month, Violet relin-
quishing her bedroom for the occasion. The building overlooked the
noisy Paddington Goods Station, but Althea was at peace there, in the
heart of the busy city. She could smoke a cigarette, drink a glass of
whiskey—always in moderation: her idea of training—and croon nightclub ballads in the bath.

In retrospect, they were seldom happier. Their rented cars waiting in
a nearby outlet of the Blue Star garage chain, Angela and Althea would
eat a hearty English breakfast prepared by Violet, then set out for
Queen's Club and practice indoors on the slippery wood surface that
played like grass. It was Angela's idea: if the rains came, they'd still be
able to get their time in. Then Angela would head off to work her hours
at Lillywhites, and Althea would take in a movie, which she still insisted
on calling a "flicker." Once Wimbledon started, they learned their
match times from the newspaper each morning. They'd practice at
Queen's Club, then head to Wimbledon in caravan. They'd park on
Church Road and walk along the sidewalk to the All England Club,
alongside the ticket-holders who were doing the same. In these uncom-
plicated times, there were no security guards. Nobody bothered them,
except to shout a "Good luck!"

Their friendship didn't go unnoticed by the local media. By the time
the tournament started, photographers and reporters were practically
camped out in front of the door to the two-bedroom flat. Violet would
open it every so often and scold them. Then she'd relent and offer up a
tidbit for their eager readers. She'd tell them that the girls ate scrambled
eggs for breakfast, or that Althea very much enjoyed whatever movie
she'd seen the previous afternoon. The next day, there it was in the morn-

ing papers. Eventually, Violet would make a deal with the reporters. Angela would agree to come to the door for a quick photo session and interview, she said, but then they all had to leave for the day. They stuck to the bargain, decamping to outside the apartment and snapping their photos from the sidewalk. The following morning, it would begin again.

If Althea was the national and international story of the week, Angela was the charming local angle. Only a few months ago, it seemed, she was a game but overmatched schoolgirl. Now she was a Wimbledon seed in both singles and doubles, and had arguably the most famous female player in the world staying with her at her flat. Her father, too, was good for a feature or two. He was wealthy and opinionated, and seemed to have Hollywood connections.

As a publicity stunt, Harry had publicly promised Angela the title to the Bogner Regis pier that he had rebuilt after the war if she managed to win Wimbledon. He probably didn't mean it, and Angela had no interest in running an entertainment venue far from home. Accepting such a gift for winning a tournament, even from her father, might well have violated her amateur standing. Nevertheless, the idea of her playing for the pier was an alluring one that made its way into newspaper copy nearly every day of the fortnight.

Perhaps it was hometown favoritism, but the London papers routinely called Angela the most improved player on the women's tour. Even Maureen Connolly, writing in the *Daily Mail*, contributed a reassessment: "In the past I have had great respect for her fighting temperament, but her strokes . . . were too much like a robot—push a button and the racket went back in a stiff motion," she wrote. "This year, however, Angela has found the beauty and the rhythm of smooth, flowing strokes. Her racket glides through the air in one continuous motion. She has also developed an uncanny sense of when to strike forcefully. This is particularly apparent in her approach shots. Her volleying has also improved 100 percent."

Since it was woefully evident that Angela didn't have as much talent as some other players, journalists heaped praise on her work ethic. Taking the time to study your opponents can mean the difference between winning and losing, offered sportswriter Laurie Pignon. "This is proved by our own Angela Buxton—the girl they laughed at last year and fear this," he wrote. Pignon picked Angela and Althea as favorites in the doubles, seeds notwithstanding.

Angela's job at Lillywhites, which she continued throughout the Championships, was trotted out as evidence of her girl-next-door qualities, and her swift rise from anonymity taken as a sign that she was somehow fated to succeed. A poignant story in the *Mirror* outlined how Angela had all but decided to quit the game three years ago, but she rallied because of the support of a friend. The writer knew the unnamed friend well. Both were Jimmy Jones.

Jones was riding high on Angela's success. In the years that followed, he'd try the same Pattern Tennis approach with other British women, but he was never able to replicate the same symbiotic relationship that he had with Angela. Entering Wimbledon, he liked her chances. Nevertheless, under his byline of C. M. Jones, he predicted victory in the Gentlemen's and Ladies' bracket for both No. 1 seeds, Lew Hoad and Louise Brough. He could hope all he wanted for Angela's success, but as a journalist, he had a reputation to uphold.

IT WAS TRADITION at Wimbledon that the defending Gentlemen's Singles champion began play on the first day of the tournament, and the defending Ladies' Singles champion followed on the second day. On the morning of Tuesday, June 26, Louise Brough arrived at the All England Tennis and Croquet Club in a gingham dress and a cotton cardigan. That afternoon on Centre Court, she needed thirty-four minutes to dispatch Jean Forbes, the talented sixteen-year-old South African, in straight sets. Forbes was the youngest player in the draw, so young that she'd been barred from competing at Wimbledon because of her age the previous summer.

The same afternoon, the oldest player in the draw nearly ended Angela Mortimer's Wimbledon before it began. Thelma Long of Australia—thirty-eight or thirty-nine years old, depending on which newspaper you were reading—had been winning tournaments against all comers since 1935 in her native New South Wales. She split the first two sets with Mortimer, then had her at 3–2 and 40–0 in the third. Ever the fighter, Mortimer rallied, but her performance didn't impress the press box wags, who now seemed to believe that England's best hopes rested with the other Angela. "What a difference a good service would make to Miss Mortimer's game!" Tingay wrote in the *Telegraph*.

Neither Angela nor Althea played until the following day, Wednesday, June 27. Though Althea was the higher seed, she had a first-round match to contest, while Angela had drawn a bye, meaning she advanced directly into the second round. (Oddly, Fry and Mortimer also had first-round matches, while the unseeded players positioned on either edge of the bracket didn't.) Angela and Althea checked the newspapers that morning to learn their schedules. Althea was playing Edda Buding, the Romanian-born, Argentine-raised German, in a match scheduled for Court 2 early in the afternoon. She plotted her schedule accordingly.

Informed that she would be debuting on the most hallowed patch of turf in the tennis world, Wimbledon's Centre Court, with former U.S. President Harry Truman attending in the Royal Box, Angela promptly lost her voice. It was comical at first, as she croaked out her breakfast order to Violet, and then it wasn't. Clearly, her nerves were manifesting themselves by shutting down her vocal chords. "I have a very vulnerable chest," she says now. "I'd get a sore throat, I couldn't speak, I'd get laryngitis. As soon as I was under any kind of psychological stress, I'd lose my voice." It would happen again several years later, on the eve of her wedding to Donald Silk. When the time came, she could barely say her vows. "It's because it was the wrong marriage," she says. "My body was telling me not to do it."

Her voice reduced to a whisper on this bright Wednesday morning, she and Althea walked to the Blue Star garage. They wished each other luck, then set out for Wimbledon, one after the other, each in her own rented car.

ANGELA'S CENTRE COURT JITTERS manifested themselves deep into the first set of her match against Suzanne Le Besnarais. At one point, her clumsy attempt at a volley carried her racket past the net, handing Le Besnarais an undeserved game. With the score tied at four all, she couldn't help but wonder if the fourteen thousand spectators in attendance were in for a grand disappointment. Then she snapped to attention and won the next eight games in succession, blanking Le Besnarais in the second set. She stepped off the court and learned that Althea had won her first-round match against Edda Buding.

The Gibson-Buding match on Court 2 prompted the most interest of any that day. Women, especially, were eager to see this slender American Negro play her singular brand of tennis, and they crowded into the standing-room section in all their Wimbledon finery. Althea struggled against her own nervousness, ceding four games in the first set before settling in and winning the second 6–2. Still, she managed to impress a crowd that hadn't seen such powerful strokes since Connolly. Her game wasn't all power, either. All the gains she'd made as a thinking player since her last appearance at Wimbledon were on display against Buding. In London's *Daily Herald* the following day, Clifford Webb listed her weapons. Althea had the hardest serve of any woman in the tournament, the best overhead, but also the most effective drop shot. "She feints an all-out smash and drops the ball in the forecourt," he wrote.

Angela's surge against Le Besnarais had impressed the *News Chronicle*, which now couldn't praise her enough. "Miss Buxton, more than any other English player, has the stuff of latent greatness," wrote Gerald Walter. Over breakfast on Thursday morning, Angela and Althea read their reviews. Others were evidently reading them, too. A photo of them in the *Evening News*, which hit the streets at about eleven in the morning, was captioned by the information that they'd be debuting as Wimbledon doubles partners later in the day. That match, too, was held at Centre Court, but the national football stadium at Wembley would have been a better venue. More than 23,000 fans pushed their way close to viewing distance, forcing the authorities to close the gates. There, they saw the newfound darlings of the tournament show no signs of their difficulties at Queen's Club, easily beating an overmatched Norwegian pair to advance.

After beating England's Peggy Wheeler, a qualifier, Althea played Anne Shilcock in the third round on Centre Court. With the wind gusting, she emerged from the locker room in a pristine polo shirt, a pleated white skirt and a belt. She started the match playing poorly, unable to find her rhythm. She thumped one ball after another off the wooden frame of her racket as Shilcock won the first set 6–4. Then Althea, remembering Richardson's advice to vary her attack, started to lob. Up 2–1, she broke service in the fourth game and never looked back. She won the second set 6–2, and the third set 6–1, in a glittering display of all-around tennis. Still, even after Althea closed out her victory with a flurry of winners, nobody did more than clap ever so politely. "To pretend she's just another player is to bilk the truth," Peter Wilson wrote after watching the match. "She is the first colored player ever to 'invade' a game which is riddled with snobbery, even if your skin is the same colour as the majority of the other players in it." For an outsider such as Althea, he suggested, acceptance was out of the question. Fortunately, she didn't yearn to be accepted, only to win.

In Angela's second match of the tournament, she beat Lisa Gram Andersen of Denmark, 6–3, 6–2. This put her in the Round of 16, where her fortunate draw would continue. While Fleitz, Fry, and Althea were matched against formidable opposition, Angela's next opponent was the least likely of all the remaining players, a provincial player from Hertfordshire named Elaine Watson. Angela won the first set 6–4, but Watson raced to a 3–0 lead in the second set by keeping Angela constantly in motion. Angela looked uncomfortable racing around the court "like a scared giraffe," as one onlooker later described her, and it seemed as though some genuine drama might follow. Then Watson realized where she was and what she already had accomplished. Something within her decided that was enough, and the winners she had been hitting turned into tentative slaps at the ball that Angela handled easily. Angela equalized at 4–4, won her service game, then broke Watson for the match.

For the second consecutive year, Angela had advanced into the Final Eight, this time with three other Englishwomen and four Americans. It was quite an honor. But this year was far different from a year ago, Angela couldn't help thinking. Last year, she hadn't been prepared for such success. The Angela of 1955 had been satisfied with merely getting so far at the world's most prestigious tournament. In 1956, she intended to win it.

Looming ahead was Fleitz, Angela's first genuine test of the tournament. With her blond hair of 1955 dyed a handsome auburn, the second seed had sailed past Suzi Kormoczi, 6–0, in the first set of her Centre Court match, and raced to a 3–1 lead in the second. She looked unbeatable, but Kormoczi chipped and sliced her way back to 5–4, then broke Fleitz and held serve to take a 6–5 lead. Fleitz noted a queasiness in her stomach—she hadn't felt quite right since crumpling in a faint in Lugano weeks before—but stayed back at the baseline and played her game. Hitting her line-drive forehands from both sides, she rallied to win, 8–6. She, too, was determined to improve on her performance of a year ago, when she'd lost in the final. This was her year to win, she felt. She was still young, but she didn't know how many more chances she'd have to get this far at Wimbledon. She and John already had one child, a daughter named Kimberly, and they'd lost a second after a difficult pregnancy. It would soon be time to stop traveling and concentrate on having a family.

ALTHEA, TOO, went through to the Final Eight, but not without another of the turns on the roller coaster that marked her career. She won the first set 6–0, against Hird, and then, as though a switch had been flipped, could barely win as much as a point in each of the next four games. It had little to do with Hird, whose style of play could best be described as innocuous. Hird was there for the taking. But Althea was making unforced errors on nearly every point. "I thought, 'Whoa, this is fine!'" Hird says now. "I was coming to net, volleying, having a great time." As suddenly as Althea's slide started, it stopped. With no noticeable change in her strategy or her demeanor, she ran off six straight games and won the match.

Such inconsistency hadn't been seen before in a player of such stature. That tendency Althea had to let her game veer off the road and into the underbrush caused observers to wonder how she would ever put six consecutive matches together to win a major title. More insidiously, it played to stereotypes: that somehow this black woman wasn't trustworthy enough to handle the immense talent she'd been given, or intelligent enough to harness it. But then, she already had harnessed it,

in Paris the previous month, and she'd won more championships—and
more matches—than anyone else so far that year. That she happened to
play in streaks, losing four games in a row, then winning six, masked
the fact that she reached the same place in the match as did a consistent player who held service each time but managed just a single break
during the course of winning a set 6–4. That was the conventional way,
the tidier way, *the way a white person would do it.* Something about
Althea's all-or-nothing game was unseemly, the British crowd thought,
and so was her manly way of dressing, and the way she carried herself.
They had seen enough to satisfy their curiosity, but Althea was no
favorite of theirs.

CHAPTER 13

Wimbledon

Violet Buxton was enjoying her daughter's tennis success immensely, and not just because of the tennis. She herself had become something of a minor celebrity. When Angela and Althea declined to come to the door and answer questions, the reporters interviewed Violet instead. She had a telepathic link to Angela, she told them. When Angela was on the court, she could send her support and encouragement through the ether by the force of her will. At night, when the girls had gone to bed, she'd sit at her desk and write poems to commemorate the occasion. It was as though she, too, realized that this wouldn't be the first of many fortnights like this, but perhaps the only one.

Harry Buxton was also getting everything he could from Angela's success. In truth, he'd been waiting for something like this all his life. Each day that Angela played, whether singles or doubles, he'd roll up to the Church Road entrance in that secondhand Rolls-Royce, purchased from Holland's Queen Wilhelmina. The likes of Harry Buxton couldn't easily get Centre Court tickets—there were some things in those days that money couldn't buy—but, invariably, he'd bluff his way in, alongside an advertising executive named Barney Goodman, who had been dating Angela for several years.

Barney called Violet "Mum" (as opposed to Althea, who called her the American "Mom"), and he and Harry had quickly become fast friends. Harry had more in common with Barney than he did with Gor-

don, his own son. Harry and Barney would take a day off of work and head to the horse track, a couple of pals out on the town. Unlike tennis, horse racing was a sport that Harry understood. At least, betting on horse racing was. It was just like the stock market, Harry liked to explain. You put your money on something when it was cheap, and you hoped it gained in value by winning. Tennis had an incomprehensible scoring system and endless rallies, and it bored him. Barney had to frame each match in horse racing terms to keep him engaged. "It's 4–1 against Angela now," he'd say if she fell behind late in a set. Harry would nod knowingly, then take a quick look around to see who else was at the matches that day.

ANGELA AWOKE ON JULY 2 to sage words from Bill Talbert, a multiple doubles champion and two-time Forest Hills singles finalist. "Angela Buxton is getting closer to the top and could go all the way," he wrote in the *Daily Mail*. "She has the right approach. She's intense, hard-working, and concentrates on tennis above everything else." But Talbert wondered if perhaps Angela was *too* committed to tennis. He invoked boxer Gene Tunney, whose stunning upset of Jack Dempsey in September 1926 had earned him worldwide fame. Tunney was one of the most "concentrated sportsmen of all time," Talbert wrote, but he took care to keep boxing in perspective. His favored method of relaxation was to read Shakespeare. Talbert didn't necessarily advocate that for Angela, but he felt strongly that some kind of diversion would loosen the tension and make her a stronger player.

It was a provocative thought, and Angela made a mental note to talk to Jones about it when she saw him that afternoon. Still, with Beverly Fleitz looming, this hardly seemed a suitable time for relaxation. Angela and Jones had been watching films of Fleitz, and they believed they knew how to beat her. It was vital to draw her away from the baseline and up to net, where she was most vulnerable. "Like a blind man without his white stick," was how Peter Wilson of London's *Evening News* described Fleitz's net game. Angela had patterns in her head that could accomplish just such a task, and she'd been practicing them daily with Jones at Queen's Club.

She wasn't daunted that nearly every prognosticator picked Fleitz to beat her, just as Fleitz had done at Wimbledon the previous year. Certainly, Angela had improved since then; nobody doubted that. But Fleitz had improved, too, and a feeling was growing that perhaps this would be her breakthrough tournament. Angela was the grinder, whose diligent practice habits had earned her significant success; as Tingay would write in the *Daily Telegraph*, "I doubt if any British player ever applied herself to the dull preliminaries with equal resolution." But Fleitz was a genuine talent, a player who could eventually collect major singles titles a handful at a time, like a Brough or an Osborne.

Angela's match with Fleitz was set for Tuesday, July 3. It would be the second match on Centre Court after Althea's quarterfinal against Fry. But first, Angela Mortimer and the unseeded Pat Ward did battle the day before to see who would be the first Englishwoman to advance into the Wimbledon semifinals since 1939.

Angela had a vested interest in the match, because she would play the winner if she managed to get past Fleitz. Having never beaten Mortimer, she much preferred to play Ward. But in order to have a Buxton-Ward match, she well knew, two improbable results had to happen, and that was unlikely at this stage of the tournament. Fleitz and Mortimer were two of the best players in the world, and they would make worthy combatants in a Wimbledon semifinal. That was the conventional wisdom. Instead, Mortimer came out with a case of big-match jitters, failed to hold service even once, and lost in two brief sets to Ward. It was a shocking development. Pat Ward, the London-born twenty-seven-year-old who looked like everyone's stern homeroom teacher, had advanced into the Wimbledon semifinals. The luckiest woman at Wimbledon, all agreed, was Fleitz, who by merely beating Angela and Ward would advance to the Ladies' Singles final for a second consecutive year.

BUT SOMETHING WAS WRONG with Beverly Fleitz. She'd fallen faint in Lugano, limited her Wightman Cup participation to doubles, felt queasy all week long. Now she was holed up in room 742 of the Cumberland Hotel with "flu-like symptoms." "My doctor says I must not leave the bed for at least two days," she told Darlene Hard, her doubles

partner. If she followed the advice, it would mean defaulting her quarterfinal match against Angela. That morning, Fleitz's illness was a topic
of conversation throughout the city. Would she defy doctor's orders to
play her singles match? Hard knew as little as anyone. "Beverly has
been in bed for forty-eight hours," she told reporters. "She's got the flu,
or something."

Fleitz suspected otherwise. She and John had been trying in earnest
to have another child. According to what she remembered from her
earlier pregnancies, this wasn't a bout of influenza or anything else. The
timing couldn't have been worse, but tennis was an ephemeral pursuit,
while a family meant forever. Though she'd only be in the second
month, she didn't dare risk losing the fetus, not after already having
miscarried once. She'd called the doctor over the weekend and been
thoroughly examined, but now it was Tuesday and her nausea was getting worse. She was leaving her quarterfinal match, she felt, in the bottom of a hotel toilet bowl. Then four men arrived unannounced at the
door of the hotel room, wearing black frock coats and hats. "I thought
they were there to tell me I was dying," she says. Instead, they told her
she was, indeed, pregnant. The doctors strongly advised her to cease all
physical activity until her condition stabilized.

That was what women did in 1956, even if they were second-seeded
at Wimbledon and two matches—two relatively easy matches—from
the final. Some might even reach the same decision today. The previous
year, Fleitz had been the first mother since 1920 to reach the Wimbledon final, and that had occasioned comment enough. To play now
would be terribly irresponsible, she and her husband agreed. Accordingly, Fleitz telephoned in her withdrawal from the Ladies' Singles
bracket, handing a walkover to Angela. She told Hard she'd be unable
to play their scheduled doubles match that afternoon. She was going
home to California to rest for the summer. If her math was right, the
baby would be due in late January.

The newspapers heard the news from the tournament director, and
before long it was literally on the street. The newsboys hawking the
Evening Standard, which hit the streets in the late morning, wrote it on
their placards as the lead story of the day. "Mrs. Fleitz Expects a Baby,"

the headline screamed. Lunch hour had barely come and gone before the newsmen had packed the hotel corridor. They were carrying bouquets of flowers and begging for an interview. John Fleitz called the front desk to ask for a vase, and when the maid knocked, the newsmen hovered, looking for a glimpse of Beverly. But John extended an arm, grabbed the vase, and slammed the door.

By then, Althea and Fry were already on Centre Court. It was a match of the hottest female players on the tour, and the players with the most contrasting styles. Fry, whose father had been preparing her to win Wimbledon since she was nine, was a dogged retriever, "one of the greatest of the era," Maureen Connolly had said. She would stay at the baseline and float those softball backhands over the net all day, until her opponent didn't have the stamina to send them back any longer. She'd grown up playing on clay in Akron, three courts side by side with almost no room between them, "so you had to learn to run and cut off angles," she says now. "I was always determined to get to every ball because that's what I was taught by my father. You can get to *every ball* on the court." Through the years, Fry came to favor three-set matches, particularly in the heat of a summer afternoon. Even after coming out of retirement, she felt it was to her advantage to play long matches, because pure talent wilted, but stamina and determination didn't. "I didn't mind staying out there forever in the heat," she says.

Althea, for whom training was a particularly distasteful pursuit, was vulnerable to just that type of player. Yet her strengths, especially the power with which she hit nearly every ground stroke, confounded Fry. Aside from the 1951 Wimbledon semifinal, which she won in two sets, Fry had managed little success against Brough, the finest serve-and-volley player of her era, and the nearest analog to Althea the game had seen.

Beyond the difference in their playing styles, Fry and Althea were about as unlike each other as any two women on the tour. Outwardly, at least, Fry was so modest as to seem disingenuous. Years of traveling the world as Doris Hart's sidekick had given her a diminished sense of her own importance in the tennis world; it's hard to consider yourself "the greatest," as Althea was fond of saying, when you weren't even the best

player in the front seat of your rental car. When she played Hart in the
Wimbledon final in 1951, everyone she encountered told her that they
were so happy Hart finally had broken through and was in a position to
win Wimbledon. By the end, Fry says, "I wanted her to win, too."

Fry deflected any credit that came her way as luck, or at the most
the product of a prodigious work ethic. She liked to quote Abraham
Lincoln about working hard and putting yourself in position to gain
good fortune. When her tennis career came to its second and final end,
she left it behind. She remembered which matches she'd won and
which she'd lost, but little else about them. And when a representative
from the city of St. Petersburg, Florida, called a few years ago, determined to give her a plaque to celebrate her various triumphs, she tried
hard to convince him not to. "That was years ago," she told him.
"Nobody even remembers anything I did, much less cares about it. Isn't
there someone else you could honor?"

FRY STARTED HER QUARTERFINAL against Althea inauspiciously, losing
the first game with a double-fault. She broke Althea's serve in the second game, then double-faulted twice to lose her serve again. At best,
Fred Tupper of the *New York Times* wrote, Fry's serve is fast and flat. "In
the first set, it was flat, slow and often into the net." This was not the
way to beat a player as talented as Althea Gibson, Fry knew. And once
she had that 2–1 advantage, Althea began to play impeccable tennis.
Her long legs seemed to cover half the court in two strides. No matter
how she angled her ground strokes, Fry couldn't hit a ball outside
Althea's reach. And each time Fry allowed her to get to net, Althea
invariably won the point. She took the fourth game with an artful volley
that seemed to fall dead over the net, then stayed on serve. She served
out the tenth game to win the set 6–4.

Fry came out for the second set determined to change the dynamic
of the match. She sensed a weakness in Althea's forehand that she
believed would expose itself as the match continued. It was a tenuous
hope, but proceeding the way she'd been going, she knew, was a subtle
form of surrender. She began to hit every ball to Althea's forehand,
some with pace (or what passed for pace in her repertoire), some with-

out. With the second set on serve after five games, the "first gentle breeze" began to blow in Fry's direction, the *Times* of London wrote the following day. Althea double-faulted twice to give Fry a service break and a 4–2 lead.

Energized, Fry scampered around the damp grass like a teenager, but hit her shots with the guile of a veteran. She double-faulted to hand Althea the seventh game, but immediately broke back to take a 5–3 lead. Then she won the set on an uncharacteristic overhead putaway. By then, both players had been turned inside out. Althea was ready to abandon her attacking game. She had been playing such steady tennis, aiming her drop shots and angles with the precision of a marksman, but now she felt that her best strategy was to outwait Fry. Aware of the criticism against her, she was determined that she wouldn't be the one to make the mistakes. Perhaps because she'd adopted a defensive mind-set, her booming first serve abandoned her. The first seven games of the third set were service breaks, and that suited Fry fine. If she could take Althea's serve out of the match, she knew, she stood a far better chance of winning it.

To Fry's astonishment, Althea continued to linger at the baseline. She was running down Fry's shots with a consistency that she hadn't displayed before, but playing that kind of tennis minimized her own talents. She chopped and lobbed, but showed little of the sustained power that had won her so many matches over the previous months. At 4–3, Fry served out a love game to move within hailing distance of the semifinals. She steeled herself not to let a single ball pass her, repeating her father's words in her mind. She ran down whatever Althea sent her way and sent long, looping returns back, balls hit with such little force that they seemed to pause at their apex. Still, Althea refused to come to net and put them away. Fry won the first three points of the game, which gave her three match points at 0–40. Althea saved the first, then saved the second, but she couldn't save the third. Her long winning streak had ended.

Shirley threw her hands up and shouted "Yippee!" like a schoolgirl. Then she met Althea at the net. They turned and walked off together, Althea a head taller; her arm extended over the net in deference. Althea was magnanimous after the match. Seated with a cup of tea in a formal interview room, she fielded questions from a room full of reporters. "It was easier to beat small fry elsewhere than big Fry at Wimbledon," she said, keeping a poker face at her pun. There was no animosity, none of the bitterness that characterized so many of Althea's defeats—and fueled so many of her victories. She knew she'd been outplayed by a more experienced opponent. After only five minutes, the solicitous press officer ended what had been a restrained session with a rhetorical, "Will that be all, gentlemen?" Althea still had a doubles match to play.

For her part, Fry professed to be shocked at the result. She was so accustomed to losing the matches that mattered, she couldn't believe she'd finally won one, especially at Wimbledon. But the previous generation of champions was gone now, and Fry was playing as well as she ever had in her life. "Althea played so well in the last set that the pressure was on me," she said. "But she got scared. If she had crowded me at the net when I expected, she [would] have won. But she hung back, through nerves, I guess. I felt sorry for her because I know how it feels."

THE LONDON PAPERS praised Fry for her smart, gutsy performance, but they also blamed Althea. They couldn't help but think that, though she'd played with a marvelous consistency, she had lost the match more than Fry had won it. It was an old criticism of Althea, that she couldn't handle adversity. "Once things began to go askew, even slightly askew, something drained out of her slowly," the *Times* wrote.

More likely, Althea was beaten by Fry's superior ability to adapt to the circumstance. Fry knew just how to nudge the match in a direction that would play to her strengths, and Althea was just stubborn enough—and just proud enough of her newfound consistency—to go along. That angle was lost on nearly all the newspapermen, who must have been occupied thinking up new synonyms for dark skin. Althea was "the dark star," "the naturally talented Negress," "the coloured girl from Harlem." Not a single account of the match in the London papers failed to mention Althea's race, as though it had somehow mattered in the outcome. Frank Rostron of the *Daily Express* was even more direct, casting Althea as the representative of Negroes everywhere: "Shirley

Fry . . . yesterday crushed the hopes of millions of coloured folk by putting Harlem's 30-year-old [sic] challenger, gangling Althea Gibson, out of the Wimbledon Women's Singles."

The last time she'd lost a match of this import, at Forest Hills the previous summer, she was thinking about quitting the game and joining the WAC. It had been a marvelous run since then, a romp through Mexico and then Asia and Europe and even North Africa. She'd been playing a tournament most every week and winning all but four of them over the last six months, but now it had ended, and soon she'd be heading home. She had won the French singles championship; she was the holder of titles from the English countryside through the European continent, all the way to Delhi and Calcutta; she had made the memories of a lifetime; but she hadn't won at Wimbledon.

Though it seemed as though her career as a world-class player was only beginning, Althea was already a few months shy of her twenty-ninth birthday. She was anything but a fitness fanatic, and she was short on money. She still had the opportunity to make a little money playing professional tennis, matched against a drawing card like Maureen Connolly or even Karol Fageros, the golden-panties girl. In all likelihood, she was nearing the end of what had been a historic but ultimately frustrating amateur career. In that sense, the defeat *was* crushing.

If Althea wanted to be certain of having a Wimbledon championship to brag about, her best chance was in the Ladies' Doubles. She and Angela had cruised through the first two rounds, winning twenty-four games and losing only four. Having showered and changed from one Fred Perry shirt into another, Althea now had to join Angela back on Centre Court for a third-round doubles match against Dottie Knode and Christiane Mercelis. The way that Angela and Althea were playing together, they could have sleepwalked through it. They finished off the Frenchwoman and the American in less than an hour, winning 6–3, 6–2.

Betty Rosenquest Pratt and Thelma Long were waiting in the doubles quarterfinal. But before that, Angela had a semifinal singles match to play. No matter what happened the following afternoon, Britain was assured of its first Ladies' Singles finalist since Kay Stammers in 1939. It would be Angela or Pat Ward, and the winner would advance to face the winner of the match between Fry and Brough. In the *Daily Sketch,* Laurie Pignon's article raced past Ward to consider the possibilities. "It's Angela's Big Chance to Wear the Crown," the headline screamed. "The girl they said was useless can make Wimbledon history." Behind the hyperbole was a salient fact. Only a few weeks before, Angela had beaten Fry but for the incorrect line call in the Wightman Cup. Now they were each a semifinal away from meeting again.

THE EMPATHETIC FRY felt bad for Althea, and she felt bad for Louise Brough. Brough was still winning tournaments, and she was seeded No. 1 for this Wimbledon, but Fry knew she was far from the same player that she had been. In her best days, Brough's high-kicking American Twist serve, the engine behind her vaunted serve-and-volley game, would drive an opponent off the court in pursuit of the ball. If someone managed to return it, it left them at a significant tactical disadvantage, scrambling to get back into position. Now that serve was all but gone; Brough was having more trouble all the time simply getting the ball in play. "She was shaking while she tossed the ball in the air," Fry remembers. "She'd have to catch it and start again, over and over. It wasn't the same Louise, not at all."

Brough had always looked her years and more. She seemed more matronly than most of her peers, but she'd played the game with an unquenchable energy. At thirty-three, she acknowledged that she felt tired. She'd lost the will to practice, and she found herself snapping at slow-moving ballboys, willing the match along so she could get off the court. "I didn't enjoy playing anymore," she says. "I was almost counting the days until it was over. Some days, I didn't even feel like I could pick up my feet." Nevertheless, Brough remained a formidable player. She'd swept through the bottom of the draw, losing only eight games in three matches before her three-set quarterfinal with Bloomer. In all, her track record at the All England Club was remarkable. She'd won in 1948, 1949, and 1950, lost to Connolly in the final in 1952, 1953, and 1954, and beaten Fleitz for her fourth singles title in 1955. Since 1947, nearly a decade before, she'd advanced to the Wimbledon final in every year but one.

But in that one year, 1951, she was upset in a semifinal by a lesser talent who played almost a perfect match. That player was Fry. And in Fry's mind, the 6–4, 6–2 victory of five years prior would be the template for this match. Fry would vary the pace of her ground strokes in an attempt to keep Brough off-balance, she'd lob to prevent her from camping out at net, she'd run down every ball on the court, and resist whatever urge she might have to come to net.

That was exactly how this semifinal played out on July 6. The wind was gusting, which made Brough's toss all the more erratic. By the middle of the first set, she had all but abandoned her serve as a weapon. Those who had seen Brough in her prime couldn't help thinking that she'd lost just enough off her serve that the aces of previous years were now being handled rather easily by Fry, and it seemed to make all the difference, at least in the first set. Fry won it 6–4, but then Brough stiffened and started hitting the ball with pace toward the sidelines, and won the first four games of the second set even without a formidable serve. Fry then fought back magnificently, pulling within a point of five all, before faltering.

Brough eventually won the set 6–4, but the momentum had turned. As they prepared to play the third set, Fry realized that the match was hers to win. From then on, she moved as well as she ever had. Her backhands didn't have much power, but she hit them low and frustrated Brough's attempts to take control of each point. Brough didn't go down easily, but both over the course of the years and the course of the afternoon, Fry had become the better player. She won the deciding set 6–3. It was, all agreed, the match of the day.

Fry had come of age just after World War II, a game but not especially gifted player who toiled in the long shadows cast by her peers. She'd waited patiently as Betz, Osborne, Connolly, and Hart had won their titles, then moved on—to careers, marriage, the occasional tennis exhibition. Now, having returned to England for a final try as "more of a lark than anything else," as she puts it, she'd beaten Brough and advanced to the Wimbledon final. She couldn't describe how happy she felt, though she still didn't quite believe she deserved it.

Having assumed she was done with the hope and the glory when she'd accepted the job with the St. *Petersburg Times* some nine months before, she now found herself a single match away from the biggest prize in her sport. She'd face Angela or Ward in the Wimbledon final on Saturday afternoon. She tucked into a Centre Court seat and waited to see which one it would be.

ANGELA'S SEMIFINAL OPPONENT was as solid—and as uninteresting—a player as her straightforward, two-syllable name: Pat Ward. She seemed to surface with a strong match against quality competition once or twice a year. In 1955, for example, she somehow had advanced to the final of the U.S. Championships. Her masterful Wimbledon quarterfinal against Mortimer two days before would probably stand as her finest match of 1956. Even she knew she wouldn't have that kind of success against Angela.

In Bournemouth the previous year, Jimmy Jones had spotted a weakness in Ward's game. Ward was a large, slow-footed woman, and he noticed that she had a difficult time reversing direction and returning to the spot she'd just vacated in time to set herself and strike the ball. Jones advised Angela to hit behind Ward, away from the direction she was moving, whenever possible. "We worked on the sequences," Angela said. "Short across court, then long across court, then up to the net. It worked. She was always running in the other direction." After that, Ward couldn't beat Angela. She knew exactly what Angela was doing, but she wasn't nimble enough to stop her. When Angela learned that Ward had upset Mortimer, she jumped from her chair with excitement. Because of the strategy she and Jones had worked out, she says, "I knew exactly how to beat her. It was my ticket to the final."

By then, Jones had abandoned much of the pretense that he was a disinterested observer. Everyone knew he was Angela's coach. They'd scout the other women together, figuring out which patterns might work best against each opponent, and then Jones would go to the press room and write up the match he'd just seen, once and twice and sometimes even three times, for the different papers he was freelancing for across the globe. Pat Hird remembers seeing them at a match together at Wimbledon and shaking her head. "They had stacks of paper, and they'd be working out strategies," she says. "And the rest of us had nobody behind us! Our parents, of course, but nobody who was interested in us the way Jimmy was interested in her. I would almost call him a guru, and she was the follower."

By then, too, Angela had another adviser. While practicing at one of the Queen's Club indoor courts early in the tournament's first week, she'd come across Harry Hopman, Australia's Davis Cup captain. Hopman served as a combination coach, drill sergeant, and father figure for several generations of Australian male players, from Lew Hoad through Open Era champions Rod Laver, John Newcombe, and Ken Rosewall. He was a small man, but he had an imposing presence. Recognizing Angela, he stared at her with his penetrating eyes and offered up a suggestion. When she came to net, he wondered, why not stand about a foot closer? That way, the volleys that he'd seen her slap directly into the net would be transformed into winners. When Angela wondered if stepping up several steps would leave her too vulnerable to a lob, he sneered. "What's the matter with your legs?" he asked. "If that happens, turn around and run after it."

Angela tried his suggestion and found that it worked. It helped her serve-and-volley game, and it helped even more in doubles, where she spent half the time—whenever she wasn't serving or returning serve—away from the baseline. She was five-foot-nine, with good instincts, and she should have been a formidable net player. By moving two steps forward, Hopman's keen mind had seen, she would instantly become one.

In her semifinal against Ward, Angela played with the self-assurance of someone who was reading from a well-studied script, which in a sense she was. She overwhelmed Ward. She still seemed somewhat robotic in her movements, the opposite of a natural athlete, but she was gaining believers by the match. "Miss Buxton is a vastly improved player this year," the New York Times would write, invoking the three-set Wightman Cup matches against both Brough and Fry as evidence. Her ground strokes were "sound and severe," her service the best of the English players. Angela won the first set 6–1, in unremarkable fashion, keeping each ball in play until Ward would hit it out. Then she closed out the match with an error-filled 6–4 second set, flung her arms in the air, sat down on the court, and ran her fingers through her hair. For once, she'd been rendered speechless.

Afterward, she showered, changed into a white tennis warmup suit available only at Lillywhites, and basked in the glory due a Wimbledon finalist. "I think I stand a very fair chance," she said to her inquisitors, then allowed herself a moment of candor. "My parents didn't actually think it possible that I would reach this far, but here I am."

With champion Shirley Fry

CHAPTER 14

Angela's Ashes

ANGELA MARCHED INTO Lillywhites that Friday, the day of her doubles semifinal, and asked for a raise. She was still earning the same five pounds a week she'd been earning since she started the job three years before, but now her profile was higher. At least two pounds a week higher, she figured, and probably more.

It was prohibited for newspapers to mention the name of the store at which she was employed, lest it profit by her tennis success and thereby jeopardize her amateur status, but intelligent readers weren't fooled by euphemisms like "a West End sporting goods emporium." Anyone who'd been paying attention knew she worked at Lillywhites, and she wore their store-brand outfits on the Wimbledon grass. She had helped Lillywhites more than anyone could have imagined when she'd signed on. The least it could do, she figured, was pay her a decent wage.

Angela couldn't get much accomplished that morning. The whole world seemed to know her schedule, and to want to talk to her about the singles final the following day, as well as her doubles semifinal that afternoon. Some people appeared to have come in just to see her. The managers didn't mind the disruption. It made sense to show her off, maximize the affiliation. Still, that didn't mean the store wanted to pay her two pounds a week more. "We'll talk about it next week," she was told. "You have enough on your mind right now." She never did get a raise.

That day was both the longest and the shortest of her life. Her every activity was chronicled, related, examined. Knowing you were going to play in a Wimbledon singles final must be like being engaged to be married, she figured. It defined you. After a matter of hours in that condition, you find it hard to believe it wasn't always that way.

She'd practiced with Jones and Howard Walton at Queen's Club at 9:30, then stood outside in a plaid dress and long black gloves signing autographs. She'd put in her brief shift at Lillywhites ("I felt duty-bound," she'd say to the papers), then arrived at Wimbledon in time for her and Althea's late-afternoon match against Brough and Fry.

Fry hated the idea of losing to Althea, even in doubles, and this match had her worried. Brough and Fry weren't working out well as doubles partners. It wasn't a question of styles. Brough's power game complemented Fry's run-and-slap just as well as Doris Hart's slow-footed slugging had. Instead, their problem was psychological. For years, they had played against each other as the subordinate halves of the two pairings in one of the great rivalries in tennis history. Now Brough and Fry had trouble thinking of themselves as partners. Teaming with the enemy was unfathomable, like Jackie Robinson getting traded from the Dodgers to the Giants. (When that happened to Robinson, he chose retirement rather than face the psychological discomfort of pulling on the despised orange-and-black uniform.)

Brough and Fry had passed through the first round with a bye, easily beaten inferior opposition in the second and third, then routed a French pairing in the quarterfinals. Up to that point in the tournament, they'd lost a total of two games together. But Fry wasn't fooled. "I knew from the beginning that we wouldn't play well," she says. "We were opponents, not teammates. We'd both lost our captains, and we were trying to be teammates after all those years. I knew it wouldn't work."

Althea was still alive in the mixed doubles, teamed with Mulloy, but her focus now was on winning the Ladies' Doubles with Angela. It showed on the court. Her serves kept Brough and Fry on the defensive, and when Angela served, Althea waited at net to poach winners. Her ground strokes were nearly impeccable, and her decisions invariably correct. With all that, the match was close. Althea and Angela needed a late service break to win the first set 7–5, and they captured the second set by a single break, 6–4. By winning, Angela qualified for her second Wimbledon final of the fortnight, and Althea for the first Wimbledon final of her life.

Then they learned that Fay Muller and Daphne Seeney had upset defending champions Mortimer and Shilcock, adding a sweet coda to what already ranked as the best forty-eight hours of Angela's life. She would be playing in two finals the following day, and all those other British Wightman Cup players—Mortimer, Shilcock, Ward, Hird, Bloomer—would be in none.

WHILE AT WIMBLEDON that afternoon, Angela and Violet stopped by the Lawn Tennis Association office, located near the main entrance to the grounds. They wanted to pick up an extra ticket for the annual Wimbledon Ball, which was scheduled for the evening of the last Saturday of the Championships, at London's fancy Grosvenor House hotel on Park Lane.

Traditionally, the winners of the Ladies' and Gentlemen's Singles were paired off, like bride and groom, for a ceremonial first dance. If it was Angela, who would stand as the first British woman to win Wimbledon in decades, Violet couldn't imagine not being there to see it. Even if the unthinkable happened and Angela had lost to Fry earlier in the day, Violet wanted to go to the ball. More than that, she felt she was entitled to. She had been in on the ride from the beginning. She wanted to see it through to its conclusion. But no, she was told, there were no more tickets to be had—not even for the mother of a Ladies' Singles finalist. "I'm very sorry, Mrs. Buxton, but I'm afraid we have none remaining," the functionary said. In fact, she didn't sound sorry at all.

Angela's relations with the LTA had never been good. It was the LTA, above all other organizations, that she felt she needed to surmount if she wanted to succeed at tennis. Still, it was the power at hand, and any tickets to the Wimbledon Ball came from that office. Whether it was a matter of not wanting an additional Jew at this most conservative of

London social occasions, of resistance to Angela's wilfullness through the years, or simply of a stubborn adherence to protocol, she didn't know. But the LTA's answer was firm.

If it had been up to Angela, she would have retreated with a shrug of her shoulders and counted it as another wound to nurse. But Violet put up a fight. Never afraid of making a scene, she figured she'd use the ammunition she had at hand. "Well, I'm sorry, too," she said, as Angela looked on in horror. "In fact, I think I'll keep my daughter in tomorrow afternoon. Good day! Come on, Angela." She grabbed her daughter's hand and strode out the door.

It was typical Violet. "Her mother would say what she thought," Shirley Bloomer recalls. "Angela always had two barrels firing, hers and her mother's." But the outburst could hardly have come at a more difficult time for Angela. Controversy on the eve of her two finals was something she certainly didn't need.

Yet Violet did have leverage. Keeping Angela at home, if she were to follow through on her threat, would have canceled two-thirds of the following day's program. The LTA's representative realized this as Angela and Violet left the office. She came dashing after them, offering a whispered invitation to follow her into the LTA's back room. She not only magically procured Violet a ticket for the ball, but an additional one for an escort.

Mollified, the Buxtons headed home. Angela arrived at Rossmore Court, stepped around the waiting reporters, then sat down to play "Whispering" at the piano. "Whisper and tell me you adore me," she sang softly to herself. "It helps to soothe my nerves," she told the *Daily Mail* reporter listening outside the door—and by then, her nerves needed soothing.

FRIDAY MORNING, Angela had been photographed at the door of what the papers called "her mother's luxury flat in Park Road NW," but was really the same rather shabby apartment on Rossmore Court. She took care to pose in an elegant striped dress of white and navy blue. The *Daily Sketch* ran the photo with a feature on her workaday life. "Before going to Wimbledon today, she will board a tube train and report for work," it related. "Angela, who designs and often makes her own dresses, prefers to work for her money, though her father owns cinemas in and around Manchester."

Fry was having rather a different Wimbledon experience. She was staying at the Westbury Hotel, sharing a room with Betty Rosenquest Pratt. Every morning, the transportation desk would arrange for a car to retrieve them at the proper time. It was a Bentley or a Rolls-Royce, invariably, and it had the purple-and-green Wimbledon flag affixed to the fender. The cars would roll through Central London in stately fashion, and fans would spot the flags and wave and wonder which tennis star had just rumbled by. And then, a few days before the end of the tournament, Pratt was called home to Jamaica to deal with a minor emergency. That left Fry alone in the hotel suite, and she relished the space. She was accustomed to traveling with Hart all those years— and she knew she couldn't easily afford a room by herself—so she'd arranged to share with Pratt. But now she was within a match of winning the Wimbledon title, and it felt good to have a room in which to think.

Fry didn't have the photographers hounding her the way Angela did. She wasn't a hometown hero, trying to bring the championship back to England for the first time in decades. She wasn't a dark-skinned novelty, a defending champion, or even a pretournament favorite, and she hadn't learned of a pregnancy in the middle of the fortnight. (That morning, a newspaper photo showed the Fleitzes, looking harried, waiting to board their Pan Am flight back to New York.) As had happened so often during her career, Fry had slipped through the cracks. Her ability to wait in the shadows, all but unnoticed, was serving her well.

THE BUXTONS HAD ONE TELEVISION in the house, a large black-and-white console in the living room. In the mixed doubles semifinal, Althea and Gar Mulloy were playing Daphne Seeney and South African Trevor Fancutt, Seeney's future husband. Shirley Fry and Vic Seixas already had advanced from the other side of the bracket.

Angela was sitting out the mixed doubles—Jones had limited her to two events to conserve her energy—and now she sat down and watched

Althea play on the BBC. It was an opportunity to scout Seeney, half the doubles pairing she'd be playing the following afternoon after her singles match. She noticed that Seeney was skilled at taking a hard serve, from Althea or from Mulloy, and liked to return it with a lob over the head of the opponent standing at net. It was a smart shot, because it forced the opposition to rotate, the server racing over to handle the lob in the backcourt, the player at net sliding on the grass to cover the vacated half. She made a note to talk with Althea about that.

Althea played doubles with Mulloy the same way she played it with Angela. "I'd like to say she was dominant," he would say later, "but she was domineering." An overhead would go up, and "she would say 'Mine!' before it could be determined who should take it." Despite such unorthodoxy, Mulloy and Althea advanced in two sets.

That night, Violet and Harry took Angela and Althea out for dinner at Le Coq d'Or in Mayfair, just opposite the Ritz. The staff fussed over Harry, who was a regular there, and over the two celebrity guests. For the first time, perhaps, Angela was the featured attraction, not Althea. "She didn't like taking a back seat, but she did it with good humor," Angela recalls. On the eve of her singles final, Angela ate chicken-and-beef soup, lamb cutlets, and fruit salad, all prepared in the butter-and-cream style of French food of that era. "I love substantial meals, and I've simply got to have them," she explained to the papers. Her every move was being chronicled for posterity. That surely would have become tiresome before long, but for a day and a half, Angela was loving it.

So was Violet. In a long interview that day, she explained the importance of her role in her daughter's tennis success. "Angela will not play unless I am there," she said. "I feel her every move. If I get depressed, Angela's game falls off." She also divulged details of Barney Goodman's insistent courtship. He was thirty, she noted, and had been waiting for Angela for years. "She won't admit romance," she said, "but he calls me 'Mum.'"

After dinner, the doubles partners spent an hour discussing strategy. They'd been using what was called an Australian formation for their service games. The player standing at net positioned herself not in the opposite corner of the court from the server, as is typical, but almost directly in front of her. The two partners needed to be certain of which way the other would break, to the right or the left, following the serve. With Jones's help, Angela and Althea had worked out a set of signals they could use on the court to keep themselves informed and their opponents ignorant. Now they reviewed them to make sure they were on the same page.

The impending doubles match had an air of anticlimax to it, and not only because Angela would be playing the singles final the same day. "We had already beaten the top team in the semifinal," Angela notes, "and Seeney and Muller had beaten the holders, Shilcock and Mortimer." Yet somehow, Althea was as energized for the doubles match as Angela had seen her. She'd spent half a year living from a suitcase, she felt, and she wasn't about to come home from Wimbledon empty-handed. Althea hadn't been able to win at Wimbledon in the years between her debut there in 1951 and the trip to India in 1955, a stretch of time that Angela always thought of as Althea's first career. But the partnership with Angela had brought on a new day. "Now she was about to embark on this doubles final and probably win it," Angela thought.

It was odd to be ruminating on her doubles partner's career while lying in bed on the night before her own Wimbledon singles final, but Angela felt especially introspective. She wanted to be certain to appreciate every minute of this experience as it unfolded. It was clear that this was the climax of something—a beginning, in a sense, but also an end to a marvelous adventure that had begun when she and Althea became friends over those two weeks in India. She knew that she would rarely in her life feel as excited, as alive, as she felt on this night.

Angela's room, tiny but comfortable, overlooked the Paddington Goods Station. Freight cars would rumble in and out all night. Angela was a sound sleeper and rarely heard them, but as this Friday night became Saturday morning, she lay in her bed and listened to every one.

BY SHORTLY AFTER TWO O'CLOCK the next afternoon, she was standing at Centre Court, perspiration trickling down her arm and onto her palm, wondering how she was going to make it through the match. The day was as warm as anyone could remember for a Wimbledon final. It was seventy-six degrees in the shade, the official records indicated, but far hotter on the court and in the stands, where spectators had covered bare heads with paper cones to keep off the sun. Angela had awakened, heard her name on the television news, gobbled down a breakfast. She hadn't stretched, hadn't exercised—which, in retrospect, might have helped to calm her nerves. She had chosen an outfit from Lillywhites to wear while practicing at Queen's Club, and two more to wear on Centre Court that afternoon, one for the singles and one for the doubles. Then she walked to the Blue Star garage, started her car, and headed off.

There had been quite a scramble after the gates had opened, Angela learned later. Some four thousand fans flooded through, and many of them had been waiting all night. Children were knocked over, a few injured badly. It had been seventeen years, nearly a generation, since an Englishwoman had a chance at a Wimbledon singles title. Tennis fans had learned the game, played through an adolescence, married and started families without ever experiencing such a thing.

Angela had come on court wearing a pair of mannish shorts, as short as she could get them within the bounds of propriety. As befitted a dress designer, how she looked always mattered to Angela. It was an advertisement for her work, and an advertisement for herself. She never had a hair out of place. "She was always so elegant," Pat Hird recalls. "I remember sharing a room with her and seeing all her clothes beautifully packed, wrapped in tissue paper. She was just immaculate."

Yet at a time when so many other players were doing their best to appear as demurely feminine as possible on the court, Angela dressed as functionally as she could. Her hair was short and severe, in the manner of a rural librarian. She didn't make herself up for matches like many of the other women. For the final, she'd chosen no lace panties or frilly skirts but these severe-looking shorts that were almost inappropriate for a Wimbledon final. It wasn't by chance. Angela had discussed it at length with Jones. She was a big girl with a long backswing and she feared catching her racket in the folds of a skirt. Jones agreed. "One point," he'd told her, "might mean the difference."

She had won the first game against Fry, holding serve, and felt no more than the normal jitters a player feels at the beginning of an important match. But sometime during Fry's first service game, the sweating started. The Centre Court crowd of some fourteen thousand had pulled off jackets, loosened ties, and was down to shirtsleeves—but, beyond that, it slowly dawned on Angela and every nerve in her body that she was playing in the Ladies' final at Wimbledon. Three games in, Fry broke Angela's serve by popping a volley over the net. As she did, Angela could feel her nerves beginning to get to her. She was getting more nervous, not less, as the match progressed. Even if it hadn't been such a stifling hot day, she remembers thinking at one point, she would be sweating, regardless.

Now, as the perspiration began to show against her shirt, she asked for time to dry her racket and to steady her nerves, the first of many times she would do that over the course of a match that wouldn't even last an hour. Fry held serve to go ahead 3–1, then Angela pulled back within 3–2. She was still down only one service break, but she sent a backhand straight into the net to end game six. On her serve in the seventh game, she missed an easy putaway at net, but managed to hold off Fry at deuce and hang on. It was 4–3.

Those early games were marked by long rallies, from baseline to baseline. Usually, such points—which showcase an array of shots from a variety of positions—help to dissipate nervousness. It didn't work that way for Angela, who had been conditioned to keep her mind in the match. She couldn't stop thinking, and she couldn't stop obsessing about the perspiration. She always wanted things just so: clothes wrapped in tissue paper, every hair in place. She was bothered by the idea of feeling so disheveled. She couldn't get comfortable.

Then Angela took a 15–40 advantage on Fry's serve. It was her finest moment of the match, the only time she could see her way clear from where she was to a championship. She had two chances for the equalizing break, but Fry drew her to net with a short forehand, then deftly passed her down the line. At 30–40, Angela came to net again. "Forehand long, come to net," she intoned in her head, then she hit a lovely forehand all the way to the baseline and marched forward. On the defensive, Fry countered with a lob, but she couldn't loft it deep enough. Angela stood at net, waiting, with the court spread open before her. But she heard the crowd, she felt the sweat, she sensed the weight of England's tennis history sitting on her shoulders. By the time the ball came, she could barely lift her arms. She smacked it straight into the net for deuce. Fry won the next two points and the game.

Down 5–3, Angela then benefited from a fortunate line call. A ball she hit long was called good, and it gave her a 30–15 lead in the ninth game. Had she gone on to win the game and the set, it might have served as a neat counterpoint to the Wightman Cup call that went the other way. But she couldn't hold the advantage. Fry won the game— and, with it, the first set, with a backhand to the far corner of the court that Angela could only flail at as it went by. Fry 6, Buxton 3.

Those were the details. What was happening inside Angela's head was even more dispiriting. As she watched the match unfold, she knew she should be able to win it. Fry wasn't even playing as well as she'd played during the Wightman Cup. This was Angela's chance, and she was squandering it. The patterns had flown from her mind. Her serve had become tentative. Her body didn't obey the commands that her mind was sending it. She felt like she was running underwater. And she was so hot, the sweat seemed to be pouring down her face. She sat on the umpire's stand for a moment to catch her breath and noticed that Fry seemed cool and collected, the picture of a champion. Suddenly the emotions that were welled up inside Angela needed an outlet. She couldn't hold them back. Tears began streaming down her face. She steadied herself, walked to the far court, wiped the tears away with the sweat, and started the second set. But in her heart, she was already beaten.

AT HER SUMMER HOME IN CHESHIRE, near Manchester, Angela has a videotape of the final against Fry that one of her sons asked to be copied from the BBC archives. She has never watched it. She can't bear to see herself in the second set, standing still as a traffic cone as the balls fly around her. She can't bear to hear the commentary that aptly describes the state of affairs as Fry raced to a 5–0 lead: "A picture of dejection . . . terribly, terribly tense." She can't understand why she wasn't able to handle Fry's looping serves, balls that seemed to have the consistency of a pat of butter. She remembers a court that seemed as large as Regent's Park, and Fry placing balls here and there, always way beyond Angela's reach. She doesn't want to see it again.

A few days before, the news had reached Florida that Harry Buxton had offered the Bogner Regis pier to his daughter if she could manage to win the Ladies' Singles at Wimbledon. The mayor of Fry's adopted hometown, St. Petersburg's S. G. Johnson, sensed an opportunity for publicity. He held a news conference and proclaimed that if Fry won the tournament, he'd give her the key to the St. Petersburg pier, which was a darn sight prettier than that English pier anyway. To his astonishment, it was coming to pass. Fry was playing as if she meant to come home and claim her prize.

In one game alone, the third game of the second set, Angela stopped play three times to wipe her hands on a towel. She was obsessing about the perspiration now, thinking that if only she could control that, she could begin to control Fry. With Fry ahead 5–1 and 30–0, two points from winning the match, Angela stopped play again for a towel break. It was getting ludicrous. Even her own fans felt that it was becoming unseemly. "Miss Buxton has much to learn regarding her conduct on the court," the *Daily Telegraph* would write, wondering if the frequent breaks could be interpreted as gamesmanship.

They had only been on the court for some forty-odd minutes when Fry reached match point. Up 5–1 and 40–30, she drove a forehand a few inches long. Two points later, she had another, but hit wide into the alley. Still, there couldn't have been a single spectator watching inside the grounds, or as part of the BBC audience throughout England, who had any hopes of a reversal. Angela had shown so little that a comeback was beyond the bounds of possibility. When Fry gained her third match point in the match's fiftieth minute, everyone watching knew it was over. She won the match, and the Wimbledon title, with a cross-court smash that left Angela rooted in the backcourt, unable to move. At 6–3, 6–1, it was a merciful end.

In the press room, Jimmy Jones started feverishly composing a new story for the *Mirror*. In the one he'd written in advance, lacking all but the salient details, Angela had won the championship. "Bad luck for Miss Buxton, she wasn't quite up to the big event," the BBC commentator intoned, but it wasn't luck. On this day, Angela was out of her league. She'd been playing above her level for the better part of two years, beating nearly everyone below her in the rankings, but she never managed a breakthrough against one of the top players in the world. Jones's strategies could take her so far, but no further. She was a fine singles player, and she maximized the athleticism and the ability that she'd been given, but she was never meant to be a Wimbledon champion.

Neither was Fry, she'd figured all these years. It was her tenth Wimbledon. She hadn't figured on playing it, let alone winning it. Now she had won, and she was caught between tears and laughter. The duchess of Kent, looking overheated in a long coat, appeared and presented the Venus Rosewater dish to Fry. Then Fry headed up to the BBC booth.

"How many Wimbledons have you played in, Doris?" the interviewer asked. Even in her moment of glory, Fry still couldn't step out of Hart's shadow.

"Doris? That's my doubles partner."

"Sorry. *Shirley.*"

The *New York Times* was kinder. "In ending Althea Gibson's winning streak, eliminating the defender, Louise Brough, and defeating Angela Buxton in the final, she achieved the pinnacle," Allison Danzig's copy read. "She is one of the most tenacious fighters in women's tennis." Soon a telegram arrived from Hart, offering congratulations. Fry set off to find a dress for the Wimbledon ball, where she would pair with Lew Hoad in the first dance. "I've always wanted to dance with Lew," she said, tears streaming down her face. She had the mixed-doubles final later in the afternoon against Althea and Mulloy, but she found time to send a cable to Mayor Johnson. It read, "COMING SOON TO COLLECT MY PIER."

AT THE END OF THE YEAR, after she had added the Forest Hills title to the Wimbledon prize, before she journeyed to Australia for the championships there and won that tournament, too, this unlikely hero would set down her thoughts for posterity. Fry would write of losing to Hart and Margaret Osborne du Pont and Louise Brough and Pauline Betz as a young player, playing close matches but never managing to win any. "I believe it was a mental block which kept me from realizing that I could possibly beat these people," she wrote. "Too many youngsters are beaten before they go on the court, just because the opponent is seeded. It took me a long time to believe that all players can be defeated no matter who they are. A close three-set loss proceeded to be the story of my tennis for the next ten years. I seemed satisfied to reach my seeded position, and then winning or losing was irrelevant."

Over the preceding months, Althea, too, had finally passed that stage. It had taken her even longer than Fry to do it, in part because— occupied by getting a college degree and then earning a living—she was playing many fewer matches each season. Though Althea, unlike Fry, was never satisfied with simply reaching her seeded position, the process of learning how to win proved far more difficult than the process of learning how to play well. Fry would complete the graduate course she was teaching Althea by beating her at Forest Hills, and then one last time at the Australian Championships in Melbourne at the end of the year. After that, she would step aside, and Althea would stand alone as the finest player in the world in 1957 and 1958. All of that was yet to come.

Nearly a decade younger at twenty-one, Angela was still at the start of the same process. She had made tremendous strides in a year, and "leapt to the front," as the *Dunlop Lawn Tennis Annual* put it, by virtue of her advancement to the Wimbledon finals alone. But it is important to remember that future champions such as Althea and Fry, each now approaching thirty, were not nearly as advanced as Angela when they were her age. She had come a long way, though she still had a long way to go. She moved stiffly, as if her joints needed oiling. Her ground strokes were ordinary, her net game only a cut above, and there probably wasn't a slower player in tennis, unless it was Pat Ward. Angela had the tendency to lose her voice from the stress, collapse under pressure, even burst into tears when events went awry. In short, she was far more like an ordinary twenty-one-year-old woman—still living with her mother, working as a filing clerk in a department store, and starting a career as a dress designer—than our classic notion of a tennis champion. "Miss Buxton must strive for the poise and staunch qualities of past champions," Roy McKelvie intoned in the *Daily Mail.*

But there was no reason to believe that she couldn't get there, if the next few years were to prove anything like the one she had just completed. "I was just starting out," she says now. "I had my whole career ahead of me." That career began, in her eyes, with the doubles final against Muller and Seeney. It wasn't so much a chance for redemption as the start of the next chapter—and this one would be a winning chapter. Her doubles partner would see to that.

CHAPTER 15

A Black from Harlem, a Jew from North London

ANGELA ARRIVED at the ladies' cloakroom in a daze, craving a warm bath despite the oppressive heat. The first person she saw was Althea, who wrapped her in an embrace. "We'll get them in the doubles, don't worry about that," she said. Althea knew she needed to get Angela back among the living. Otherwise, they'd have little chance against Muller and Seeney, and Angela would end the day a double loser.

By then, Althea had come to appreciate the value of a doubles partner. If she still seemed domineering to Gardnar Mulloy, much of that was bravado. She had all the confidence in the world in her own ability, but she knew that even she couldn't carry a partner at the level of a Wimbledon final. And Muller and Seeney had emerged as a dangerous pairing. Unknowns when the tournament started, they hadn't lost a set all the way to the final. Unlike Angela and Althea and Brough and Fry, Muller and Seeney knew they weren't good enough at singles to get far in the tournament, so they'd placed their emphasis on the doubles from the start. Of course, they had entered the Ladies' Singles—Muller had lasted to the Round of 16 before Bloomer beat her in straight sets; Seeney had been beaten by Komorczi in the previous round—but for more than a week, they'd had nothing but doubles on their minds. They would sit for hours and study the other pairings, looking for ways to

Celebrating with friends

win. "We were cheeky, we were young," Seeney says. "We were going to grab every opportunity we had. We had nothing to lose."

In some ways, they were an unlikely team. Muller had started her career as a backcourt specialist who hated coming to net. She'd grown up in Palmwoods, Queensland, and didn't take a tennis lesson until she was fifteen. A year later, she'd moved to Brisbane, where she would watch the finest players of the day on the newsreel. "Hart, Brough, du Pont," she says. "I'd watch them and I'd say, 'That's what I want to be.'" As often happens, her game was a reflection of her personality. Her strokes were classical—"I was described as 'copybook,'" she says now—but her demeanor was naturally passive. She enjoyed tennis the way a prima ballerina enjoys the dance.

Seeney, the tomboy from the outback whose siblings had helped scrape together the funds to get her to Europe, was a spirited left-hander who wanted to win each point and cared little about how she looked doing it. They'd started playing together in Australia with mixed success. They couldn't get their minds around each other's styles. "Look, we'll give it a few more chances," Seeney finally said to Muller, "but if you won't come to net, I'll have to find a partner who will. I need to play with someone who isn't afraid to come to net." After that, Muller tried hard to adapt. Still, at some point every couple of matches, Seeney still had to remind her to stop sitting back on her heels. Seeney was the stronger-willed of the two, the leader. At a crucial point in the match, she'd invariably sidle up to Muller. "Serve four medium-paced balls over the net, and it's *over*," she'd say. "I will kill the ball."

Seeney wasn't the most mobile player. She'd damaged the cartilage in her right knee before leaving Australia—working as an usherette during a Davis Cup tie, of all things—and hadn't completely recovered. She needed surgery, the doctors kept telling her, but she refused to have it. Once you do, you're in for a lifetime of it, she believed. She'd never known anyone who had just a single knee operation. One always meant two, and then three, and then four. So she played on, often in pain. She couldn't bear to return home to her siblings and say, Well, that's that. You saved your money and sent me overseas, and I played one season and now I'm ready to come home. She was driven by a sense of responsibility, and it would be quenched only when she won something important, something memorable. Like a Wimbledon title.

After a year in Europe, playing the likes of Althea, Seeney had come to understand that such success wasn't going to happen in singles. So she put pressure on her partner, and on herself. This was supposed to be fun, of course, but it was also serious, she'd tell Muller. The idea was to win.

ANGELA HARDLY REMEMBERS where the time went between her matches. She soaked in the bathtub, and it helped clear her head. She pulled on a tennis dress with a dropped waistline, pleats, lime-green piping. (It was on sale at Lillywhites, for anyone who cared to find it.) Althea guided her out of the locker room. Before Angela knew it, she was standing in the front court again, peering over her shoulder as Althea tossed the ball in the air for the first serve.

Althea started the match playing against the two Australians by herself, or so it seemed. When she wasn't performing acrobatics at net, she was tomahawking winners with her overhead, or unleashing a heavy serve that seemed to have Seeney and Muller rooted to the grass. "We were intimidated," Seeney says now. Seeney had played Althea in Bristol and been overwhelmed. More recently, she'd seen how Althea comported herself in the semifinal of the mixed doubles, and it had only built on the lasting impression she'd felt seeing her that first time in the locker room in Naples that spring, zipping up the front of her shorts. Serving first may not have helped Althea's mixed-doubles pairing win— she had a terrific serve, but certainly not the equal of Mulloy's—but her serve awed this young girl from the Australian bush and set the tenor of the match. "I'd never beaten her, of course," Seeney says. "And when you walk out on the court thinking the way I was thinking, it means that she's halfway home."

Muller can't recall many details of her tennis career, but she never forgot her matches against Althea. "She was so tall, so athletic," she says. "Taller and slimmer than Louise Brough, and more of a natural athlete. And such power! I have to say she was awesome to play against."

From one-armed Fred Johnson's rudimentary instruction through the pointers gleaned from Jimmy Jones, Althea had developed a style all her own. Her serve was cracking, her net game subtle and highly intelligent. At her best, she knew just where to put the ball on every point. During the first set of that Ladies' Doubles final, she played so well that she brought Angela along with her. Angela served effectively, won points at net, kept rallies alive, and seemed an entirely different player from the one the capacity crowd at Centre Court had seen earlier in the day. In a sense, it made the loss to Fry that much more heartbreaking. If this is what she was capable of, you can easily imagine an English tennis fan thinking as he watched Angela stroke a backhand winner past Muller down the line, why wasn't she able to show it when it mattered?

Because Althea had raised Angela's level of play, Angela was there when Althea needed her. Angela and Althea won the first set 6–1, but Seeney and Muller hadn't come this far to roll over. They started the second set as if they'd been given new life. You can do that in tennis, if you have a mind to; there's no clock, and no cumulative score other than the number of sets. At least once a season, someone will win a tournament final despite having lost more games than his or her opponent. Each set is a fresh start, and the most experienced competitors can usually manage to put the previous set's result out of their heads and begin again.

That's what the Australians did that afternoon. Neither of them had played a match on Centre Court during the entire tournament, but after a set spent feeling like fish in a fishbowl, they'd gained a measure of comfort. "It took us a while to adapt, but eventually we did," Muller says. They did their best to ensure that the second set looked nothing like the first. Seeney would rush the net at every opportunity, and Muller started hitting crisp ground strokes from the backcourt, then coming to net behind them. These women were scrappy, eager, and they made their opponents work. As the second set wore on, they gained confidence. With Angela and Althea up 4–2, they came within two points of breaking Althea's serve, steeled themselves for the two biggest points in their careers—then were handed a gift-wrapped service break when Althea double-faulted twice.

That broke the spell. The Australians held serve to even the set 4–4, and then Angela won her service game. She was the steadier of the two now; Althea had fallen into one of her funks. Behind Angela's ground strokes, she and Althea advanced to match point, but still Muller and Seeney wouldn't capitulate. Five times they saved the match with one magical volley after another. Finally, on an ad point, Seeney rifled an overhead winner and broke into a smile big enough to be seen in Brisbane. It was 5–5, and a long way from over.

Moments later, the Australians almost broke Althea again, but Angela saved a point at net with a dainty volley and secured the hold. The set stayed on serve from 6–5 to 6–6 to 7–6, and then the sleepwalking Althea awakened. Suddenly, she was flying around the court like a superhero, slapping a winner with an overhead from the middle of the service box, then angling a winner after charging the net. She and Angela broke service to take the second set 8–6 and win the match. With a certain astonishment despite all their expectations, they turned toward each other. And then the Wimbledon Ladies' Doubles champions, a black from Harlem and a Jew from North London, embraced.

SET AGAINST THE HEIGHTS that Althea eventually scaled in her career, including five major singles titles, it is difficult to put that first Wimbledon doubles title in its proper context. It was as difficult then as it is now. "Doubles gets you on the board, but it isn't like winning the singles," Angela Mortimer says; she eventually managed to do both at Wimbledon. In Althea's autobiography, there isn't a word about the 1956 Wimbledon doubles final. When you've just won the singles at both Wimbledon and Forest Hills two years in succession, as Althea had when that book was published, some two-year-old doubles title hardly seems crucial anymore.

As Angela drove home to Rossmore Court that night, after dancing at the Wimbledon Ball and visiting a Berkeley Square nightclub with Althea, winning the doubles wasn't foremost in her mind. She'd awakened that day with a chance to be the Ladies' Singles champion—quite a good chance, she'd believed—and she'd managed one of the poorer showings since Fry herself was steamrolled by Hart in 1951. The doubles seemed like a lovely consolation prize, but a consolation prize nonetheless. Fry had danced with Lew Hoad at the Grosvenor House that night. Angela could only sit idly at a side table beside Barney Goodman, now officially her fiancé, and watch it happen.

Althea had similar thoughts. Following her match with Angela, she had returned to Centre Court with the forty-two-year-old Mulloy to face Vic Seixas and the ubiquitous Fry. A nationally ranked doubles player as far back as 1936, Mulloy was gliding through the tournament. "I think Gar felt that he had a lock on the mixed doubles because he was playing with Althea," Seixas says now. "He was willing to let her do whatever she wanted." It had worked, for a while. Mulloy and Althea took the first set 6–2, using that inverted style that only Althea employed. "Strangely enough for mixed doubles, it was Mulloy who was setting up the shots and Althea who was taking the overheads," Fred Tupper wrote in the *New York Times* the next day.

But Fry and Seixas had a plan. "Keep lobbing," Seixas told Fry. Make her hit one overhead after another, if she wants them so badly. Drive her crazy. "As much as Althea liked hitting overheads, if you threw up a few and she missed them, she'd lose her confidence," Fry remembers. So Fry would throw up moonballs from the backcourt and Althea would rush to net and whack at them. She hit some winners, she hit some out. The strategy effectively removed Mulloy from the match.

Through the first half of the decade, Seixas had played mixed doubles with Doris Hart. In five years, they'd lost one match—to Fry and Mulloy, as it happens, at a tournament at the Caribe Hilton in Puerto Rico. When Hart retired, Seixas inherited her best friend and doubles partner. This meant he had to change his game entirely, for Fry and Hart were opposites as players. Hart didn't get to many balls, but when she did, Seixas says, "there was almost nobody better." As a doubles player, Fry had a game that was similar to Seixas's own, but he had to play the power role when he teamed with Shirley. By the second set of the final, he had it down.

Serving at 6–7 of the deciding set, Althea double-faulted to give her opponents match point. She served, and Seixas hit a return up the middle. Accustomed to taking a subordinate role, Mulloy pulled his racket back and let the ball pass, but he was stunned to find that Althea hadn't moved from the baseline. "She'd been coming in on nearly every point," Mulloy remembers. "On match point, she served and I could have—and should have—poached, but I hesitated. It was the only point in that sequence she didn't come in. As a result, we lost."

Althea was shocked. At the end of her tour of Europe, six months with a different bed in a different hotel or home nearly every week, she had a Wimbledon Ladies' Doubles title to show for her efforts and nothing more. Angela had the same. Althea may have gone to sleep that night with a strong feeling that, despite her loss to Fry, she was the finest female tennis player on the planet, but in point of fact, Wimbledon finalist Angela had come closer to showing it than she had.

In retrospect, the final against Seeney and Muller marked both an end and a turning point. It was the last time that Althea and Angela would play as doubles partners together. The partnership had reaped dividends for both of them, beyond etching their names in the Wimbledon championship rolls. Angela had learned how to think like a champion from Althea, and she'd gained the confidence to stand up for herself the way Althea always did. And though Althea may not have noticed it at the time, and certainly didn't remark on it to Angela, she eventually came to realize that she'd been given a stirring lesson in how to turn the theoretical into the actual by this tenacious Englishwoman. Angela was anything but graceful on the court, but she was officially and forever more a Wimbledon champion, just the same.

WHEN ALTHEA'S PLANE touched down at New York's Idlewild Airport later that month, executives of the ATA were waiting to greet her. Nobody had bothered to come representing the USLTA, on the other hand, and that would rankle for years. New York's mayor, Robert Wagner, received her at City Hall to commemorate her success. Since she'd last set foot in the city, she'd won the singles at the French Championships and the doubles at Wimbledon. She'd emerged as one of the two or three best players in the world in anyone's estimation. That year's U.S. Championships at Forest Hills, coming up the following month, would be the seventh she'd played in succession. This time, though, she'd be favored.

Fry returned home to St. Petersburg and was gifted with the honorary ownership of the new million-dollar pier that jutted into Tampa Bay, and a ticker-tape parade that may have been the city's first. Seemingly unretired now, at least for the rest of the season, she resumed playing tournaments.

So did Althea. On July 23, she won the Pennsylvania State Championships at Haverford over an aging Margaret du Pont in straight sets, then staggered into the U.S. Clay Courts without the benefit of a respite. She had become so accustomed to playing every week, she didn't know what to do with herself when she wasn't. In the final at River Forest, she held a 5–2 lead on Fry in the first set when she crashed. Fry won five straight games to take the first set, then cruised through the second set 6–1. Knowing that Althea's legs carried the weight of six months of continuous play, Fry lobbed at every opportunity.

After that, Althea returned to New York for a few weeks of needed rest. She relaxed with Llewellyn, who was still technically her coach, and Billie Davis at Llewellyn's apartment. They'd eat dinner, then talk tennis late into the night, skull sessions that ranged from the theoretical to the practical. By early August, she was playing again, staying with her good friends the Darbens, while taking the Eastern Lawn Tennis Championships, the most important tune-up for Forest Hills, with an easy victory over Brough.

Angela arrived in America intending to play the Easterns. She'd traveled to Sweden just after Wimbledon and won a tournament there, then joined the official British contingent for the flight to New York and the sequence of tournaments before Forest Hills. She was staying at the team's headquarters hotel as a matter of protocol, but intended to spend much of her time with Althea, who introduced her new best friend to Rosemary Darben. The three of them may have gone out for a dinner, joined by Will Darben, who had taken a shine to Althea. They certainly made plans for the weeks to come. This was Althea's territory, which suited Angela fine. Without the pressure inherent in being an Englishwoman at Wimbledon, she believed, she had a chance to win at

Forest Hills. Althea would be her strongest competition, along with the indefatigable Fry.

And then it stormed one day before the tournament started, and everyone stayed inside and missed a day of training, and the next morning Angela woke up in her hotel room and found that her right wrist had swelled to double its normal size. She rushed to a doctor and had her arm put in a sling. With orders not to play tennis for several weeks, she made the agonizing decision to fly home. If she couldn't compete at Forest Hills, there was little point staying in America. She was young, and she always had next year, and the year after that.

When she flew back to England, photographers met the plane. Her injury was big news. Harry reveled in the publicity, telling Angela, "See how important you are?" Angela couldn't listen; she was heartbroken. She visited a top orthopedic surgeon in Park Street, the same man who had treated Maureen Connolly for shoulder trouble several years before. He put her in a plaster cast for six months, ending her season. It was the first time she had heard the word tenosynovitis, a rheumatic complaint. An irritation of the tendon sheath caused by repetitive motion, it is most commonly encountered in the wrist or the hand. It usually lasts a few days or even weeks, but in some cases can linger for months.

Not long afterward, Angela's fiancé, Barney Goodman, fell ill. His older sister, Rhoda, walked the hallways of the hospital in anguish. For lack of a better target, she turned on Angela. "It was the pressure of all your tennis that did it," she screamed. She ordered Angela out of the hospital; Angela threw her engagement ring at Rhoda as Barney looked on. Barney recovered, but the relationship didn't. In a matter of weeks, Angela had lost both her tennis and her impending marriage. A year that had started so promising was shrouded in gloom.

BEFORE FOREST HILLS, Althea won another ATA women's singles championship, her tenth in succession—and her last. She had outgrown Negro tennis. Unlike some of the other civil rights pioneers, she felt no obligation to continue to help organizations such as the ATA once they were no longer useful to her. The best thing she could do for blacks in tennis, she felt, was to win tournaments. If she played well enough, it would become clear that skin color had nothing to do with any success a person might have in the sport.

"She was not a crusader, not a Jackie Robinson or even an Arthur Ashe," says Bill Hayling, for years Althea's personal physician, who later was instrumental in forming a national society of black business-men and social leaders, 100 Black Men. "She wanted to be a tennis champion, and that was all. She wasn't getting into the racial politics at that time, though there were people who thought she should have." Even during the civil rights crises of the 1960s, Althea refused to take a stand. Her weapon was the tennis racket, she felt, and her golf clubs. She'd leave the politicking to the politicians.

She did feel pride in her connection to Harlem. Several days before the start of the U.S. Championships, the Paddle Tennis Association feted her with a luncheon as one of their own. She likely hadn't played a single competitive match in that sport since taking up tennis, but it didn't matter. It was an excuse to celebrate the gains that she had made, and blacks had made in her name. All her staunchest supporters attended: Sarah Palfrey Cooke, who had accompanied her on her first tour of Forest Hills; her good friend Karol Fageros, the other American woman on the State Department tour of Asia; Ren McMann, who had approached her at Forest Hills the previous summer with the initial invitation for the trip. Their faith in her had been confirmed. "In a short six months," *World Tennis* noted, "she has risen from a First Tenner to the No. 2 player in the world." It was remarkable, but it wasn't enough. More than ever before, Althea was hungry to be number one.

To do that, she had to win at Forest Hills. Althea roared through the early rounds as if she couldn't wait for another chance at Fry. She still couldn't comprehend how a player with Fry's strokes and athletic ability could have beaten her—both on the grass at Wimbledon, and then the slow clay at River Forest. She beat Nell Hopman in straight sets, beat Fageros in straight sets, beat Hard in straight sets. She beat Betty Rosen-quest Pratt in the semifinal, though she wasted seven match points before winning a 10–8 second set and the match. Entering the final against Fry, she'd looked vulnerable in places, yet she still hadn't lost a set.

By contrast, Fry had needed all she had to beat Shirley Bloomer in a 6–4, 6–4 semifinal that easily could have gone the other way. Yet she arrived for the final utterly calm, while Althea seemed tense. Fry had adopted a mindset that served her well even in the most important matches. No matter what happened in 1956, she still thought of herself as a copy girl on holiday, though the holiday was lasting the better part of a year. The wind was gusting that day, and Althea couldn't find the court with her ground strokes. When she lost her touch at net in the first set, she didn't have a chance.

Fry had been the youngest entrant in the history of the U.S. Championships in 1941, a mere fourteen. She'd returned to Forest Hills fourteen years in succession without winning the event. This was her sixteenth trip in all—most likely her last, she knew—and she was determined to give it one last, best effort. She spent the first set attacking, the second set defending, and won the match 6–3, 6–4. Althea kept her defeat in perspective; she'd come to understand that it was simply Fry's year. "I won't pretend that I wasn't bitterly disappointed," Althea wrote, ". . . but I was a long way from wanting to hang up my racket."

Instead, she barely paused to catch her breath. She flew to Toronto, where she beat Bloomer in the final. From there, she went directly to Denver, where she beat Knode and sang at the Tennis Ball. Once again, she was integrating a tournament—and a country club—that had never entertained a black player. This time, it was captured by a four-man film crew dispatched by the NAACP. The film has disappeared, but the memories linger. "It was a strange scene," recalls Jack Phelps, who served as tournament director. "It was a novelty to have a female, black, nationally ranked player come through. There was a huge curiosity factor. Nobody had ever seen anything like it before."

Then she traveled to Los Angeles and became "the first girl of her race ever to reach the Pacific Southwest final," according to *World Tennis,* as if that honor might conceivably have fallen to anyone else. More than six years after integrating Forest Hills, Althea was still the only African-American—or black of any nationality, for that matter—in every locker room she entered. The records from that era are woefully incomplete, but as far as anyone can tell, she never played another black woman in a USLTA event at any time in her career.

In Los Angeles, Althea beat the ageless Dodo Cheney in the semifinal, then conquered her old nemesis, Nancy Chaffee, in the final. Chaffee had married baseball's Ralph Kiner and was nearing the end of a fine, if not quite historic, career. She'd had two children and was making a comeback, but she found out during the tournament that she was pregnant again. Unlike Fleitz, she didn't withdraw, but she did find herself tiring easily. She took the first set from Althea 6–4, but Althea won twelve of the next fifteen games and the match. Movie star George Murphy handed Althea the championship trophy, and then she headed to the airport again.

She alighted next in Mexico, beating Hard for her fourth championship in three countries since Forest Hills. It was the North American version of her European tour. Then she accepted an invitation to travel with Fry to Australia and play in her first Championships there. She was going to chase Fry around the globe, it seemed, until she could beat her.

Althea's year would finally come in 1957—but not before one final loss to Fry. By beating Althea in Melbourne 6–3, 6–4, Fry gained the only major championship she hadn't won. It was a remarkable story, the third major championship in succession for a player in the twilight of her career who'd only ever won the French prior to that. With that victory, she lost her initiative to compete further. She'd not only won everything she'd set her sights on, but far more.

While Fry was playing at the New South Wales Championships in Sydney early in their four-week Australian tour, she'd met a J. Walter Thompson advertising executive temporarily stationed there, and fallen in love. By the end of her scheduled stay some weeks later, she'd cabled her parents in Akron and told them she was staying on to marry Karl Irvin. By then, she'd become close to Althea, and even asked her for advice about Irvin's proposal of marriage before she accepted it. As two of the only American women competing in Australia that year, they'd learned to separate one relationship from the other, to the point that Fry invited Althea to stay in Australia and attend her wedding. But

Althea had made a commitment to return to Ceylon, off the Indian coast, and defend the title she'd won there on the State Department trip the previous year, and she did exactly that. "Maybe I couldn't win Wimbledon or Forest Hills," she noted wryly, "but I was hell on wheels in the Far East."

ANGELA'S CAST had been removed by then, and she returned to tennis in tentative fashion. The tenosynovitis was still latent, her doctor warned her, and could manifest itself at any time. Eager for matches, she booked passage away from the dreary London weather for the balmy Caribbean, where she'd play the annual tournaments in Puerto Rico, Jamaica, Barranquilla, and beyond. It would be good for her wrist, and for her psyche. She needed to prove to herself as quickly as possible that she still could play competitively.

Her first stop was Panama. She'd been contracted by the *Manchester Evening News* to send dispatches from her trip, a coup for that newspaper, and she approached the job with the utmost seriousness. With her tennis future uncertain, she could take nothing for granted. Almost immediately, she wrote about a seventeen-year-old Brazilian named Maria Esther Bueno, whom she'd discovered, just as she would later write articles about Chris Evert, Jennifer Capriati, and the Williams sisters early in their careers. Angela was a star, promoted as such by the tournament, and Bueno followed her everywhere, asking questions, looking for pointers. Within two years, this Maria Bueno would be the top-ranked player in the world. In 1958, she'd eventually win the same Ladies' Doubles title at Wimbledon that Angela had won, and with Althea as her partner. Angela's dispatch to Manchester may have been the first article written about her anywhere outside her native Brazil, and almost certainly the first in English.

But Angela's tennis didn't go as well as her journalism. On February 26, 1957, she lost to Mary Ann Mitchell, and the tenosynovitis returned. Devastated, she flew home a month early. The headlines that greeted her on her return only exacerbated her dismay. Even now, her face darkens when she pages past one such headline in her scrapbook.

"ANGELA BUXTON MAY HAVE TO GIVE UP TENNIS," it reads, in a type size previously reserved for the Battle of Britain.

To help her stay active, Jones soon had her learning the game left-handed. Of all his experiments, this was the most embarrassing for Angela. She played in the park on weekend afternoons when she didn't have commitments to Lillywhites, and took care to see that nobody she knew was watching. (That hardly mattered, of course; everyone knew *her*.) It was pitiful. Here she was, not a year removed from playing in the Wimbledon final, and she looked like she was new to the game. She couldn't manage to keep a ball on the court.

Being Angela, she persevered. Later, she would enter the Wimbledon warmup at Beckenham, a handicap tournament, as a left-hander—and she'd even win an open Chandos tournament at a Jewish club in Golders Green. It was just to keep her name in the public eye, Jones assured her, and shine a spotlight on her fortitude and endurance, but she couldn't help feeling shamed. She decided that if her wrist didn't heal soon, she would abandon tennis and turn her competitive instincts elsewhere.

Fortified by her experience with Jones, Angela held an enormous respect for the power of perseverance, far beyond that of natural ability. In her head, she had turned her liabilities into assets. Excelling at a discipline simply meant putting your mind to it, as she believed she and Jones had proven. One can only imagine Althea, who could have beaten Angela at nearly any athletic competition ever devised, erupting in laughter at the thought. But that was Angela, and such thinking helped to explain the success she'd had.

Now it served to brace her against the news that her tennis career might, indeed, be coming to a premature end. It was too bad about her wrist, Angela figured, but it wasn't the end of the world. If she couldn't play anymore, perhaps she might try track and field. That she was slow and awkward even for a competitive tennis player concerned her not a bit.

With Shirley Fry

CHAPTER 16

Althea's Championship Seasons

Intent on winning Wimbledon, Althea returned to London on
May 28, 1957. Her Pan American Strato-Cruiser flight had been paid
for by the USLTA, a significant difference from her two previous Wimbledons. Angela met her at Heathrow Airport in a new Morris Minor.
She'd rented a car against her parents' wishes the previous year, and
found she enjoyed the freedom it gave her. She felt she should have one
for her own, and Harry—always a soft touch—agreed to buy it. Angela
named it Agatha III (the first two Agathas had been bicycles, tributes to
a nun who'd been her favorite teacher in South Africa) and, just for fun,
painted it bright pink with the name stenciled in Olde English letters on
the back. Arriving at the airport to meet Althea in this miniature pink
convertible, her boyfriend of the moment in tow, she must have looked
quite a sight.

Bringing the car to collect Althea was a symbolic act. "Never depend
on anyone else," Althea had advised the previous summer, and in recent
months the philosophy had resonated with Angela. She was on her own
now, with a broken engagement and a tennis career stuck between past
and future tenses. Her mother had moved out of Rossmore Court to
marry her boyfriend, Percy Rubin, and the cozy apartment suddenly
felt quite large. It made her feel, for the first time, as if youth was over
and adulthood had begun.

Althea was the reigning champion, yet she had chosen to skip the French Championships earlier that month. "The clay court doesn't suit my game," she explained, though it had suited her game well enough the previous May for her to win both the women's singles and doubles. In truth, she wanted to concentrate on winning Wimbledon—and after that, Forest Hills and perhaps Australia, all tournaments at which she'd lost to Fry the previous year. Now the path was clear. Fry had married Karl Irvin in Australia the previous February 16 and retired to have a child. Louise Brough was still playing but showing her age. Angela Mortimer had struggled through a difficult spring, battling stress and injuries. Althea would be seeded first at Wimbledon, ahead of Brough, Bloomer, Knode, and Hard, with Mortimer seventh. She looked up and down the draw and couldn't find anyone who could give her trouble. Her biggest concern was what to wear to the Wimbledon Ball, where she sensed that her striped jerseys and battered raincoat would hardly be appropriate. "I don't even know where to start," she said to Angela, who assured her she'd design a dress especially for the occasion.

Angela had signed up to work Wimbledon as a broadcaster for ITV, England's independent network. She suffered pangs when she saw the draw. She would have been the third seed, she figured, and she plotted her way through to a meeting with Althea in a semifinal from there. It was a delightful fantasy, but it wouldn't happen. Instead, she'd do television reports from Wimbledon, and newspaper writing, and watch her friend compete.

Althea won at Surbiton, she won at Manchester, and she won at Beckenham. She then skipped the Queen's Club singles as she'd done the year before to save her strength, and headed into Wimbledon as the favorite. After a first-round bye, she pushed past the always difficult Suzi Kormoczi, 6–4, 6–4, then glided into the semifinals without dropping a set.

Her semifinal opponent was Christine Truman, a sixteen-year-old English sensation. Six feet tall, rangy and strong, Truman was already making English tennis fans forget all about Angela Buxton, the papers said. But Truman was intimidated by the prospect of playing Althea— and she had reason to be. Althea was at the top of her game. She seemed to play like a natural, those who hadn't seen her before remarked, but it had been more than a decade in the making.

Truman was young, talented, and eager, but she was overmatched. Althea won a pair of 6–1 sets to advance to her first Wimbledon singles final against the fifth-seeded Darlene Hard, her doubles partner for the tournament, who had survived the other half of the bracket by toppling two higher seeds. For the second consecutive year, 97 Rossmore Court was home (at least temporarily) to a Wimbledon finalist. Angela well remembered what it felt like, and she tended to Althea as best she could, bringing her tea in the morning. Then she left for Wimbledon in her Morris Minor to perform her broadcast duties, telling Althea she'd see her after she won.

That Saturday afternoon was even hotter than the previous year's final. Contemporaneous reports put the temperature at ninety-six. Queen Elizabeth, who had been coronated four years before, in June of 1953, was making her first visit to Wimbledon as the reigning monarch. She arrived at the Royal Box moments before the Ladies' final, in time to see Althea win the first four games. "There is something about a hot, still day that brings out the best in your shots," Althea wrote, though Hard might disagree. Her face drained of color by the extreme conditions, Hard could do little more than lob off of Althea's explosive serves, and had trouble taking control of her own service points. The set lasted only twenty-five minutes, with Althea winning it 6–3.

Hard did no better in the second set. She never found a way to sustain an attack, and Althea's serve never wavered. "I felt all along that it was my day," Althea would write. Nearly every time Hard advanced to net behind one of her thumping serves, Althea calmly passed her with a stinging forehand or a perfectly placed backhand. Each of Althea's winners would leave Hard nodding distractedly to herself, deep in an internal monologue, the sweat beading on her brow. (Now on the administrative staff at the University of Southern California, Hard declines to discuss the details of that 1957 Wimbledon final, nor any of the other matches during her career.) As the games passed, her nods began to look sadder and sadder, until Hard's expression showed nothing more than resignation. On her best day, the stocky

Californian wasn't a player of Althea's caliber, and this was far from her best day.

Less than an hour after the match started, Althea accepted the trophy from the queen. "At last! At last!" she said. And again, "At last! At last!" Nobody within earshot had to be told what a long journey it had been.

Fred Tupper's story in the *New York Times* captured the import of the moment. "Althea Gibson fulfilled her destiny at Wimbledon today and became the first member of her race to rule the world of tennis," he wrote, well aware that her triumph had implications beyond the personal. It was one in a series of barriers being broken that year. A month later, President Eisenhower would push through the Civil Rights Act of 1957. That fall, integration would begin at Little Rock's Central High.

Althea and Hard then teamed to win the doubles, beating Mary Hawton and Thelma Long. Angela saw it all from the press seats, then found Althea, drenched with sweat, in the ladies' No. 1 cloakroom. Althea had earned a dance with Gentlemen's Singles winner Lew Hoad at the Wimbledon Ball, which she attended in the strapless, floral-patterned dress with a bow below the bustline that Angela had designed for her. Althea wore a choker of white pearls and glittering earrings, and she had fluffed out the curls in her hair. She looked like a champion.

She not only danced at the ball, she sang, too. First she gave a speech, as all winners do. She quoted Churchill, she thanked Doctors Johnson and Eaton, the one-armed Fred Johnson, and Syd Llewellyn. She mentioned the USTA and the ATA, she referenced her opponents and the "good people of England." And she didn't forget Angela, thanking her for her support, then making the quip about Angela forgetting to bring in the milk. After that, she sang two songs—"If I Loved You" and "Around the World"—and headed out to a nightclub with Angela, Angela's latest boyfriend, and Dorothy Parks, a WAC captain stationed in West Germany. By the time they returned to Rossmore Court, they could see the sun rising over Baker Street. It was even later than they'd been out after the ball the previous year, which was only fitting. This time, they had a Wimbledon singles champion numbered among them.

· · ·

THE REACTION TO Althea's Wimbledon title was immediate. New York's Governor Harriman sent a telegram. Eisenhower sent a letter. A crowd of reporters met her plane at Idlewild Airport. So did Althea's mother, who has been out of our story since the beginning. Never estranged from her daughter, Annie Gibson had neither the time nor the energy to be actively involved in her life. She was proud of Althea, but her pride was passive, not proprietary. She knew Althea had made the life she had on her own.

The next day, the City of New York threw her a ticker-tape parade. Thousands of New Yorkers lined the streets to see her. Among them were Harlem friends like Adeline Matthews, her old basketball teammate from the Mysterious Five, who hadn't set eyes on Althea for a decade. Althea saw her from the convertible in which she was riding, and her eyes grew as big as moons. "I could hear her yelling, 'Hiiii!'" Matthews recalls. "And then she was gone."

The day's festivities included a luncheon at the Waldorf-Astoria, then even more than now a symbol of New York luxury. With Sarah Palfrey Cooke, Bobby Riggs, and others looking on, Mayor Wagner presented Althea with a city medallion. She was thankful, but struck a cautionary note. "Whenever I hear anyone call me 'champ,' I think there's something behind it," she said.

She had reason to be careful. For everyone who helped her get to the top, there was someone ready to pull her down. Race continued to be an issue. In 1953, Lorraine Bryant had won the USLTA's national junior title and was heralded as the next Althea, but five years had passed and, still, few blacks were playing at the sport's highest level. Despite the fetes and luncheons, Althea continued to get treated by the tennis hierarchy like one of the help, not the premier attraction of the day. At Chicago that summer for the U.S. Clay Courts, Althea was unable to rent a hotel room in upscale (and utterly white) Oak Park. The Pump Room at the Ambassador East Hotel did its best to sabotage a luncheon being held in her honor, refusing to take reservations or divulge rudimentary information about when it would be held.

Althea responded, "I'm playing tennis to please me, not them," and she carried that attitude everywhere she went. For the first time, she'd been chosen to represent the United States in the Wightman Cup. It was held at the Edgeworth Club in Sewickley, Pennsylvania, on August 10 and 11. Margaret du Pont was again the captain, and she watched Althea split sets with Shirley Bloomer in her first singles match. In those days, the women were entitled to a rest after two sets if both wanted it, and du Pont advised Althea to ask for one. Bloomer had won the second set and seemed the stronger player, and du Pont felt a change of clothes and a respite from the sun would aid Althea. "I was the captain, and that was my advice," she says now. Althea ignored it. She insisted on completing the match without a break. Althea won the third set easily, and du Pont could only shrug. Later, Althea beat Christine Truman as the United States yet again retained the trophy, six matches to one.

Althea won the U.S. Clay Courts, then skipped the ATA Championships for the first time since 1944, causing comment in the black tennis community. "They say I'm bigheaded, uppity, ungrateful," she wrote. But majority opinion was that Althea was doing what Althea needed to do. She was the Joe Louis of tennis, an African-American who had reached a preeminent position in her sport but declined to use that position for the betterment of her race. Louis didn't want to disturb the white oligarchy that ruled the most political of sports, for fear that it would turn against him. Althea had no such fears, but she'd worked hard and long, and she didn't feel obliged to share her spoils with anyone. She had exceeded by two Ora Washington's record of eight ATA women's singles titles. Now she had the sense that ATA events were losing in currency by the year, what with her winning first the French and now Wimbledon against all comers.

Instead, she traveled to Manchester, Massachusetts, two weeks before Forest Hills, and beat Brough and Hard to win the Essex County Club Invitational. It was the same event that the USLTA players had competed in seven summers before while Althea was at Wilberforce, wondering if an invitation to Forest Hills was imminent. Now she was making her decisions on the basis of her tennis, not race. Essex was a sedate event that lacked the frenzy of the ATA Championships, and it provided her with a better class of competition to play against before

Forest Hills. That was the only event left that she yearned to win, and she believed that she was overdue.

Althea was convinced that Fry had beaten her the previous year with the mind as much as the racket, and she was determined not to let it happen again. She filtered out all possible distractions. Rather than bunk with Rhoda Smith, as she usually did, she booked a room at the Vanderbilt Hotel in downtown Manhattan and rode a USLTA courtesy car to Queens every day. She had built on the momentum of Wimbledon, and she was ready for her coronation. As the U.S. Championships opened, her boyish, neatly trimmed Afro and wary smile adorned the cover of the August 26 issue of *Time* magazine. "She may not belong to any of the clubs that run the tournament," it said, "but this year the tournament belongs to her."

Althea played two competitive sets against old friend Karol Fageros in the first round, winning both. Then she lost a total of only twelve more games in the four rounds that followed. She ended up in the final against Brough, a full seven years after their dramatic confrontation at Forest Hills in 1950. The morning of the final, she journeyed to Harlem to get her hair done by a friend of Sydney Llewellyn's, lingered over breakfast, then drove to Forest Hills in Llewellyn's car, relaxed and ready. Her match against Brough was almost as leisurely as her morning had been. "Louise just didn't seem to have it anymore," Althea would write. She won easily, 6–3, 6–2, to complete "a year of almost uninterrupted conquest," as Allison Danzig of the *New York Times* would put it in the day's paper.

Ren McMann, who had saved her career by inviting her to Southeast Asia two years before, introduced Vice President Nixon, who handed her a championship trophy filled with gladioli and red roses. She made a speech about humility and gratitude that was followed by, in Danzig's words, "the longest demonstration of hand-clapping heard in the stadium in years." It seemed like an eternity to Althea, a thunderclap of sound that rolled on for minutes, but she sure didn't mind. "Nothing quite like it had ever happened to me before," she wrote, "and probably never will again."

. . .

ALTHEA NOW RANKED among the biggest black celebrities in America. She had brought more interest to bear on tennis than the sport had seen in years. Wherever she went, she was recognized. She returned to Denver for the Colorado State Championships, but this time she was paid a thousand dollars, which served to cover her expenses and beyond. She arrived "floating around," still on an emotional high from winning Forest Hills, remembers Denver's Joanie Birkland, who faced her in the first round. Without time to adapt to the mile-high altitude, Althea was hitting every ball six inches longer than she intended. She swiftly fell behind by 5–3 to Birkland, a glorified club player who was amazed to be serving for the first set.

It put the Denver Country Club members in a quandary. "A lot of my friends wanted me to win," Birkland says, "but they sure didn't want Althea to lose in the first round, because she was the star." They needn't have worried. Althea started coming to net, spreading her arms wide, and before long Birkland was flummoxed. "Oh, my God, there's no place to hit the ball," she remembers thinking. Althea won the match, 8–6, 6–4, and eventually the tournament.

A few weeks later, she was in Kerhonkson, New York, at Peg Leg Bates' Country Club, which billed itself as the largest resort in America that catered to blacks. Ray Robinson was staying at nearby Greenwood Lake, training for what would be a September 23 loss to Carmen Basilio, and Althea had come up from the city for rest and relaxation.

Clayton Bates was a tap dancer who would eventually make twenty appearances on the *Ed Sullivan Show*. He'd lost a leg in a cotton gin as a youth and learned to dance with its wooden replacement. From 1951 through 1987, he owned a Borscht Belt resort that catered to blacks instead of Jews, and drew all the top black celebrities at one time or another. We can see Althea there, posing for pictures with Peg Leg, enjoying her status as the most prominent female athlete of the day, black or white.

She ended up on the court at Bates's club, giving a lesson to a couple of aspiring welterweights who were being managed by Harold Wiley, Robinson's trainer. It was nothing advanced, just how to hold and swing a racket, but it was given by an icon of the black community. It's a compelling scene to picture, these two powerfully built 147-pounders submitting meekly to tennis instruction from a woman who stood nearly a head taller, but such was the spell Althea cast. "Unforgettable," Dino Woodard, one of the welterweights, says now.

Billie Jean King, then Billie Jean Moffitt, was equally reverential when she saw Althea that September at the Los Angeles Tennis Club. (Althea could no more qualify as a member of the LATC than Angela, but the club was willing to admit blacks and Jews during the week of the Pacific Southwest, especially when they were certain to boost interest and attendance.) Moffitt was thirteen, still four years away from her first Wimbledon, but already a promising player. Althea caught her eye not because of her fame as the reigning Wimbledon and Forest Hills champion, but because she was one of the first blacks Moffitt had ever seen on a tennis court. Like Alice Marble, Moffitt had grown up watching and playing team sports, and she knew that there were blacks competing at the highest levels in baseball, basketball, and football. "Seeing Althea made me wonder why there weren't people of color playing tennis," King says now. "In that sense, she was a symbol for me. She was different. And the older I got, the more I wondered why that was."

Yet all her talent and all her charisma didn't make Althea rich. In fact, it barely paid the bills. She was affiliated with the Harry C. Lee sporting goods company, earning seventy-five dollars a month. The money was paid to her for serving on its advisory board, at least theoretically, but the photographs of her during that period show the Harry C. Lee name prominently displayed on her racket cover, a side benefit to the company that was in only tenuous compliance with the USLTA's eligibility rules for amateurs.

The truth is, Althea needed that seventy-five dollars to live. Her tiny New York apartment at 461 Central Park West was outfitted with a certain flair, but it hardly seemed the domicile of a famous athlete. She had a striped chair and matching settee, a console television with trophies sitting on top, stacks of books and magazines resting on a side table, a dresser in a closet, clutter on her desk, and a couch that converted into a bed at night. It was a substandard way for a professional woman in her thirties—let alone a world champion—to live. As Shirley

Fry recalls, "The poor girl was trying to make a career out of tennis when there really was no money in it."

For some time, Althea had pondered generating income with her singing. She'd been singing in the bathtub, singing at tennis balls, singing in nightclubs with jazz combos. Eventually, she decided to start a singing career. Llewellyn tried to dissuade her, saying it would detract from her tennis, but she insisted. Angela provided the connection: an actor and singer named Jerry Wayne, who had played the role of Sky Masterson in the London run of *Guys and Dolls*. With Wayne's backing, Althea had made her first, tentative foray into a recording studio in London in 1956, met some prominent record-industry executives, and gradually became convinced that she could succeed as a professional singer.

By late 1957, she was working on improving her voice with a professor at Long Island University. In May of 1958, she'd released a monaural disc on the Dot Records label from a session recorded at the Apollo Theatre. Called *Althea Gibson Sings*, it showed off on its cover an Althea nobody had ever seen. She wore a sleeveless plaid dress with a tight collar. Her lipstick was the color of a cherry lollipop, and her hair had been teased and treated until it shone. It was a look she would cultivate after her tennis career.

In her nasal baritone, she sang such standards as "Around the World" and "September Song." Her voice might have been terrifically impressive if you'd heard it coming from your bathtub, but wasn't especially enjoyable on a disc. It was clear that, despite the lessons, she was largely untrained. She sang in French with a New York accent on "Don't Say No," and negotiated her way through a syncopated version of "Dream a Little Dream of Me" that sounded like a bad Sinatra imitation. Still, she had a name, and the record attracted interest as a curiosity. On May 25, 1958, she appeared on the *Ed Sullivan Show*, with Frankie Lymon, Georgie Kaye, and Wayne & Schuster. She'd make a return visit several months later with Lymon, Alan King, and Hermione Gingold. In between, she appeared as the mystery guest on *What's My Line?*

Between entertainment commitments, she found time for tennis. Earlier in the year, she had played the full Caribbean circuit for the first time. At the Caribe Hilton, she lost in straight sets to Beverly Fleitz, now the mother of two, who was attempting a comeback. That was about the only stress of the trip, which was being funded by the tournaments. At Montego Bay, she lay on the beach, giggling at the pale-skinned white players who were so intent on getting tanned, working so hard "just to look like me," as she put it. In Caracas, she beat Brazil's Maria Bueno, Angela's discovery from the previous year, in the final after double-faulting to lose the second set. "She was beating everybody pretty badly," Bueno recalls. "I was able to take her to three sets, and that made me feel pretty good about my chances." As a direct result of that match, Bueno decided she was ready to travel to Europe and play Wimbledon for the first time.

Some months later, Althea would approach Bueno and ask if she wanted to play doubles together. "Imagine, my first year in Europe, and the best player in the world comes and asks me to play doubles with her," Bueno says. "It was wonderful." Though Bueno barely spoke English and was in those days reluctant to say anything to anyone in any language, she and Althea would win at Queen's Club and then at Wimbledon. It was Althea's third Ladies' Doubles title in succession, with three different partners, another bit of tennis history. Only one other woman, Elizabeth Ryan, had done that before.

ARRIVING IN LONDON in June of 1958, Althea stayed at Rossmore Court for the third consecutive year. It seemed like a second home to her by now—or a third, if the Darbens' house in New Jersey ranked as her second. Angela had given up on tennis, at least temporarily, and was determined to make her name as a dress designer. She created outfits for Althea to wear at Wimbledon, where they would be seen by thousands, and at some of the social events surrounding the tournament. On the afternoon before the start of the Championships, they attended a garden party given by Lady Crossfields, and were photographed for the newspapers as the height of fashion. At some point during her stay, Althea received a visit from a man who must have been her old boyfriend from Jefferson City, a major in the army who arrived "wearing epaulets, and with his medals, flashing," as Angela remem-

bers. He and Althea ensconced themselves in the bedroom for the better part of two days. Angela left meals outside the door and came back
hours later to find the empty plates stacked up.

Violet had been gone for two years, though she'd stop by regularly,
and Angela had made the apartment her own. Harry passed through
London when he could manage. He was getting more eccentric as the
years wore on. He'd phone from Manchester late on a Friday afternoon.
"Angela, I'm on my way down, make me chicken soup," he'd say. "Some
baked apple, barley water, you know what I like. I'm on my way to the
aeroport." Angela would cancel her plans, make a rushed trip to the
market, throw the pots on the stove, and wait. The next she'd hear of
him was the following morning, when she'd get an apologetic phone
call from somewhere like Cannes. "I got to Heathrow and changed my
mind," he'd say.

Althea was expected to successfully defend her Wimbledon title by
all but the most fervent of British fans. Truman, now seventeen, was
seeded second; she was seen as the only other potential champion in
the field, though the clearest-eyed observers knew she was still several
years away from making a championship run. Dottie Knode was seeded
third, while Bueno, playing in her first Wimbledon, was fourth. As the
defending champion, and the top draw besides, Althea would play all
her singles matches on Centre Court. That alone was a measure of how
far she'd come. She was tested during the fortnight, but was never in
danger of losing. Yola Ramirez extended her to 9–7 in the first set of
their third-round match, but Althea won the second set easily. Later,
she needed three sets to put away the fifth-seeded Bloomer. She
advanced to defend her title not against Truman, who had been upset
early on, but Angela Mortimer.

Mortimer had been fourth in the world in 1955 and 1956, the highest ranking by an Englishwoman since Kay Stammers in 1939. Then
she'd faded from sight. She battled injuries and her own demons, but
her competitive urges drove her back into the fray. She entered the
Wimbledon draw unseeded and began to build a comeback against a
United Nations of opponents on a series of side courts. She beat Chile's
Carmen Ibarra, South Africa's Sandra Reynolds, Germany's Edda Bud-

ing, Belgium's Christiane Mercellis, and another unseeded relic of a previous era, Margaret du Pont, who had last seen the Wimbledon quarterfinals in 1954. Then Mortimer routed Hungary's Kormoczi, who had won the French Championships that May at thirty-two and was playing the best tennis of her interminable career, by 6–0, 6–1. Out of nowhere, she had gained her first Wimbledon final.

London's dailies treated Mortimer's reemergence as a miracle, the second for British tennis in a matter of weeks. The previous month, Britain had astonished everyone by finally winning the Wightman Cup. Even more surprising, considering she was the best player in the world, Althea had been blamed for America's defeat.

The countries had been tied at two matches each on the second afternoon when Althea took the court against Truman. It seemed a likely mismatch. Althea had beaten Truman easily each time they'd played. Now she won the first set by 6–2, in just nineteen minutes. But unlike each of their previous matches, Truman wasn't cowed. She won the first three games of the second set, added another break to go up 5–1, and evened the match at one set each when Althea hit a forehand that curved past the sideline.

The deciding set was spectacular tennis, made all the more compelling by the stakes at hand. At 4–4, Truman broke Althea for the fourth time with a series of cross-court winners. Ahead 30–15 in the following game, she hit a winner with a ferocious forehand, and now she had two match points. After a double-fault, she caught her breath, engaged Althea in a brief rally, then won the game and match when Althea slapped a backhand out.

Later, Althea would anger American tennis officials with the claim that she'd been experimenting during the Wightman Cup matches, trying to linger at the baseline rather than play the attacking game that was her forte. Whether that was true or not, the long English drought was over. And when Mortimer ascended to the Ladies' Singles final, it could be said that England had finally overcome the effects of World War II and gained something close to parity with the Americans. The top-ranked player in the world, Althea, was American, but the sheer dominance of America's postwar generation of female players—Betz and Connolly, Brough and du Pont, Hart and Fry—had officially ended.

Angela had had a hand in ending it, but she'd arrived a year or two too soon, and departed too early. She could only sit in the grandstand at Wimbledon and watch it happen. Her emotions were mixed, and not merely because Althea was a great friend. "I always felt that I opened the door for British tennis after the war and led the way, and yet I never got the credit," she says. She wasn't wrong about the latter, at least. Each year since 1951, the Lawn Tennis Writers Association of Great Britain has given an annual award to the individual who has made the greatest contribution to English tennis. When Mortimer finally won Wimbledon in 1961, she received the award, and when Greg Rusedski didn't win it in 1997, he received it anyway. Yet in 1956, when Angela became the first British player to reach the Wimbledon final since World War II, the award was left vacant for one of only two times in half a century. Whether it was because of anti-Semitism, a dislike for Angela's willingness to flaunt convention, or something more benign is unclear. No explanation was ever given.

THE 1958 WIMBLEDON FINAL was a last act of closure for Althea, just as defeating Brough at Forest Hills had been the year before. Not only did Mortimer epitomize exactly the sort of player that the less mature Althea had been unable to overcome—someone who couldn't come close to matching her in talent, but whose fortitude and steadiness somehow enabled her to triumph regardless—but she herself had managed to beat Althea most consistently. She'd mastered Althea in Mexico, in Sweden, in Cairo, in Alexandria, and battled until the end at the French Championships. Mortimer knew that Althea had matured as a player almost beyond recognition since then. Those erratic patches, game after game when she'd played in a private funk, were long gone. Consistency was now a strength of Althea's. Still, Mortimer nursed the belief that she could wait out anyone. The longer a set continued, she figured, the better chance she had.

In the final, Mortimer was helped by a recurrence of a foot-fault issue that had plagued Althea in the past. It was a question of how closely the line judges monitored where Althea's toes were placed when she hit her serve, and on this afternoon that placement was monitored with particular care. Althea was called for foot-faults—the equivalent of a fault on a serve, no matter where the ball lands—eleven times in the first set alone. Up 5–3, Mortimer had a set point. But Althea served her way out of the mess, pulled to even at 5–5 and 6–6, added a service break, and overpowered Mortimer to win the set, 8–6.

This time, it was Mortimer who sagged. For so long, she'd been clawing her way through matches she had no right to win, and now she was trying to do it in a Wimbledon final, with all the pressure on her that the other Angela had felt two years before. It was too much. The first set had been hers to take, and, by losing it, she had squandered her chance to win the match. Althea swept through the second set, 6–2, and received the winner's dish from the duchess of Kent. She stayed on to win the doubles with Bueno. Then, with Angela by her side once more, she danced and sang late into the night at the Wimbledon Ball and in the streets of London beyond. It had become a habit.

The Silks

CHAPTER 17

Second Careers

FOLLOWING HER VICTORY at Wimbledon in July 1958, Althea won her second singles title at Forest Hills, beating Truman, Fleitz, and Hard in the last three matches, the latter only with some difficulty. "[Hard] came out attacking me, serving, volleying . . . outwitting me, outplaying me and everything else," Althea told journalist Stan Hart in 1985. But she won the match and the championship—3–6, 6–1, 6–2— and accepted the trophy from Secretary of State John Foster Dulles. Then she told the gallery she was finished with amateur tennis.

She was thirty-one years old, so it wasn't a shock. She wanted to earn money from tennis while she could. Because no professional contracts were pending, she called it a hiatus, but she had no intention of playing on the amateur circuit again. But it was an uneasy time for African-Americans. A black woman looking to tour the country playing tennis for pay was not the most salable of commodities. On September 20, a few weeks after Althea was honored with a second ticker-tape parade in New York, this one even larger than the first, Martin Luther King Jr. was stabbed with a letter-opener while autographing books at Blumstein's department store in Harlem. Advancement for blacks came as slowly as Althea's tennis had progressed, a few steps forward, then a few steps back. Promise was undercut by reality.

What Althea needed, she knew, was a white costar. When Fry returned from Australia later that year, Althea proposed traveling with her on a tour with the Harlem Globetrotters. They'd play a set before the Globetrotter games, which were already booked into the best arenas throughout America. Because of her success against Althea, Fry was one of the few opponents who would have helped draw crowds in city after city, but she longed to be nothing more than Mrs. Karl Irvin, a Connecticut housewife. She had spent the last two years doing her best to retire, and now, after winning consecutive majors of the Grand Slam, she'd finally managed it. She had a new life and a one-year-old son. She wasn't about to get on a bus bound for Everywhere, USA, tennis dresses folded neatly into a traveling trunk.

For more than a year, from the fall of 1958 until late in 1959, Althea languished. She was working for Harry C. Lee, the sporting goods manufacturer, as a spokesperson, but earning little. She played the role of Lukey in *The Horse Soldiers,* a John Ford movie about the Civil War that starred John Wayne and William Holden, but she didn't exactly light up the screen. (She wasn't even the most prominent Gibson in the movie; it was silent-screen cowboy Hoot's last credited appearance.) She was earning more money than she had earned playing amateur tennis, but not by much. The year 1958 marked the first time in her life that Althea filed an income-tax return. Before that, she'd never amassed enough in a calendar year to warrant one.

Althea could feel her fame and her marketability slipping away. Finally, she convinced Karol Fageros to turn pro and tour with her and the Globetrotters. The announcement came at a luncheon in midtown Manhattan on October 19, 1959, complete with tennis rackets and basketballs. Althea signed a "near-$100,000" contract to play ninety matches. It was by far the most ever paid to a female player, but the money she'd actually receive would depend on gate receipts. Fageros, billed as the "Golden Goddess," was promised thirty thousand dollars. For the same reason that the State Department had wanted this butterscotch-haired Floridian and Althea to be seen representing the country together, they made an attractive pairing as touring professionals, at least until each night's match started. But Fageros could hardly compete with Althea on the court—and Althea, to her credit, wasn't about to lose for the sake of promulgating a rivalry.

From the end of 1959 through 1960, they traveled with the Globetrotters, playing a set before each game. Billie Davis, Althea's old friend and doubles partner, came along to construct the net and lay the lines of the court atop the hardwood. Althea ended up earning about eight hundred dollars a performance, the most money she'd ever had in her life, and she beat Fageros in 114 of 118 matches. When the Globetrotters decided not to renew her contract, Althea and Llewellyn concocted the idea of a competing tour. This time, she'd be the featured attraction, and the basketball game would be the sideshow.

She and Fageros toured for several months more, but with drama utterly lacking, crowds were sparse. Althea had invested most of the money she'd earned while working with the Globetrotters in the second tour. She wound up all but broke again.

ANGELA WAS STILL BIG NEWS in London in 1959. She'd been supplanted by Christine Truman as the most successful British woman player of the day, and the importance of her trip to the finals in 1956 had been mitigated by Mortimer's emotional run in 1958. But she'd made the newsreels when she announced her engagement to Donald Silk, and their wedding that February was covered in all the papers.

She'd met Silk in September at a speech she was giving. He was the secretary of the Zionist Federation of Great Britain, and a political comer. They'd been introduced once before, when she was fifteen, and disliked each other on sight, but now each felt an intense fascination with the other. It had the capability of manifesting itself as either revulsion or love. Angela's brother, Gordon, remembers her saying with disdain that she'd run into that Donald Silk again. Then Gordon left on a holiday. By the time he'd returned, he was perplexed to find them discussing their engagement.

Silk was six years older than Angela, and immersed in Jewish politics. He felt that Angela's name recognition, especially in the Jewish community, could only help him. A Magdalen College School and Oxford graduate, he was something of a prodigy. He came from a world entirely different from Angela's. "I've never played a game of tennis in my life," he said. "About the only thing we have in common is that we both have convertible cars." He was kidding, yet he wasn't. The two were a mismatched set, and even Angela knew it. Before the wedding, she was sick for a week, losing her voice again. A photo of her lying in bed, the unlucky bride-to-be, appeared in the papers. Her illness threatened the wedding, but in the end she had enough strength to step to the altar. They were married on Sunday, February 8, 1959. He was thirty, she was twenty-four.

They lived at Rossmore Court together until a house could be finished in Hampstead, then moved there early the following year. By then, they had established a kosher household. All the time Angela had been playing tennis, no one would have guessed that hers was the apartment of a Jew. She was Jewish in the most secular sense, having embraced the religion as a cultural heritage, if at all. Now she used separate sets of dishes for milk and for meat. They'd go to services on all the important holy days; it helped Silk politically to be seen there.

She was designing clothes for a living, but still thinking about tennis. She'd been doing some informal coaching, helping a junior champion from Nottinghamshire named Carol Webb. Eventually she hit on the idea of getting Webb some Wimbledon experience by entering the doubles competition with her. Webb had little chance of making the main draw on her own, but Angela was a Wimbledon singles finalist and a doubles champion. She figured she had enough cachet to earn a wild card into the draw. The tenosynovitis hadn't returned, and Angela's doctors told her to refrain from putting the stress on the wrist that she'd previously done. To her, that meant playing doubles instead of singles.

Althea had retired, so she wasn't competing at Wimbledon in 1959. Like so many former players before her, she was fronting a newspaper column, in this case for the *Evening Standard*. So Angela was playing, and Althea was writing about it! Once again, they'd gracefully shifted their positions like a do-si-do in a square dance.

First, though, Angela had to qualify. She was astonished that the tournament director didn't grant their pairing an exemption, but Webb was young, and 1956 was three years distant by then, and Angela didn't exactly have friends in the LTA. So they played through the qualifying, and landed in the Ladies' Doubles draw for Angela's Wimbledon coda. They won one match, then lost to Sheila Armstrong and Margaret O'Donnell. Concurrently, Angela also played mixed doubles with John Maloney of South Africa, winning two matches in straight sets before losing to Truman and her brother, Humphrey, 7–5, 8–10, 6–3. A month later, she would learn that she was pregnant, which ended any thoughts of a repeat visit in 1960.

Her Globetrotter tour in full swing, Althea would again return to Wimbledon for the *Evening Standard* the following June. She showed up at the Silks' Hampstead house like a tornado, full of vigor and good cheer. She emptied what seemed like three weeks' worth of laundry in the middle of the hall, then looked in the kitchen cabinet. "Tell Don to get more whiskey," she said, a twinkle in her eye. "You're out of it."

This time, Richard Evans, later to become the most prominent of the British tennis writers, served as her ghost. He'd just returned from the army the week before and knew nothing about tennis. His editor Charles Wintour, whose daughter, Anna, would dominate the American fashion community in decades to come as the editor of *Vogue*, sent him off to Queen's Club to meet Althea. They spent an afternoon together at the Silks' house in Hampstead, along with couturier and tennis personality Teddy Tinling. Evans was charmed by Althea, who taught him the intricacies of tennis during their series of interviews. "In a way, she's responsible for pulling me into the game," Evans says. "She was totally cooperative, and she taught me a lot about tennis because she was analyzing the other players."

Althea even invited a wide-eyed Evans to accompany her to the Wimbledon Ball, and he accepted with alacrity. He lived with his mother, not far from the Grosvenor House, and felt it would be only decent to ask Althea over for cocktails beforehand. That was a traumatic evening in the Evans household. "My mother had never entertained a black person in her life," Evans says now. "The social etiquette was so much more rigid then. For normal families, there was a strict social order, and the opportunity to do such a thing would simply never arise. From that generation, you just didn't have black people over for drinks."

The engagement was emblematic of those Althea had been faced with over her entire career—and, as usual, she handled it with aplomb. It wasn't overt prejudice she was battling in most cases, but lack of experience. At nearly every tournament she entered, she was breaking a barrier. She was the curiosity, the conversation piece. This wasn't the same as being called "Nigger!" by players on opposing teams to provoke a fight, something Jackie Robinson had faced, but it did get old. "Althea came round and was absolutely charming, and my mother was charmed," Evans says. Then they headed to the ball, where Evans danced with a woman taller than he was for the first time, another barrier broken.

Between columns, Althea tried to drum up interest for her professional tour. The tennis world was the only one in which she had currency, and currency was just what she needed. But the visibility afforded by the *Evening Standard* column ended when the popular Jaroslav Drobny, the 1954 Gentlemen's Singles champion, became available as a commentator. Althea wasn't invited back for 1961, and she wouldn't return to Wimbledon again under any auspices for two decades.

DONALD SILK WAS AN ATTORNEY, but he spent most of his time working for the Zionist Federation. It was his life's work, though he'd later serve two terms as a London alderman and "fight an epic battle to bring voter power to the governance of the City of London," as the *Times* would write in his obituary on June 27, 2002. Angela became a housewife, and she had a mail-order business selling maternity clothes that she had designed. It was profitable, and it gave her an outlet for her creativity.

In 1967, Egypt invaded Israel and started what became known as the Six-Day War. By then, Silk had advanced to Zionist Federation president. At a rally held at the Royal Albert Hall in support of Israel, he declared that he was moving there to serve on a kibbutz and join the fight. Angela was aghast. She had two young boys and a baby girl. She wasn't going to be left alone in London while her husband chased trouble halfway around the world. Silk told her she could stay in London or get an apartment in Tel-Aviv, far from the kibbutz. "I didn't like either choice," she remembers. She put her business on hiatus, locked up the stock, and took the three children to the kibbutz with her husband. It never occurred to her that her father had sent her and her mother to South Africa before the bombs started falling on London nearly three decades before, and now she was running after a war, and with children in tow. They were a family, and what families did was stay together, she believed—though her father hadn't taught her that, either.

Two of their au pairs came with them as volunteers. It looked odd, like driving a Cadillac to a campground, but Angela didn't care. For five months, they lived on the kibbutz near Lake Tiberius. A palpable sense of danger was in the air. Syria was just over the next hill, and snipers were everywhere. They picked fruit, did laundry work, and the community helped care for the children. At one point, a newspaper learned that there was a Jewish Wimbledon champion living in its midst and someone called to interview her. Asked what she missed most, she named a hot bath, a haircut, and a game of tennis. So they flew her to Tel-Aviv and arranged them all, including a match against an Israeli standout named Tovah Epstein. Donald wasn't amused. He reminded Angela that they weren't there for fun.

It is probable that Althea never knew Angela had gone to Israel. They were out of touch to that extent. After the failure of her second tour with Fageros, she'd taken stock of her options. By this time, the civil rights movement was gaining momentum, but the equal rights movement wasn't. Althea was being held back more because she was a woman, she realized, than because she was black. She was one of the best female athletes around, but true professional tennis was still several years away. She tried to open a tennis club, but didn't have the money to make it succeed. She had signed a $25,000 annual contract to represent Tip-Top Bread, but that was a stopgap. She needed a career, and she had little more than her athletic skills to offer.

In the early 1960s, only one sport afforded women the chance to earn a living. Althea had picked up golf at college in Tallahassee; it is said that she broke one hundred the first time she played eighteen holes. Now she set out to qualify for the Ladies Professional Golf Association tour, which had been founded as the Women's Professional Golf Association during World War II. In two decades, it hadn't had a black member. (The men's PGA Tour had admitted its first black, Charlie Sitton, in 1959, but he only played a portion of the schedule, eschewing anything south of the Mason-Dixon Line.) As with tennis, most of the LPGA tournaments were held at private clubs, and in many cases they didn't admit blacks. Not only did Althea have to learn a new sport, she once again had to integrate it.

Golf brought all her competitive instincts flooding back, and all her insecurities with them. In 1962, she played the National Amateur Championships in Rochester, Minnesota. One or two blacks had entered that event during the 1950s, but organizers were still concerned that an unruly mob would follow Althea up and down the fairways, disrupting play. It didn't happen, of course. In match play against the wife of famed golf-course designer Pete Dye, Althea held a narrow lead through fifteen holes. Then she hit a ball downhill and pulled it to the left. "I won the hole and she became very upset at herself," Alice Dye remembers now. "I was surprised. Here was this two-time Wimbledon champion getting flustered over an amateur golf tournament." It may have been amateur, but Althea felt her future livelihood was at stake. Dye won the match, and Althea offered a limp hand. "I'll be back," she said, as if it were Forest Hills all over again.

In time, she became a formidable golfer. She earned her card as a touring professional, and started playing LPGA events in 1963. "Everyone admired her tremendously," Dye says now. "Here was this person at the very top of her sport who was starting over again with golf. We all appreciated that, and tried to help her however we could." If Althea—and, later, Renee Powell, the LPGA's second black member—was denied access to a clubhouse or anywhere else at a club holding an LPGA event, the other women would usually refuse to play. In that sense, they were years ahead of the men. Nevertheless, Althea often stayed at different hotels, changed into her golf shoes in the car or on a sidewalk, and was occasionally denied an invitation to tournaments.

Althea started her LPGA career in 1963 and finished for good in 1978, with time as a sports consultant for the Essex County Parks Commission and a two-year term as New Jersey's athletic commissioner in between. She never won a professional tournament, but played in 171 of them. Her best finish was a second-place tie at the Immke Buick Open in Columbus, Ohio, in 1970, where she lost in a three-way playoff to Mary Mills.

Several years before, Mills had hosted an invitational event in her home state of Mississippi that carried $15,000 in prize money, a formidable amount. To mollify the Jim Crow element, which likely would have disrupted the proceedings or worse, Althea wasn't invited. "I was a young kid in my early twenties, and I wasn't a political activist," Mills says now. "I felt it was an injustice, but I had to take it."

She'd felt pangs of conscience ever since—but on the course at Columbus, she pushed it all from her mind and putted as if her life hung in the balance. "I felt sorry Althea didn't win, but you can't roll over and give somebody a tournament," she says. Still, Mills was impressed by the way Althea handled what must have been a devastating loss. Althea had been a professional golfer for seven years without winning, and this was her opportunity.

Althea's formidable strength was being wasted by bad mechanics. She had a flat swing, by most reports not unlike the swing of former Olympian Babe Didricksen. In both cases, it was the result of a background playing a variety of sports. "We had other girls who came from various other sports—a rodeo rider and an Olympic javelin thrower," Mills recalls. "They all came to golf to make money, and they all found it very difficult."

Twice Althea finished with yearly averages of fewer than seventy-six strokes a round. From 1964 through 1969, she played in tournaments at least seventeen weeks a year and as many as twenty-five, her expenses partially defrayed by friends, including future New York mayor David Dinkins. She ranked among the LPGA's top fifty in each of those years. Yet she earned only $24,437 from golf—for her entire career; less than a single year of endorsing Tip-Top Bread. There was money in the game, but only for the leaders.

In those days, players would pay their own expenses, driving from tournament to tournament and eating sandwiches along the way. Tournaments would often provide housing at members' homes for the white players—and the blacks, too, "if they didn't have a lot of bigots," says Powell, the LPGA's second black player, who joined Althea on the tour in 1967. Powell had started in golf at age three and grown up with the game; she knew the other players, and they knew her. Althea had come in from the outside, bearing the burden of fame and expectations. Her ability to intimidate opponents, which served her so well in tennis, didn't come into play in golf. "You can't intimidate the course," Powell says. "You're playing the field, not one on one, and you have no idea what the other women out there are doing. It's a different mindset." Having said that, Powell recalls that mental strength was Althea's greatest asset. By this time, she knew how to compete. She didn't win tournaments, but she didn't embarrass herself, either.

While on tour, Althea had little time for contact with the tennis world, except when she happened to pass nearby. Each time the LPGA came through Phoenix, she stayed with Flo Blanchard, who had umpired many of her matches, and she always saw the Darbens in New Jersey. Rosemary was like a sister to her, and her relations with Will seemed to alternate between friendship and romance. And then, after years of turmoil in their relationship, he finally became her husband.

Will Darben was a production analyst with Bendix Aviation, an engineer's assistant though he'd never been to college. Two years older than Althea, meek and mild in her presence, he was devoted to her cause. "I always picture him as carrying Althea's tennis rackets and bags wherever she went," says family friend and former personal physician Bill Hayling. He had supported her tennis career and now he was supporting her golf career; Althea couldn't make up her mind if he was a lover or a terrific friend. Perhaps for that reason, and possibly an ambiguity that several intimates from the tennis world and beyond have reported regarding Althea's sexual orientation, her relationship with Darben was tempestuous. She broke one engagement with him in 1958, saying she was too busy to prepare a wedding, and another in the spring of 1961 for unspecified reasons.

Finally, on October 17, 1965, they were married at the home of Las Vegas dentist Arnold DeVoe. Althea sent Angela a wedding invitation, but with young children and her mail-order business and Donald's pre-occupations, Angela never seriously considered coming. They hadn't seen each other in five years by then, and they wouldn't for many more.

After the wedding, Will and Althea moved to 69 Pleasant Way in Montclair, New Jersey. In a matter of days, Althea had returned to the golf tour. The marriage would last a decade and end in divorce after accusations of infidelity on both sides. "He saw it coming," his sister, Rosemary, says. "She was traveling all over, she had made mistakes. He couldn't establish a home with her. She wouldn't stay still."

ONCE ANGELA HAD RETURNED to England from Israel, she prepared a series of lectures about her life. She gave presentations on what it was like to live in Israel in the aftermath of war, or play on Centre Court in Wimbledon, or meet Hollywood stars like Katharine Hepburn and Walter Pidgeon. She was adept at pulling together and packaging bits of her past. Today, labeled as a motivational speaker, she could earn good money extrapolating advice for businesspeople from her own curriculum vitae. But this was the mid-1960s, and youth-oriented London was "swinging like a pendulum do," as the song went. A housewife who'd played some tennis years before wasn't exactly considered an authority on how to live a life.

By then, Angela's relations with Donald had deteriorated. They'd seen a therapist, but Donald's mind was elsewhere. He hadn't taken the idea of therapy seriously; it wasn't as readily accepted then as it would come to be later. He didn't have the attention span to engage the idea, either. He had his work to do.

As a response to his lack of interest, Angela had thrown herself back into tennis. She wanted to coach, so she studied for her official certificate. Pat Hird was doing the same, and they reconnected. For this task, she was an ideal doubles partner. Hird remembers sharing a room with

Angela at the Lilleshall Sports Centre in Shropshire, where they'd gone to take the exam. They were two tennis professionals, a scrapbook of Wimbledon memories between them. Yet there they were, awake at two in the morning, memorizing the size of the tennis court. "We'd been playing all our lives," says Hird, who coached for years on the Isle of Wight. "Now we had to know the height of the net, which we'd never paid any attention to. It was hysterical. We had a wonderful time."

Not long after, with her marriage to Donald in trouble, Angela attended the British Junior Indoor Championships at Queen's Club with her two sons. By happenstance, she bumped into Jimmy Jones. Immersed in life with Donald, she'd lost touch with Jones, just as she'd lost touch with Althea. It was understandable. They were of different generations, and their social circles didn't overlap. Now Jones wanted to catch up on more than ten years all at once, but watching tennis matches is hardly the venue for a reunion. So he invited her to tea on the spot, and she accepted. He sat down and looked her over. When he asked, "So, how are you, Angela?" she burst out crying. With Benjamin and Joseph there, she couldn't go into detail about her troubles, but Jones had spent enough time with her to know without asking.

He was a shoulder to cry on. She might have been talking to her father. At fifty-seven, Jones had been married to his wife, Heather, for a quarter-century. He had retired from newspapers and moved to Suffolk, where he'd bought a house for his family and a nearby bungalow where he'd do his magazine work. He had three children and what appeared from the outside to be a settled life.

But then so did Angela. And beneath the veneer of a thriving life as the wife of a politician and activist, she eventually told Jones, she felt woefully dissatisfied. Silk's yearnings weren't her yearnings. He wanted to start a political dynasty, and was handcuffed by appearances. "Do it this way, that's how the Kennedys do it," he'd say. Angela tried, but she didn't have the soul of a conformist, let alone a Kennedy. His work also left little time for the solicitous moments that sustain a marriage. His emotional tank was always dry. He'd come home exhausted on Friday nights and head straight to bed, then take his meals in bed Saturday and Sunday and be back hard at work on Monday morning. Angela didn't understand what it was all for.

Silk was of her religion and her generation, but Jones spoke her language and thought her thoughts. At some level, he'd been in love with her all along. He'd wanted a romantic relationship a decade and a half before, but she'd subconsciously put him off, not daring to let herself decode the signals he was sending. Back then, the idea had seemed preposterous to her. He was married, for one thing. He wasn't Jewish, and neither was he the upwardly mobile businessman or lawyer—a Barney Goodman, a Donald Silk—that her father would have seen as a suitable match. More than that: at seventeen, a forty-year-old man hardly seemed attractive.

Fifteen years later, that had changed. She'd lived almost another full life from when she'd known him, and learned a great deal about what she wanted. She realized that Jones validated her quirkiness, just as he had all those years ago. She was an outsider, and he was, too. He made her feel as though her unconventional way of approaching life, whether striding through the hotel lobby in India to hit tennis balls in the blazing sun or repudiating the upwardly mobile conventions of her husband, was perfectly fine. He didn't pass judgment. His fondness for her was unconditional. "You're OK," he'd say in words, but more tellingly in how he treated her. "In fact, you're more than OK."

In early 1970, under pressure from Angela, Silk moved out of their Hampstead house. By then, Jones was spending much of his time in London. On Heather's insistence, the Joneses had adopted a fourth child, a six-year-old daughter named Melanie, and suddenly he couldn't make ends meet with the occasional magazine piece and lecture. He had to return to Fleet Street and a regular writing career. So he'd rented a room in Bayswater and lived and worked there Monday to Friday. He would have dinner with Angela several times a week, and phone her daily. "He was very worried about me," Angela remembers, and why shouldn't he have been? She had no income, and no way of earning money beyond the occasional tennis lesson.

Jones had no money to give her, but he could help her create money.

He had the connections and the ideas. They worked together, traveling the country, giving talks at Rotary Clubs and workshops, collaborating on articles. "A thousand different things," Angela says. "He had a very inventive mind." Along the way, they started to see each other as something more than traveling companions. Eventually, Heather Jones realized that something was amiss and bustled her husband off for a holiday. Jones was never reticent, and his pining for Angela was hard to hide. He had worked himself into a quandary, and now he didn't know of a noble way out.

He returned from the trip on Easter Sunday, 1971, and called Angela from his bungalow. His voice was ominous, and he talked of ending his suffering by suicide. Angela called Heather immediately and told her to send police to the bungalow and break down the door. The attempt was averted, and Jones stayed on with Heather for several more months. Finally he worked up the courage to leave and move in with Angela.

That didn't work, either. She was planning bar mitzvahs for her sons, Benjamin and then Joseph, and Silk had put a private detective on their trail with orders to barge in at three in the morning and generally be as disruptive as he could. "I can't continue with this," Angela told Jones. So he moved out—but, to her surprise, he didn't go home. He rented a house and lived there alone, like a recluse, doing little other than work. Eventually, Angela found him a room fifteen minutes' walk from her Hampstead house. It was an acceptable compromise. He'd come over for dinner a night or two each week, and when the children left to see Silk on the weekends, he'd stay the night.

Later, when all the children had moved out (the last, Rebecca, as a runaway), Jones moved in again. He would stay five years, until his death in 1986. At his funeral, Jones's daughter would approach Angela and say a remarkable thing: "I would never be disloyal to Mother, but those five years he spent with you were the happiest of his life."

CHAPTER 18

Together Again

I N J U L Y O F 1968, Billie Jean King and her husband, Larry, created a two-day professional tennis tournament at the Oakland Coliseum Arena. Prize money totaled five thousand dollars, a pittance, but it was the philosophy behind the event that mattered. Althea was in the midst of her golf career, and she was a month away from her forty-first birthday, but King felt it was only right that she be invited, along with top players of the moment, such as Rosie Casals and Françoise Durr, and Pancho Gonzalez, Andres Gimeno, Roy Emerson, and Rod Laver. If she was worried that she'd embarrass herself, King told Althea, she shouldn't feel obligated to come. Althea scoffed at the notion. As always, she felt she was as good as or better than anyone playing the game, though she'd hardly had time to practice in years. As it happened, she didn't win a match, but that hardly daunted her. If such an event was held again, she let it be known, she wanted to be included.

By 1972, King, Evonne Goolagong, and Margaret Court were starting to make relatively good money at women's tennis. Althea saw the headlines, heard the numbers, and contemplated a comeback. She wasn't winning golf tournaments—and even at forty-four years old, she still considered herself better than all the other women out there playing tennis. It was just a question of getting into shape. "I hope to play in a few tournaments before the year is out," she told the *Sporting News* that June from an LPGA event in Sutton, Massachusetts. She men-

tioned teaming with her old partner Gar Mulloy in the mixed doubles at Forest Hills. "That could be my jumping-off place," she said.

It was the first in a series of attempted comebacks that would punctuate the middle of her life. She couldn't give up the idea that she'd been the premier female athlete of her time and, in any material sense, profited little from it. She'd signed on as program director of the Valley View Racquet Club in Northvale, New Jersey, but that was short-lived. She missed the limelight. "I'd like to be associated again with the sport that made me popular," she said at the time. She also had Sydney Llewellyn pushing her. And money remained an issue, she admitted. "The opportunities in tennis now are greater than they've ever been. The girls are playing for large sums of money . . . Now the money in tennis provides an opportunity for a girl to make a fair living out of the sport. Maybe if I concentrate on it, I might even get a piece of it."

As Althea Gibson Darben, she teamed with the apparently ageless Mulloy at the U.S. Open in 1972, losing in the first round of the mixed doubles to Gene Scott and Ceci Martinez, but winning the first set. A year later, she was Althea Gibson again, and back at Forest Hills. She and Arthur Ashe made a historic pairing; between them they owned all four U.S. singles titles won by blacks. But Althea was nearing fifty, and even the formidable Ashe couldn't carry her. They lost in the first round to Marita Redondo and Jean Chanfreau, 6–2, 6–2. Athea also reunited with Darlene Hard in the women's doubles, but didn't get any further, losing in three sets to a Japanese pairing in what must have been one of the odder-looking matches at the West Side Tennis Club that year.

She always had considered herself an all-around athlete, but as the years passed without significant success on the golf tour, her achievements in tennis loomed larger. They were the sanctum for her pride; whatever she did or didn't accomplish, no one could dispute that for two years, at least, she had been the best female tennis player in the world.

In 1974, she was invited to participate in a ceremony honoring past champions at a clay-court tournament in Fort Lauderdale. In the professional event, Chris Evert and Kerry Melville advanced to the final, but Melville stubbed a toe and had to withdraw. To have something for the fans on finals day, promoter George Liddy asked Althea if she wanted to play a single-set exhibition against young Evert, not yet twenty, who recently had turned professional. With Goolagong and King, Evert was already considered one of the world's top women. That year would be the first of five in succession she would be ranked first in the United States, a feat nobody had accomplished since Alice Marble. Althea was forty-seven, a name from the past. She readily agreed to play, but warned it would be no exhibition. She was out to win.

Evert was a teenager, but she handled the situation with grace. She was accustomed to rallying with players who weren't her equal, since by that time almost nobody was. Against Althea, she hit ball after ball down the middle of the court, giving her opponent every chance to look good. Given opportunities to end points with winners, Evert often kept rallies alive, knowing that it was what fans wanted to see. She hit no drop shots, sent no drives deep into the corners. Still, she won easily, ceding a game at the most.

Althea was far from humiliated. She was so proud as to be almost delusional, as Nancy Chaffee, who was also being honored there, remembered later. "I know I can beat her," she whispered to Chaffee after she'd come off the court. "She's not so terrific. If I could get her on my home court, on a hard court, I'm sure I could beat her." It was the same old Althea after all those years, never admitting any task was too much for her. Her attitude caused some rolling of the eyes in Fort Lauderdale, as it had in many places before. But it was what had made her great.

In 1975, King was asked to participate in the first Women's Superstars competition, a made-for-television event on ABC that had been invented by former figure-skating champion Dick Button. The male version had successfully showcased the world's finest athletes beginning in 1973, and now its spinoff would pit some of the best female athletes against each other in ten events, including tennis, rowing, bowling, basketball shooting, a softball throw, and an obstacle course. King, who had beaten Bobby Riggs in tennis's Battle of the Sexes two years before, agreed to compete—it could hardly have been held without her—but only if Althea was eventually included. Always ready to champion a cause, King believed that Althea was a heroic figure who had been lost in the mists of history, and she wanted to do what she could to both bring her back into prominence and help her earn some needed money.

The following year, with King now serving as a commentator on the telecast, Althea was one of two dozen women flown to Rotunda, Florida, by ABC to compete for nearly $70,000 in total prize money. The list included Martina Navratilova, then an emerging tennis star, as well as golfers Jane Blalock and Amy Alcott, drag racer Shirley Muldowney, diver Micki King, distance swimmer Diana Nyad, surfer Laura Ching, speed skater Anne Henning, skier Kiki Cutter, and track star Wyomia Tyus. At forty-nine, Althea was two decades older than most of them, but she held her own. With more people watching her on television than during her entire tennis career, she won the bowling and basketball-shooting events in the preliminary competition and, remarkably, was one of five athletes from her group to advance to the ten-woman final, televised the following week. In the final, wearing tortoise-shell sunglasses, she struggled through the sixty-meter dash and over the obstacle course, but finished second in bowling and basketball. She earned $4,200 for her efforts: far less than the $30,000 of winner Henning, but a substantial payday nonetheless. Althea never acknowledged King's efforts in getting her an invitation. But she enjoyed herself and performed well, especially in bowling. All those midnights at the lanes with Gloria Nightingale had finally paid off on national television.

With her fifty-first birthday approaching in 1978, she was back to playing golf. She had won Wimbledon and Forest Hills, but it galled her that she couldn't manage a single tour victory on the LPGA circuit. "I am closer than most people think," she said after failing to qualify for the third and fourth rounds of the LPGA Championship in Mason, Ohio, but in truth, that wasn't the case. Mason was the thirteenth consecutive tournament at which she failed to make the cut. Soon after, she retired again.

ACROSS THE OCEAN, Angela was back in the limelight. By the late 1970s, she and Jones had established a thriving tennis academy together in Hampstead Garden Suburb. Called the Angela Buxton Centre, it served four thousand students of varying ages, from young children to elderly matrons. It operated seven days a week from March to October, sunrise until dusk. Angela ran it from her house while Jones did his magazine work and wrote tennis for the *Daily Mirror*, tennis and bowls for the *Sunday Telegraph*, and freelanced throughout Fleet Street. She'd traverse the village on a bicycle delivering invoices and receipts, a one-woman show.

Jones's ideas had gained currency through the years. In matters such as fitness and nutrition, the world had come around to his point of view. The advent of professionalism meant that, at least for some, tennis could be undertaken with the seriousness of a profession. That didn't happen overnight—precious few players could actually make a living at the game, for one thing, and the old habits died hard—but by the end of the 1970s, the application of science to the sport was no longer as outlandish a concept as it had previously seemed. Jones hardly noticed. He was too busy communicating in ideas, doing experiments on reaction time and flexibility, timing serves with a rudimentary speed gun, teaching tennis, writing tennis books.

For several weeks each year, he and Angela traveled to Israel together to lead a conference at the Wingate Institute. Their goal was to teach every child in the country to play tennis. They'd also met up with Paulina Peisachov, an Israeli visiting London. A fine player, she was aiming at the top twenty when the Israeli Army came calling. In those days, there were three ways for a woman to avoid the country's mandatory military service: marriage, pregnancy, or desertion. Peisachov decided on pregnancy, which should have been a warning about the depth of her commitment to tennis, but Angela persuaded her to get married instead. As Paulina Peled, and under the direction of Jones and Angela, she rose to No. 19 in the world. She won a match at the U.S. Open in 1974 and seemed full of promise. Then she left Jones and Angela for another coach, the celebrated 1959 Wimbledon winner Alex Olmedo, who had a bigger name and lofty ambitions. Jones was sharp with her. He predicted her demise and told her not to bother to come crawling back when she failed with Olmedo. It all unfolded almost exactly as he had said it would, which impressed Peled, but impressed Angela even more. A quarter-century after Pattern Tennis had carried her to the Wimbledon final, Angela saw that Jones still had a certain prescience about the sport.

By then, their relationship as lovers was public knowledge. Nobody found it strange; indeed, many wondered why it had been so long in coming. In September 1980, they decided to sneak away together for a long weekend in New York and see some U.S. Open matches at the new Flushing Meadow facility. A pupil of Angela's had done it years ago, and it sounded so marvelously decadent. They arranged their schedules so it could work, postponed some lessons, feigned illness with others, whatever it took to clear their days. They felt like schoolkids playing hooky.

On Jones's suggestion, they called Althea. She was overjoyed to hear from them. She wanted to know where they were, what they were doing, when they could meet. Angela and Althea arranged to hold their reunion at the USTA booth at Flushing Meadow. Angela arrived early, which is her style; Althea arrived late, which is hers. They greeted each other like the long-lost friends they were, with Jones off to one side, looking on. They'd both changed partners in recent years and had suffered through various disappointments and reversals, but no more than life normally gives. They seemed healthy, if somewhat altered from the last time they'd seen each other, a decade-and-a-half before. Together, they ate lunch in a restricted-membership restaurant on the grounds, talking about their lives over roast beef and potatoes. Then they headed out to watch tennis.

At the time, the organizers had former champions sitting directly on the court, six seats in every corner, in order that the camera might catch them. As a result, half of tennis-playing Hampstead saw Angela sitting beside Althea. Some of her pupils, who believed she was ill, were angry with her, but those for whom 1956 had been little more than a rumor were duly impressed. There was their tennis teacher, right beside the great Althea Gibson, in whispering distance of Chris Evert and Bjorn Börg.

In years to come, Angela and Jones would fly to New York for a week or more during the U.S. Open almost every year. Invariably, they'd see Althea. Angela would call and say she was arriving in New York on a particular date, and Althea would be thrilled all over again. Sometimes they'd eat lunch at a diner in East Orange, sometimes Angela would visit Althea at home, occasionally they went out to see the tennis together.

Since her divorce from Will Darben, Althea had been spending more and more time with Llewellyn. Even after all these years, those who knew Althea best didn't trust his motives. Llewellyn wanted Althea to fund his various schemes and inventions, and he reveled in his associa- tion with her. Unlike Jones, his rough equivalent in Angela's life, Llewellyn had never accomplished much outside of coaching and man- aging Althea. He never was any kind of love interest for her as far as anyone could tell, and he was almost two decades older. Yet one day in 1984, she shocked her friends by announcing that she was getting mar- ried to him.

Llewellyn was a Jamaican national who had been living in New York for decades; one friend has always believed that the marriage was a sham merely to get him citizenship. "It was a marriage of convenience," he says. It also seems to have been a means to reward Llewellyn for years of assistance. That year, Wimbledon had invited all of its past female champions and their husbands to celebrate the centenary of women's play there. The All England Club offered to pay their way to London and put them up in a fancy Kensington hotel. Althea and Llewellyn weren't living together after their wedding and had no plans to do so. Nevertheless, she brought him along to England. She'd also been asked to participate in the ceremonies surrounding the 1984 Olympic Games in Los Angeles, which meant two weeks of high living at another posh hotel, and Althea knew she'd be allowed to take a hus- band to that, too. In all, it constituted a month of grand treatment for a man who hadn't seen much of it through the years.

Althea had called Angela after the invitation to Wimbledon arrived, pleased to be able to say that she was the one who'd be crossing the ocean this time. There was a fancy dinner on her first Saturday night in London, but Angela was running the tennis school and couldn't get away. It was the busiest time of year, with hundreds of pupils a day shuttling in and out. Louise Brough remembers Althea arriving at the hotel like royalty, still sure of herself after all those years. She sent her laundry out, had her hair done, lived it up. "She charged it all to the All

England Club, but she didn't get away with it," Brough says with a laugh. The other champions didn't know whether to be embarrassed or proud of such brazen behavior, but they recognized it as vintage Althea.

On the following Tuesday morning at ten o'clock, Angela was starting to give four consecutive hours of lessons to housewives when she heard a rustling in the bushes behind the court. It was Althea and Llewellyn, pushing through. They'd tracked down the location, a concealed pathway leading to the main entrance from a secondary road. It was no easy place to find—Angela had to send a road map to new pupils, or they'd lose themselves among the tangle of suburban streets—but Althea had hired a car from Wimbledon to take them there. Angela was flabbergasted. Here she was, ten minutes into a rudimentary lesson with a dozen suburban housewives, and Althea Gibson, her new husband, and a Wimbledon chauffeur had emerged through the thorns and brambles. "I decided to give you a surprise, Angie," Althea said matter-of-factly.

Althea and Llewellyn proceeded to take over the lesson. They gave pointers, then stood at the net answering questions for as long as anyone had questions to ask. The students didn't want to leave. And then the next group came, and Althea and Llewellyn stayed on and did it all again. It was Althea at her best, teaching what she knew, taking an interest, letting her charisma light up the day. It made quite an impression. Two decades later, Angela was still receiving Christmas cards from some of these women, and they still recalled the time Althea Gibson showed up at the end of the dirt path on their hidden court unannounced and gave them a lesson.

IN THE MONTHS following her accomplishments at Wimbledon in 1956, Angela had been advised by what friends she had in the British tennis community to apply for membership at the All England Club. Strike while the iron is hot, they said, because you may never get the chance again. Singles winners are automatically entered as members, but winners of the Gentlemen's, Ladies', and Mixed Doubles—so numerous by comparison—are a step lower on the social ladder. Like everyone else, they were forced to submit applications.

Angela did, but she never received a response. She thought about it occasionally through the years, but figured it hardly mattered. It wasn't as though she was about to journey all the way to SW19, where the All England Club was located, just to play a match. But once she returned to the game as a coach, it became quite noticeable that she wasn't a member. She inquired, and was told that she remained on a waiting list. This was something of an embarrassment, considering the major figure in English tennis she again had become. She'd been a Wimbledon singles finalist and a doubles champion; only Mortimer, among British women, also managed both accomplishments in the years since World War II. Now she was teaching several thousand students at her academy, many of them juniors who represented the next generation of Wimbledon prospects. Yet Wimbledon itself was closed to her. Eventually a reporter came calling to ask why. "I suppose it's because I'm Jewish," she blurted, and it went straight to the headlines. The chairman of the All England Club appeared on television hawing his way through an interview. He'd have to look into it, you know, and he couldn't really comment without more information.

Wimbledon had a few Jewish members by then, but none as forthright as Angela. In time, she was informed that she had been asked, and evidently must have declined. Now she'd have to get back at the end of the line. "That's all right, I've only been waiting thirty years," she told the bureaucrat on the phone.

Before too long, she'd left London for good. On March 22, 1986, Jones died of a brain tumor, at the age of seventy-three. They'd operated on him the previous month and sewn him up, saying he had six months left at the most. Instead, it was six weeks. A light went out in Angela's life. Within a year, she'd sold the Tennis Centre. It was too difficult, and too painful, without him. A year after that, her son Joseph came bounding up the stairs in her office in a state of agitation. He'd had his first sexual liaison, he'd explained, and the condom had broken and he'd ended up HIV-positive. "It's the most unfortunate thing ever," he said. He wanted her to believe that it happened with a woman, but Angela knew he was homosexual. There had been signs for years. To the last week, he was living in denial. He finally died in August 1995, at thirty-four. She had lost her companion and her son, and, not long before that, her mother, too.

Now she sold the Hampstead house she'd owned since 1960, and looked north, where her brother had left his wife and was living on his own in Cheshire, near Manchester. She'd had a Florida condominium since the mid-1980s, and now she bought a sizable town house. She moved the detritus of more than three decades into her new garage. Even then, her heartache didn't subside. She was only a five-minute drive from her son Benjamin, a venture capitalist, his wife, Chris, and their two daughters, Kelly and Tara, yet they'd see each other only occasionally. After years of living with Silk, she'd kept up the habit of Sabbath dinners, the occasional synagogue visit, and a strong interest in Israel. Her son evidently considered it unseemly. "I don't want all that Jewishness in my house," Benjamin told her.

"Since Jimmy died, it has all gone bad," Angela says now. Nevertheless, she has made an interesting life for herself by writing about tennis for national and international publications, cutting quite a figure in interview rooms from Key Biscayne to Wimbledon in her stylish clothes, the glamorousness of her youth still apparent. She has no qualms about asking a dozen consecutive questions of a player until she gets the information she wants. Other journalists snicker, but they write down the answers she elicits. She also helps to sponsor foreign players seeking to participate in the Orange Bowl and other junior tournaments in South Florida, and takes an active role in the social life at her Florida condominium complex. She spends time with a male companion, and plays as much golf as she can.

She even managed to play with Althea once, in the late 1980s. It was during one of her visits to Orange. They went to a public course where Althea played regularly. By then, golf had replaced tennis for both of them as their outlet for both exercise and amusement. Angela was becoming a fine player, though not on Althea's level. Still, she was nine years younger, and fit.

Over the course of eighteen holes, Angela experienced what it must have been like for Daphne Seeney, Darlene Hard, and many of the rest of Althea's tennis opponents through the years. When they'd played ten-

nis against each other those few times in the 1950s, Angela had lost but
she hadn't been overwhelmed. She'd been prepared, she'd known
exactly what she had to do, and it had been a matter of Althea's superior
talent. Now, playing a friendly round of golf with nobody watching,
Angela felt intimidated. It was a look Althea had in her eyes, a shake of
the head when one of Angela's shots would go awry, as if to say, "Gee,
I'm sorry you can't do any better than that. This sure won't be much of a
match."

Angela remembers standing at the tee, trying to hit a seven iron, and
being so flustered that she couldn't get the ball out of the tee box. "I
thought, 'What the hell is happening to me?'" she says now. Any number of Althea's opponents through the years could have told her.

BEFORE LONG, Althea and Llewellyn divorced, and she started seeing
Will Darben again. He was the love of her life, and he treated her with
the same respect and admiration the second time around. This time,
though, she was equally devoted. "She found out she really loved him,"
his sister Rosemary says. They would meet at a diner that was near the
senior citizens' center where he lived and while the hours away. He suffered from diabetes, and in the end, the complications killed him. He
would die in 1997, not yet an old man.

Althea had tried one more comeback, this time with the LPGA, but
she couldn't qualify for a tour card. It was 1990, and she was sixty-three
years old. Her long athletic career was finally over. Not long after, her
job with the New Jersey Governor's Commission on Physical Fitness
was eliminated from the state budget. Without savings and unprepared
to retire, she was out of work. Then she suffered a stroke. Her former
gynecologist, who had moved out of state, was told by the doctors who
were treating her that it was the result of venereal disease lying dor-
mant in her body for all those years. "It was the terminal, stage-three
part of her illness finally manifesting itself," he said. The venereal disease must have been treated with penicillin and cured, but the damage
had been done. Althea was never the same after that.

By 1995, she'd had enough. Her health was spiraling downward.
Her glory days were over. She had made great strides, yet she had never

received the recognition she believed she deserved. Her life had been a cocktail of success and failure, and in many tangible ways, she'd experienced more success than most. But she was accustomed to fighting for more, and she didn't know how to stop. She called Angela, who was in her Florida condominium for the season, with the grim news that she was ready to die.

In Rosemary and Will Darben, Althea had close friends who lived only a short drive away. In Billie Jean King, she had a friend who could mobilize a fight for a cause at a moment's notice. Why call Angela, a confidante from a bygone era, whom she'd seen less than a dozen times over three decades? Perhaps Althea remembered that, in the heat of competition all those years ago in Paris, Angela's instinctive reaction to Althea's distress had been to shield her from harm, even though by doing so she put herself at a competitive disadvantage. In a pinch, she could rely on Angela. Beyond that, Angela was organized, affluent, and resourceful, and Althea knew that Angela's affection for her was genuine. Long before the championship trophies started piling up in Althea's New York apartment, Angela had been in her corner.

She was calling to bid farewell, Althea told Angela. But Angela heard it, as Althea must have known she would, as a plea to live.

It is easy to see how Angela's zeal for organization would have saved her. Angela threw herself into the task of raising money for Althea like she'd thrown herself into learning Pattern Tennis. She had no qualms about being bothersome—a *nudge,* in the Yiddish of her ex-father-in-law, Bobby Silk—and talking up Althea's cause everywhere she went. When the first round of funds that had been raised became tangled in the bureaucracy of too many organizations, Angela contacted old friends and made new ones, while continuing to support Althea in the meantime. Once Paul Fein had written his plea on Althea's behalf in *Tennis Week,* new checks started arriving at Althea's home. With her name back in the news again, her achievements were introduced to a new generation, even as the Williams sisters were emerging as her sociological descendants. And as her benefactor and champion, Angela basked in the glow. The Wimbledon doubles champions had teamed up for the first time since 1956, and they'd won again.

· · ·

BY THE TIME OF ALTHEA'S CALL, Angela was living half the year in Florida. Through a contact, she managed to secure an invitation from Richard Williams to visit the Palm Beach Gardens compound where his young daughter Venus, then barely a teenager, was said to be an emerging star. Angela and Sandy Baruch, a tennis coach and part-time journalist from Connecticut, drove from Pompano Beach to the Williams home. Angela and Baruch saw Venus hit with Serena and were astonished at their ability. Richard was in mud up to his thighs from laying a clay court. His wife, Oracene, periodically delivered them cold drinks.

Richard was fascinated by Angela's connection to Althea, whom he perceived as the role model for his daughters. Angela was in frequent contact with Althea at that time, and she volunteered to call her from a mobile phone, right there in the Williamses' yard. Venus was being shy, but Richard could tell she was excited by the idea of talking to the only black woman to ever win at Wimbledon or Forest Hills. (Serena, who would later write a school project on Althea, going so far as to fax her questions to answer, sat in the background, playing with the family cat.) Angela dialed the number, spoke into the answering machine, and then Althea picked up. "Hi there, Angie," she said.

Angela explained to Althea where she was and who Venus was, then put them on the phone together, linking the past and future Wimbledon champions for the first time. Angela wrote up the story for *Tennis Magazine*, something of a scoop. Then she and Sandy celebrated their success by eating chicken soup on the beach at Pompano. It was New Year's Day, 1997.

Eight months later, Venus and Althea spoke again on the eve of Venus's startling run to the U.S. Open final. By then, Althea didn't need to be told about this African-American teenager. She thought back to her own debut at Forest Hills and the match with Brough, and how she'd won over a skeptical white public with a fearless performance. She longed to believe that the phenomenon of Venus Williams wouldn't have happened without her antecedence, and perhaps it wouldn't have. "Be who you are and let your racket do the talking," Althea told Venus. "The crowd will love you."

Althea wanted this athlete of a new generation to have it easier than she'd had it. In that sense, there was no denying the impact she'd had. By integrating what had previously been an all-white, country-club sport, Althea had paved a bumpy, potholed road. With perseverance and good fortune, this young Venus Williams would now drive right through.

Althea

IN JUNE OF 2003, just as spring is turning to summer, a phone rings in Althea's East Orange apartment and keeps on ringing. She lets the answering machine switch on, then waits to hear who wants what from her. In the final months of her life, she is living as a recluse. She rarely leaves the house, other than for doctor's appointments. She has a forty-eight-inch television screen, and she pages through the listings in the Sunday paper. She knows exactly when everything is on and sets her schedule accordingly, not just tennis and golf but baseball and basketball, too.

She has little memory of her own accomplishments; at one point, she says she can't recall anything of substance about her tennis career. For that reason, among others, she has stopped granting interviews. Even when an event is held in her honor, she almost never attends. "I want the public to remember me as they knew me," she had written in an Internet forum several years before. "Strong, athletic, smart and healthy. Right now, I don't remember everything I did, or when, or how. . . . I don't want people feeling sorry for me because of the way I look. 'Oh, look at her, she is so thin,' and other things like that. No. Remember me strong and tough and quick, fleet of foot and tenacious."

As summer comes, she weighs less than a hundred pounds, according to one account, and describes herself as having a terminal disease. "I'm the only person she allows in," Rosemary Darben boasts, and though that may be an exaggeration, it isn't by much. Her last days are witnessed by her friend Fran Gray, who runs the Althea Gibson Foundation. When Althea finally succumbs to the weight of nearly eight decades of life and dies on September 28, 2003, aged seventy-six, Angela hasn't seen her in five years.

DURING THAT TIME, Althea has been recast by Gray and others as a soldier in the war for civil rights, a cross between Rosa Parks and Arthur Ashe, until she resonates as an American folk hero. When she dies, her achievements are celebrated in every newspaper, many of which position her obituary on the front page. Her struggle for acceptance that culminated in the victories at Wimbledon and Forest Hills is presented as a morality play, and the far more nuanced story of a woman who triumphed despite her flaws is buried beneath the hagiography.

By the time of her death, the achievements of the Williams sisters have brought her nearly all the way back to center stage. After all that time, she had taken a pride of ownership in their success. Before the 2000 Wimbledon Ladies' Singles final, she had called Zina Garrison (the second black woman to reach a Wimbledon final, in 1990) with advice for Venus. It was technical stuff—move your feet, bend your knees—and Garrison didn't deliver the message until Williams had won the match, but it fortified the existing link between the two Wimbledon champions. According to L. Jon Wertheim of *Sports Illustrated,* Althea turned up the volume of the television for the presentation of the Venus Rosewater dish that year, then hoisted a glass of ginger ale in triumph.

And then, a little more than a year later, Althea watched on television as Venus defeated her sister Serena in straight sets to capture the U.S. Open. It marked the first time two blacks played in the final of one of the Grand Slam tournaments, and provided a finish to Althea's sociological journey. Though she always maintained that she played for herself, not for her race, the door she'd pushed through half a century before had finally opened wide.

Yet it would be a mistake to link the Williams sisters to Althea in any but the most superficial ways. Her importance lies not in the trail she blazed for others, but in how cold that trail was by the time anyone managed to follow. She was decades ahead of her time, to the point at which her achievements were largely forgotten by 1990, the year Garrison won just five games from Martina Navratilova at Wimbledon. Largely through Angela's efforts, Althea's accomplishments were resurrected even as her life was being saved. It was a mixed blessing; as much as Althea appreciated the help, she hated the fact that she needed it. And by promoting her cause, Angela had broadcast that need to the world.

By the end, the bitterness she'd nursed for years had passed. Picture that small apartment in East Orange, and a frail but alert old woman sitting in a comfortable chair. The sun is shining, but she doesn't see the sun. The phone is ringing, but she lets it roll over to the answering machine. Perhaps it's Angela calling on this June morning to rekindle memories of long ago. If so, Althea is unmoved. She has the time and energy to look ahead, but not behind. The only cheering in her head comes from the television, broadcasting another season's Wimbledon in real time.

Almost half a century has gone since she first won a doubles title there in 1956. Given the opportunity, Althea would have written the script of the years that followed quite differently from how they turned out. Yet from where she sits now, in the comfort of her padded recliner, life seems pleasant enough. It is the first day of Wimbledon coverage and the matches are just beginning. She plans to see them all.

Index

BRUCE SCHOENFELD, an acclaimed magazine journalist, is a frequent contributor to many national and international publications. His work has appeared in the *New York Times Magazine, Tennis, Gourmet, Outside,* and *Travel + Leisure,* and he is a contributing editor for *Wine Spectator.* As a television scriptwriter, he won Emmy awards for his work on NBC's coverage of the 1988 and 1996 Olympic Games. He is the author of *The Last Serious Thing: A Season at the Bullfights.* He lives in Boulder, Colorado, with his wife and son.